Third Edition

Implementing Organizational Change

THEORY INTO PRACTICE

Bert Spector
Northeastern University

PEARSON

Boston Columbus Indianapolis New York San Francisco
Upper Saddle River Amsterdam Cape Town Dubai London
Madrid Milan Munich Paris Montreal Toronto Delhi Mexico City
Sao Paulo Sydney Hong Kong Seoul Singapore Taipei Tokyo

For Maureen

Editorial Director: Sally Yagan
Acquisitions Editor: Brian Mickelson
Director of Editorial Services: Ashley Santora
Editorial Project Manager: Sarah Holle
Director of Marketing: Maggie Moylan
Senior Marketing Manager: Nikki Jones
Marketing Assistant: Ian Gold
Senior Managing Editor: Judy Leale
Production Project Manager: Renata Butera
Creative Art Director: Jayne Conte
Cover Designer: Suzanne Behnke
Cover Art: Getty Images, Inc.
Full-Service Project Manager: Vijayakumar Sekar
Composition: TexTech International Pvt. Ltd.
Printer/Binder: STP/RRD/Harrisonburg
Cover Printer: STP/RRD/Harrisonburg
Text Font: 10/12 Palatino

Credits and acknowledgments borrowed from other sources and reproduced, with permission, in this textbook appear on the appropriate page within text.

Library of Congress Cataloging-in-Publication Data

Spector, Bert.
Implementing organizational change : theory into practice / Bert Spector. — 3rd ed.
p. cm.
Includes bibliographical references and index.
ISBN 978-0-13-272984-0
1. Organizational change. 2. Organizational behavior. 3. Personnel management. I. Title.
HD58.8.S667 2013
658.4'06—dc23

2011043785

10 9 8 7 6 5 4 3 2 1

ISBN 10: 0-13-272984-9
ISBN 13: 978-0-13-272984-0

CONTENTS

PREFACE

NEW TO THE THIRD EDITION

Welcome to the third edition of *Implementing Organizational Change–Theory into Practice*. This edition is significantly enhanced based on recommendations for reviewers and users, as well as on new research:

- Chapter 8—"Going Green"—is completely new, covering in detail a topic that had not been included in the previous editions.
- Chapter 7—"Organizational Culture and Change"—has been eliminated as a separate chapter. Key concepts from the chapter have been integrated throughout the text.
- Five new opening cases have been included. These are all cases written exclusively for the third edition.
- Four new closing cases have been included. These are all cases written exclusively for the third edition.
- The "Theory into Practice" sections have been expanded throughout the text. At the same time, many of them have been rewritten to make even clearer the application of change implementation theory.
- New examples have been added throughout the text.
- A new framework for organizational diagnosis has been added in Chapter 3.
- A case on a not-for-profit organization—CARE—has been added to Chapter 4.
- A section on change in multinational organizations has been added to Chapter 4.
- Greater emphasis on the process of building collaboration has been added to Chapter 4.
- A case on workforce diversity has been added to Chapter 5.

Talking about what has changed in a book on change management is inevitable and important. However, I also want to make clear what has not changed. From the outset, I intended to write a text that would allow the reader to bring change management theory to implementation and practice. A COO recently told me that this was a book that he kept on his desk rather than his bookcase so he could refer to it regularly. I'm proud of that complement. I'm equally proud when students tell me that I have helped "make sense" of theory. Thanks to all of you for your input, and I hope that you are pleased with the revisions in this third edition.

UNDERSTANDING ORGANIZATIONAL CHANGE

Organizational change comes in an almost endless variety of types and approaches. Just consider these examples:

- To open new growth and revenue opportunities for the Internet-based social network company, Facebook, the CEO announces a new business model.
- To respond to shifting demands of multinational customers, the CEO of IBM attempts to achieve seamless global responsiveness in an organization long noted for its highly decentralized multinational operations.
- To encourage ongoing innovation, the cofounders of Internet search engine Google move to create greater tolerance for mistakes.

- To respond to criticism of its global labor practices, Nike commits itself to sustainable business and innovation.
- To overcome its image as a cookie cutter chain and help to recover from a recession, Macy's pushes decision making down into its regional operations.
- To improve the efficiency of software development, a small company adopts Agile, a new approach based on multiple releases in short time frames.

From multinational colossuses to small businesses, employees at all levels seek to respond to the competitive dynamics that impact their organization's performance.

Volatile swings in national and international economies, new competitive environments, shifting customer expectations, increasing pressure from financial markets, emerging governmental regulation and deregulation, not to mention dramatic and unexpected geopolitical dynamics, all demand responsiveness from today's organizations. Renewed strategies, designed to achieve and maintain a strong competitive position, demand that organizations abandon the status quo. Instead of being an occasional event, organizational change is now a way of life.

Implementing organizational change has, as a result, emerged as a core competency for corporate executives. In fact, any leader today will discover just how vital leading change is. If you're not leading change, as the saying goes, you're not leading.

Knowing that change is vital, however, and successfully navigating an organization through a change effort are quite different matters. Despite good intentions, enthusiastic support, and the availability of resources, change efforts often fall short of the expectations and promises of their champions. Frequently, the flaw can be found in the misconceptualization of the implementation process. How change is conceived and how it is implemented—that is where the barriers usually reside.

THEORETICAL ORIENTATION

The purpose of *Implementing Organizational Change—Theory into Practice* is to understand and analyze effective change implementation. In order to achieve that objective, *Implementing Organizational Change* focuses on change that can be understood as *strategically aligned alterations in patterns of employee behavior*. While recognizing the multiplicity of change efforts that span the corporate landscape, the two core concepts of that definition allow us to pay special attention to change that is strategic and behavioral. That definition shapes the core perspectives of the book, which examines change that is *strategic, purposeful,* and *behavioral*. Let's look briefly at each one:

1. ***Strategic***—the goal of change management is to help an organization support strategic renewal in order to achieve and maintain outstanding performance in the face of a dynamic environment. A *strategic* perspective focuses on aligning behaviors with renewed strategy and the requirements of outstanding performance.
2. ***Purposeful***—change can occur *to* an organization or *by* an organization, most often some combination of the two. A *purposeful* perspective focuses on explicit interventions into the organization that are designed to respond to a dynamic competitive environment.
3. ***Behavioral***—although change can occur in many forms, it is the alteration in employee behaviors—how employees conduct themselves at work—that allows organizations to implement their new strategies and achieve outstanding performance. A *behavioral* perspective focuses on the process of motivating employees at all levels of the organization to alter their patterns of behavior in ways that are sustainable, adaptive to shifts in the external environment, and will contribute to outstanding performance.

Wanting to achieve strategic behavioral change is relatively easy—implementing change is difficult. For that reason, the thread of *effective implementation* runs through the entire text. This is a book not just about *what* to change, but also *how* to change.

Implementing Organizational Change is informed primarily by the research and practice offered by the field of Organizational Development (OD). Leading writers have combined rigorous social science research with action learning to create an awareness of organizations as systems, suggesting that change efforts must be aware of the need to achieve and sustain a state of "fit" between various organization divisions and components. In terms of change processes, OD suggests that when individuals are involved in defining problems and solutions, they will be more motivated to achieve the desired outcomes.

Although richly informed by that field, *Implementing Organizational Change* is not intended to be an OD text. Instead, the book offers a view that integrates key OD insights with major perspectives from three additional fields:

1. ***Strategic renewal***—This field recognizes that highly dynamic environments require more than occasional incremental improvements in the firm's operations; new strategic directions and approaches require new ways of thinking and acting.
2. ***Strategic human resource management***—This field recognizes the requirement to align human capabilities with an organization's strategy for achieving and maintaining outstanding performance.
3. ***Leadership***—This field recognizes the role of leaders at all levels of the organization working both individually and collaboratively to mobilize adaptive behavior on the part of employees in order to drive change.

Those contributions, summarized in Exhibit P-1, will be supplemented by additional insights from fields such as organizational learning, managerial accounting, conflict management, ethics, communications, information systems, supply chain management, and organizational innovation.

Organizational development (OD)	Views organizations as open systems; sees alignment and responsiveness as necessary components of outstanding performance; emphasizes potential for collaborative effort, individual contribution, and growth.
Strategic renewal	Dynamic competitive environments often require new directions supported by new systems, structures, and processes.
Strategic human resource management (SHRM)	Emphasizes the requirement to align human resource policies and practices—both individually and systemically—with the strategic goals of the organization and the requirements of outstanding performance.
Leadership	Focuses on the behavior of leaders at all levels of the organization who mobilize adaptive behavior among employees and orchestrate effective change interventions.
Others	Sustainability, organizational learning, conflict management, ethics, communications, information systems, supply chain management, and organizational innovation.

EXHIBIT P-1 **Academic Underpinnings of *Implementing Organizational Change—Theory into Practice.***

BOOK ORGANIZATION

In order to present theories and practice of change, *Implementing Organizational Change* is divided into three sections:

- *Section 1*—"Theories of Effective Change Implementation" (Chapters 1 and 2) analyzes the forces leading to strategic renewal and organizational change, as well as the theories that form the basis for effective implementation. The section concludes with a theory of effective change implementation that combines the insights of previous works.
- *Section 2*—"Implementing Change" (Chapters 3–6) guides the reader through the theory and practice of specific methods and approaches to implementing organizational change.
- *Section 3*—"A Broader View" (Chapters 7 and 8) steps back from the specifics of change implementation to examine two larger organizational issues: the role of leadership and the change involved in "going green."

TEXT FEATURES

Because *Implementing Organizational Change* is intended for both practitioners and students of change management, the text includes a multiplicity of learning features.

- All chapters open with a bulleted list of key learning objectives. In addition, "Theory into Practice" highlights the applied, practical applications of the theories being presented.
- A short opening case study illustrates the core concepts and challenges analyzed in the chapter. These real-world examples of change implementation are referred to throughout the chapter to emphasize learning points.
- Key vocabulary items are highlighted in the text in order to help the reader develop a vocabulary of change.
- Each chapter includes a conclusion summarizing key points of the chapter and introduces key theme of the following chapter.
- Discussion questions guide readers back through key points of the chapter.
- Finally, a longer concluding case (written by the author exclusively for the text) can be used to apply and debate key points of each chapter.

The goal of each chapter is to integrate the various learning features with a presentation and analysis of influential and important theories, as well as examples of organizational change efforts. Organizations ranging from large multinationals such as Hewlett-Packard, Nissan Motors, Nike, and Cisco to nontraditional organizations such as the Rolling Stones and the nongovernmental organization CARE will help the reader apply change theories to real-world experiences.

CHAPTER 1

Organizational Change

When we talk about organizational change, we mean many different things. Calling on new technologies to improve services requires organizational change. So does offering new products in new markets. When a bank seeks greater control over employees who are making investment decisions, an athletic shoe company seeks to "go green," or a hospital decides to improve quality while simultaneously cutting costs, these, too, are examples of businesses that will need to engage in organizational change.

In order to understand and analyze the dynamics of change, and particularly the requirements of effective change implementation, it is important to sort out and distinguish the various approaches an organization can take. This chapter will explore multiple paths to change. In particular, this chapter will:

- Identify the role of strategic renewal in propelling change
- Focus on the behavioral aspect of organizational change
- Analyze the dynamics of motivating employees to alter their behaviors
- Differentiate the three faces of change: turnaround, tools and techniques, and transformation
- Understand the source of both employee resistance to and support for change
- Appreciate the importance of trigger events in initiating change efforts
- Examine the role that "going global" plays in triggering organizational change

We will start by looking at an attempt by a newly appointed chief executive officer (CEO) to revitalize the fortunes of a global leader in cell phones. As you read this introductory case, ask yourself:

- Why was Nokia eliminating jobs even though it was performing well?
- What triggered Nokia's decision to hire an outsider—an American—as CEO in 2010?
- What organizational changes will Stephen Elop need to make in order to revitalize Nokia in the United States?

ORGANIZATIONAL CHANGE AT NOKIA

As 2010 drew to a close, Finland-based Nokia, the world's leading producer of cell phones, announced the elimination of 1,800 jobs.[1] Surprisingly, the 3 percent reduction—which came a little more than one year after a previous 3 percent workforce reduction—accompanied an announcement of a strong third-quarter result. As the impact of the recent global recession slowly receded, Nokia produced strong sales and profit numbers. So, why the cutbacks?

Nokia's rise from a 19th-century paper mill headquartered in Espoo, Finland to the world's largest cell phone maker and leading employer in its native country is the stuff of business legend. In particular, its ability to overtake the previous market leader Motorola was based in large part on its early awareness of a global market for cell phones. With core competencies in production, distribution, and research and development, Nokia produced mobile phones that dominated not just Europe but also the emerging world markets.

As late as 2002, Nokia led the market in the United States as well. However, by 2009 its U.S. market share had slipped to 7 percent (from a high of 35 percent). It had been surpassed not only by its old rival Motorola but also by LG and Samsung, both based in Korea, and Research in Motion, the Canadian-based producer of the Blackberry. And then, of course, there was the hottest—or perhaps more accurately the coolest—smartphone of all, the iPhone.

In some ways, it might be said that Nokia's weakness in the U.S. market was the result of conscious strategic decisions made by the company. Nokia built its phones on the European standard GSM format rather than the U.S. standard CDMA format. This decision allowed Nokia phones ease of access to world markets.[2] By mass production of phones for a global market, Nokia lowered production costs. However, the decision limited its access to the U.S. market, where over half the phones operated with CDMA. Then too, Nokia failed to forge close ties with wireless providers, instead offering open phones that would then need to be adapted to a particular provider. Nokia's approach worked well globally. In the United States, however, wireless providers—Verizon, Sprint Nextel, AT&T, which together controlled 96 percent of the U.S. market—wanted to offer phones themselves that could be cobranded and bundled with long-term service contracts.

Perhaps most damaging, however, was Nokia's lack of responsiveness to the shifting tastes and expectations of the U.S. customers. Mark Louison, head of the North American unit, conceded, "In the past, we had a one-size-fits-all mentality that worked well on a global basis but did not help us in this market." Recognizing its growing weakness in the United States, Nokia placed an American on its management board in 2007, hired another American to be its chief development officer and moved its chief financial officer (CFO) to an office in the States.

Smartphones—phones with both Internet and e-mail functionality—represented the fastest growing and most profitable segment of the cell phone industry. As the Blackberry became a standard business tool, and the iPhone's popularity exploded in both the United States and globally, Nokia's share of the smartphone market fell dramatically. And its stock price tumbled, even after stock markets began to recover from the recession.

Many observers, both inside the company and outside, said that Nokia had become a victim of its own success, complacent and reluctant to rock the boat. In 2010, the Nokia board recruited Stephen Elop from Microsoft to transform the global giant.

Elop publicly admitted that Nokia had grown complacent and removed from customers. "It was management by committee," said one executive describing the company's approach to innovation. "Ideas fell victim to fighting among managers with competing agendas, or were rejected as too costly, risky, or insignificant for a global market leader." Elop vowed to focus on the internal barriers that existed to new product development. "Nokia has been characterized as an organization where it's too hard to get things done," he admitted. "But the board has vested in me the mandate to lead Nokia through this change." In particular, Elop said his first priority was to stem the loss of U.S. market share.

Not all news was bad. Nokia still remained the global leader in the basic phone market. In one of his first moves as new CEO, Elop announced job cuts. "The cuts were intended," he said to streamline software development for Nokia's smartphones by improving "agility and responsiveness" in the software development and Web services units.

STRATEGIC RESPONSIVENESS

Stephen Elop was just one of many business leaders facing the challenge of organizational change. Recognizing the need to change is important, of course. But it's just a first step. Next comes **change implementation**—the actions taken by organizational leaders in order to support strategic renewal and achieve outstanding performance. Successful implementation is required to translate that recognition into an effective strategic response. Poor implementation can undermine the best intentions of organizational leaders.

Building a Vocabulary of Change
Change implementation actions taken by organizational leaders in order to support strategic renewal and maintain outstanding performance in a dynamic environment.

We live in a period of rapid and dramatic change: significant alterations in customer expectations and demands, new technologies, competitors with innovative business models, shifts in workforce demographics and values, and new societal demands and constraints. Even the most successful organizations cannot stand still. They need to respond to external dynamics in order to create and maintain outstanding performance.

THEORY INTO PRACTICE

Successful organizations cannot remain static if they hope to continue that success; they must change in order to keep up with a changing world.

Building a Vocabulary of Change
Strategic renewal a change in an organization's strategy involving some combination of new products/services, new markets, and a new business model.

In response to those dynamics, organizational leaders often decide to engage in a process of strategic renewal. **Strategic renewal** involves some combination of a new product or service, a new market, and a new business model for an organization. Some companies have proved to be more nimble at adopting their strategy to shifting competitive realities:

- Amazon quickly and effectively moved from selling books online to offering eBooks on its own reader, the Kindle, while Borders lagged behind and failed to introduce an eReader.
- Netflix adapted to the world of DVDs offered through mail and video-on-demand, while Blockbuster lagged behind.
- Pandora, a Web-based music radio provider, repeatedly altered its business model in response to regulatory and technological changes, while less nimble competitors lagged behind.

Failure to adapt, of course, has serious consequences: both Borders and Blockbuster declared bankruptcy. As we saw in the opening case, Nokia found itself falling behind the more nimble Apple.

It is the ongoing demand for strategic renewal created by an ever-shifting competitive environment that creates the requirement for organizational change (see Exhibit 1-1).

THEORY INTO PRACTICE

To implement a renewed strategy, organizational leaders need to engage in a change process.

For strategic renewal to be effective, organizations need to do more than announce a new strategy. Announcements such as Elop's determination to revitalize Nokia's lagging mobile phone business in the United States come regularly.

Building a Vocabulary of Change
Organizational capabilities the collective talents and skills of a firm's employees.

Announcements such as these are useful: they alert employees, customers, suppliers, and investors to new directions the company plans to take. They are not, however, sufficient.

Leaders need to align internal processes, structures, and systems with the demands of that new strategy. New **organizational capabilities**—talents and skills possessed by employees—need to be built. Underlying all those shifts is

EXHIBIT 1-1 Strategic Responsiveness in Sample Companies.

Company	Altered Strategy
IBM	Move from product to service/consulting company
Netflix	Move from providing DVDs through the mail to providing streaming, in-demand entertainment
Renault	Move from French-based to internationally focused automobile company
Pandora	Move from selling through third-parties to selling directly to end users
Facebook	Move from restricted, college campus-only social network to become a "universal utility" open to everyone

the requirement to engage in **discontinuous change:** large-scale, long-term reorientation of most or all of the central aspects of organizational life.[3] The goal is to create lasting alterations in patterns of employee behavior in order to support strategic renewal.

Building a Vocabulary of Change
Discontinuous change large-scale, long-term reorientation of most or all of the central aspects of organizational life.

THE THREE FACES OF CHANGE

We noted at the beginning of the chapter that there are different approaches to change. Although there are many diverse methods, they can be placed within one of three broad categories:

1. Turnaround
2. Tools and techniques
3. Transformation

Let's examine each, and also take note of the overlaps that exist among them.

THEORY INTO PRACTICE

Not all change is behavioral.

To understand turnaround, look at MySpace. There was a time—the peak of which was 2005—when MySpace stood at the top of the social networking heap. Facebook had just emerged from the confines of college campuses, while major communications conglomerates entered a bidding war for the company started by Tom Anderson and Chris DeWolfe. However, soon after Rupert Murdoch's News Corporation paid $580 million for My Space, Mark Zuckerberg's Facebook emerged as its main competitor. By 2009, it was Facebook and not MySpace that had emerged as the preeminent social networking site. Perhaps it was complacency or the lack of managerial skills or the clash of cultures between MySpace and the News Corporation. Whatever the reason, MySpace began a steep decline. "MySpace was like a big party," said one media consultant, "and then the party moved on."[4]

MySpace management made attempts to respond redesigns, shifts in focus, new management, and so forth. Finally, it came time to cut costs. In January 2011, the company announced the layoff of 500 employees, over 40 percent of its total workforce. Analysts speculated that the News Corporation might be preparing to sell its once prized possession.

MySpace's most recent approach to change can be characterized as **turnaround.** Rather than focusing on new behaviors, turnaround looks at a company's assets and seeks to manage them in a new way in order to stabilize cash flow, shore up the balance sheet, and maximize shareholder wealth.

Building a Vocabulary of Change
Turnaround an attempt to improve the immediate financial position of an organization by focusing on the income statement and the balance sheet.

Turnaround can involve adding assets as well as cutting. During the recession, when many companies in the entertainment industry were cutting back, Disney grabbed the opportunity to expand. The company invested $1 billion in updating its California Adventure Park, purchased Marvel Entertainment for $4.3 billion and Playdom, a Facebook-oriented game maker, for $563 million.

This was turnaround by adding rather than subtracting. Disney saw these investments in assets as a way of ensuring continued performance of the company.

THEORY INTO PRACTICE

Turnaround may be necessary, but it is not sufficient to ensure long-term effective change.

Building a Vocabulary of Change
Techniques and tools organizational processes, mechanics, and other interactions intended to produce a product or service.

Another nonbehavioral face of change focuses on **techniques and tools**.[5] Exhibit 1-2 summarizes a number of change management tools and techniques that have been popular in recent years. Attending to techniques and tools without paying at least equal attention to the behavior of employees can be a path not just to disappointment but also to dysfunction. When employees participate in the design and implementation of new technology, they are more likely to alter their behaviors in ways that will help ensure effectiveness.

THEORY INTO PRACTICE

Effective strategic renewal efforts combine aspects of turnaround, tools and techniques, and transformational behavioral change.

EXHIBIT 1-2 Popular Change Tools and Techniques.

Tool	Key Points	Company Examples
Total quality management	Align operational processes with the requirement for customer-defined quality and continuous improvement.	Globe Metallurgical, Inc. Motorola Westinghouse
Agile development	A process for product development, mainly software, based on collaborative cross-functional team effort.	GKN Aerospace PNC Financial Acxiom
Balanced scorecard	Use of a measurement system that balances financial objectives alongside internal business process, customer satisfaction, and employee learning and growth.	VW of Brazil Ricoh Weichert Relocation
Value-chain integration	Capture value by linking and coordinating the primary activities—inbound logistics, production, outbound logistics, marketing, and sales—of the organization.	ComputerWorld IBM Electronics Microsoft
Lean	Eliminate activities that do not add value from the perspective of the customer.	Sealy Toyota Conmed
Considered design	Ecological impact is considered at beginning of new product design process rather than as an afterthought	Nike Hewlett-Packard Ford

EXHIBIT 1-3 Three Faces of Change.

Type	Target	Rationale
Turnaround	Assets	Improve short-term bottom-line performance
Tools and techniques	Processes	Increase internal efficiencies
Transformation	Behaviors	Enhance human capabilities

The third face of change involves **transformation**, a change intervention that directly targets the patterns of employee actions and interactions: *how* will employees work to meet the company's strategy and to achieve and sustain outstanding performance. Transformation, which focuses on behaviors, will be addressed at greater length in the next section and will, in fact, be the main focus for the remainder of the text.

Building a Vocabulary of Change
Transformation an intervention designed to alter patterns of employee behavior.

All three faces offer options available to leaders in search of strategic renewal (summarized in Exhibit 1-3). Although leaders may opt to approach each of these "faces" as separate and independent options, effective change efforts combine the three. We can now turn our attention to transformation.

TRANSFORMATIONAL CHANGE

THEORY INTO PRACTICE

If change interventions are to achieve significant and sustainable impact on performance, they must focus on altering patterns of employee behavior.

It's easy to think of examples of how organizations might wish to alter the behaviors of employees:

- Employees accustomed to following orders issued by supervisors might now have to make decisions on their own.
- Employees used to working as individuals might now have to work as a team.
- Employees, who have been focused purely on technology, might need to understand the needs and requirements of customers.
- Employees accustomed to working entirely within their own functional area might have to work collaboratively with people from other functions and backgrounds.

Behaviors involve how employees conduct themselves at work: what they do and how they do it, how much effort they bring to their roles, and how committed they are to achieving desired outcomes.

Behavior also involves how employees work with others: co-workers, customers, suppliers, the host community, and so forth. It is this enactment of roles, responsibilities, and relationships that constitutes employee behavior in organizations. The collective enactment of those roles, responsibilities, and relationships—that is, the *patterns* of employee behavior within organizations—constitutes the target of transformational change efforts.

Transformational change seeks more than a short-term alteration in behavior. In order to support strategic renewal and outstanding performance, new behaviors need to be *sustainable* and *adaptive* to shifts in the external environment.

The reason sustainability of new behaviors matters can be stated simply: the ways in which employees conduct themselves significantly impacts the organization's bottom-line performance.[6]

THEORY INTO PRACTICE

Transformational organizational change seeks to create long-term, sustainable alterations in employee behaviors.

Just how does that happen? How is it that of the way employees conduct themselves at work impacts a company's bottom-line performance? The key to understanding the relationship of behaviors and performance can be found in the idea of motivation.

Building a Vocabulary of Change
Motivation the degree to which employees are committed to the achievement of outstanding performance both for themselves and for their company.

Motivation refers to the degree to which employees are committed to the achievement of outstanding performance both for themselves and for their company. Employee motivation pays off in bottom-line performance. High motivation creates in employees the capability and willingness to work together to solve problems. Quality improves, customer responsiveness increases, and adaptation to shifts in the competitive environment occurs.

THEORY INTO PRACTICE

Employee motivation pays off in bottom-line performance.

Chapter 4 will examine in detail the efforts to redesign organizations to enhance employee motivation. For now, we can suggest that behaviors matter. The competitive advantage delivered by the conduct of employees can be long term and sustainable. The manner in which work is organized, information is shared, decisions are made, coordination occurs, and problems are solved are all performance differentiators.[7] Highly motivated employees can deliver a performance edge is sustainable for decades, leading to significant and often staggering competitive advantage.[8]

THEORY INTO PRACTICE

The way employees conduct themselves at work impacts the bottom-line performance of the company.

Sources of Behavior

Effective change implementation needs to start with an appreciation of the sources of an individual employee's behavior. If the goal of organizational change is to alter employee behaviors, after all, it is useful to understand why an employee behaves as he or she does.

Part of that answer resides in the individual psychology of the employee. Understanding who the individual is, what values he or she brings to the workplace, even how that individual thinks and learns can help provide insight into the question of why. But let's face it, individual psychology can be difficult to assess and slow to change.

Transformational change demands more than one-person-at-a-time change. A leader seeking leverage over the behaviors of many employees can start by focusing not on individual psychology but on the organizational context in which employees work.

THEORY INTO PRACTICE

Behavior comes from both the individual and the organizational context in which the individual works.

Building a Vocabulary of Change
Organizational context the setting and circumstances in which employees work.

Organizational context—the setting and circumstances in which employees work—exerts a powerful impact on behavior. Companies as diverse as Apple, General Electric, and Google endeavor to promote an organizational context that shapes individual behavior. They call upon organizational culture and values, the behaviors of leaders, as well as rules and procedures to define a context that shapes employee conduct.

It's worth remembering that organizational context can produce negative as well as positive results. It was a context of huge rewards for risk-taking and win-at-all-costs that led to the collapse of the financial services industry that triggered the global recession in 2008. We need to appreciate the power of organizational context to shape behaviors by examining a specific example of an employee mistake.

Sheryl Sandberg, an advertising manager at Google, made a mistake that cost the company millions of dollars. "Bad decision," she admitted, "moved too quickly, no controls in place, wasted some money."[9] Sandberg quickly informed Google cofounder Larry Page.

Employees make mistakes, even occasionally big ones such as Sandberg's. Leaders have an important opportunity to shape organizational context by the manner in which they respond to those errors. Quick and harsh repercussions—firing, for example, or demotion—will have one kind of impact on the organizational context in which employees work. That response may be justified and reasonable, but it may also work to stifle future risk-taking behaviors. Or perhaps employees will be less willing to admit mistakes, slowing down an organization's response time.

The boss may also respond in a less harsh and punishing manner. Listen to the reaction of Google cofounder Larry Page, to Sandberg's admission:

> I'm so glad you made this mistake, because I want to run a company where we are moving too quickly and doing too much, not being too cautious and doing too little. If we don't have any of these mistakes, we're not taking enough risk.

The point is not that Page's response is the only "correct" or reasonable response to the admission of a mistake. Leaders have to determine what type of organizational context they seek to create. That context will need to be aligned with the company's strategy and purpose.

Page and Google cofounder Sergey Brin believed that mistakes could provide fuel for improvements, even innovation. "We're willing to tolerate ambiguity and chaos," said senior vice president Shona Brown, "because that's where the room is for innovation." Google's leaders wanted a context that tolerated risk in order to generate innovation.

EMPLOYEE PARTICIPATION AND RESISTANCE TO CHANGE

Building a Vocabulary of Change
Resistance efforts exerted by employees either overtly or covertly to maintain the status quo.

Not all employees greet change with equal enthusiasm. It is useful, therefore, to examine the sources of employee resistance to change and the ways in which managers can overcome resistance. **Resistance** refers to action, overt or covert, exerted on behalf of maintaining the status quo.[10]

Why Employees Resist Change

You're either for this change or you're against it. That refrain may be familiar; it is not, however, accurate. Employee response to change is not either/or, not "for" or "against." Instead, it runs across a broad spectrum, ranging from "commitment" at one end to "aggressive resistance" on the other (see Exhibit 1-4). Each of these reactions to change helps shape the behavior of individuals and, ultimately, the success of a change effort.

THEORY INTO PRACTICE

Employees do not naturally resist change, but they often resist change because of the way change is implemented.

EXHIBIT 1-4
Continuum of Individual Response to Change.

Commitment	Involves a strong emotional attachment to the goals of the organization and the aims of the change effort
Involvement	Involves a willingness to participate in the behaviors, being called for by the change effort
Support	Involves speaking on behalf of the change effort without taking any other explicit actions to promote the effort
Apathy	Represents a neutral zone in which individuals know about the change effort and engage in no behavior either to support or oppose it
Passive resistance	A mild form of opposition that involves a willingness to voice reservation or even threatening to resign if the change goes through
Active resistance	Involves behaviors that block or impede change, usually by behaving in ways that contradict the goals of the change effort
Aggressive resistance	Involves purposeful sabotage and subversion of the change effort

Based on Leon Coetsee, "From Resistance to Commitment"; *Public Affairs Quarterly* (Summer 1999), pp. 204–222.

THEORY INTO PRACTICE

Managers can try to understand the reasons behind employee resistance to change.

Most attention to employee resistance has focused on how to avoid or, failing that, overcome it; which is to say, how to get employees "on board" change efforts. Managers can see employee resistance in negative terms: it is a "bad thing" that represents an irrational response to a dynamic competitive environment. In this way, employee resistance can be dismissed as invalid or disobedient.[11] Resistance to change, in this view, is a force to be overcome.

There is another way of thinking about resistance to change, however; one that may actually improve the effectiveness of implementation.

THEORY INTO PRACTICE

Employee resistance is not just a negative force to be overcome; it also presents an opportunity to learn.

How Managers Can Inadvertently Fuel Resistance During Implementation

It is tempting to believe that a certain type of individual is likely to resist change. Perhaps you've heard, or even thought, ideas such as:

- *Older workers are more likely to resist change than are younger workers.*
- *Middle managers are more likely to resist change than lower-level workers or higher-level executives.*
- *Men are more likely to resist change than women.*

Don't believe these explanations.

Study after study of employee resistance to change in organizations refutes these and other contentions that certain types of individuals are more likely to resist change than others. Individual differences may account for *some* variance in employee acceptance of or resistance to change. But the overwhelming determinant of employee reaction to change comes from how the process is managed and the degree to which employees are allowed to participate in the process.[12]

THEORY INTO PRACTICE

Resistance or acceptance of change depends mainly on how the change is implemented.

Managers do not set out to create resistance, of course, but do just the opposite. They believe that the proposed changes are being made for the good of the company and that employees will accept the need for change. Still, the manner in which change is implemented can have that effect. Here's a checklist of employee resistance and possible sources of that resistance:[13]

- ***Employees resist because they remain satisfied with the status quo.*** Perhaps management has not included employees in the diagnosis and learning process.
- ***Employees resist because they view change as a personal threat.*** Perhaps management has not offered employees the opportunity to acquire the new skills that will be required in the renewed organization.
- ***Employees resist because they see the cost of change outweighing the benefits.*** Perhaps management has not articulated the goals of the change adequately to allow a true assessment of the costs and benefits.
- ***Employees resist because they believe that management is mishandling the process.*** Perhaps employees have not been given a voice in the process itself.
- ***Employees resist because they believe that the change effort is not likely to succeed.*** Perhaps management needs to articulate why this change process is more likely to be effective than past efforts.

By looking at that checklist, we can see how often employee resistance can be understood in part as a natural and expected outcome of implementation.

THEORY INTO PRACTICE

Participation in the change process is the best way to build support and overcome resistance to change; but remember—it is no guarantee.

In treating employee resistance as a negative force to be overcome, managers risk shutting down the possibility that they can learn from resistance. When employee voice has been excluded from the change process, there is likely to be valuable data missing from the diagnostic and action planning phases of the effort. Employees may ask whether management really understands what customers expect from their products or services or what barriers the organization has erected to outstanding performance.

Even when employees question whether management has selected an appropriate strategic response, it is important for managers to learn about employee hesitations and concerns. Instead of treating resistance as a force to be overcome, managers may decide to treat resistance as an opportunity to learn from employees and improve the change process.

THEORY INTO PRACTICE

Employee resistance can offer leaders the opportunity to learn.

Not all resistance to change offers an equal opportunity to learn, of course. Eventually, resistance will have to be addressed and overcome. But when? At what point does resistance to change stop presenting an opportunity to learn and start being a barrier to overcome? We will address that question in Chapter 2. For now, let us understand employee resistance as a form of expression that is not always a bad thing and that needs to be considered and understood by change leaders.

THEORY INTO PRACTICE

There comes a point in the change process where employee resistance will need to be addressed and overcome.

Employee Participation Builds Support for Change

Change imposed from "above"—top executives telling employees that they must alter their behaviors in order to implement a new strategy or perform better under the old strategy—is likely to engender resistance. Employees often feel that they are being excluded from discussions of how best to respond to competitive pressures.

Just as there are ways in which a change implementation process may inadvertently fuel resistance to change, there are also techniques for building support. **Participation** in the process of defining problems and designing solutions will help build commitment to the new directions that result from that process.[14] By diagnosing problems, understanding their importance, and being part of the process of formulating solutions, people develop a psychological sense of "ownership" over the outcome. That ownership now creates in employees the heightened motivation to implement change in order to achieve desired goals.[15]

Building a Vocabulary of Change
Participation the process of allowing employees a voice in work-related decisions.

The difficult challenge for managers, then, becomes how and when to engage employees in the process of diagnosis, problem solving, and planning for change.

THEORY INTO PRACTICE

People don't resist change, they resist being changed.

Imposed change encourages resistance. Individuals can feel manipulated, coerced, or even ignored. When people participate in designing change, on the other hand, they are more likely to feel they are making an informed choice about altering their behaviors. Individuals can develop commitment to the choice as well as feeling responsibility for implementing that choice. When people participate in the design of change (in the diagnosis, action planning, and implementation stages), they will be more motivated to alter their behaviors.

And, to emphasize a point made earlier, employee motivation matters. New behaviors will not be sustainable if they have been prompted by manipulation or coercion. Effective change does not seek to fool employees into setting aside their better judgment. Rather, it seeks to encourage employees to find continually new and improved ways of applying their better judgment. How can internal processes be improved? What are customers telling employees about our products and services? How might we eliminate waste and improve quality? To support behaviors that can sustain outstanding performance, effective change efforts avoid manipulation and coercion, aiming instead to enhance employee willingness and ability to contribute their own judgment.

THEORY INTO PRACTICE

Transformational change seeks to motivate employees to change their behaviors; not to force, coerce, or trick them into changing.

Because motivation is internal to each employee, the manager's challenge is complex. The task involves shaping the organizational context in such a way as to encourage and support an internal desire on a large number of employees to alter their behaviors in ways consistent with the shifting demands of the new strategy.

Building a Vocabulary of Change
Trigger event a shift in the environment that precipitates a need for organizational change.

TRIGGER EVENTS AND CHANGE

Organizational change is typically initiated in response to a **trigger event**—a shift in the environment that creates a need for altered strategies and new patterns of employee behavior. For Nokia, the trigger event was the launch and overwhelming public enthusiasm for the iPhone. Often, the arrival of a new CEO—Anne Mulcahy at Xerox, Patricia Woertz at Archer Daniels Midland, and Carlos Ghosn at Nisan, for example—triggers a demand for change. The world-wide recession of 2008–2009 triggered a requirement in a wide range of companies—financial, manufacturing, service providers among them—to reconsider their strategies.

Trigger events, says Lynn Isabella, "are so named because their magnitude and potential for organizational as well as personal impact set into motion a series of mental shifts as individuals strive to understand and redefine a situation. By their very nature, they unbalance established routines and evoke conscious thought on the part of organizational members. They stir up feelings and emotions that come to affect people's reactions to the change. In short, trigger events bring people's mindsets into the arena of change."[16]

THEORY INTO PRACTICE

Trigger events, either external or internal to an organization, precipitate the need to alter behavioral patterns of employees.

GOING GLOBAL AND THE REQUIREMENT FOR ORGANIZATIONAL CHANGE

When organizations "go global," they may mean one or more of several changes:

- They may seek to outsource certain activities that had previously been performed in the home country. For example, a company moves its customer Help Desk operation from the United States to India.
- They may seek to enter new, nondomestic markets. For example, a U.K.-based grocery store chain seeks to open outlets in the United States.

- They may seek nondomestic suppliers for needed raw materials. For example, a food processor in Russia seeks wheat supplies in the United States.
- They may seek strategic alliances with related companies in other countries. For example, a French-based car manufacturer enters into an alliance with a large Japanese company.
- They may seek to locate research and development activities in multiple nations as a way of better understanding the needs of nondomestic customers. For example, a Brazilian-based jet manufacturer opens a market research office in the United States.

These are among the numerous variations on what it might mean for an organization to "go global." As varied as the opportunities are, what they all have in common is this: going global will require organizational change.

THEORY INTO PRACTICE

"Going global" takes many forms, and they all require organizational change.

Building a Vocabulary of Change
Psychic distance differences in culture, language, and the political–economic–legal infrastructure of countries that add to the complexity of managing across national borders.

Anytime an organization embraces multiple national cultures, it adds a degree of sociocultural diversity and uncertainty. This complexity is the result of what is known as **psychic distance.**[17] Differences exist not only in culture, but also in language, and the political–economic–legal infrastructure of countries. In later chapters, we will discuss the specific implications for organizational change when multiple countries are involved. The point now is that organizations will need to develop new structures, new ways of thinking, and new ways of behaving if they are going to be successful operating in a global arena.

Conclusion

Strategic responsiveness to a dynamic environment requires organizational change. Change, however, is not a singular concept. The three faces of change suggest that change leaders face options. Turnaround addresses the need to improve the balance sheet. Tools and techniques focus on improved processes. By themselves, however, neither will achieve the full, intended impact of strategic renewal. Effective change will also require attention to employee behaviors—patterns of action and interaction—no less than financial and technological effectiveness.

Not all employees will greet change efforts with equal enthusiasm. Employee resistance arises from a number of sources, some internal to individual employees and others externally located in the implementation processes of change leaders. By allowing employees to participate in the formulation of change plans, however, leaders will increase employee ownership over and support for those efforts.

Trigger events—either discontinuities in a firm's competitive environment, new leadership, or a combination of the two—precipitate the requirement for strategic renewal and organizational change. One of the most common trigger events is when organizations go global, dealing with people and organizations in multiple cultures.

Recognizing the requirement for change and being able to manage change effectively are, of course, two different matters. Chapter 2 will examine the theoretical underpinnings of effective change implementation.

Discussion Questions

1. Review Exhibit 1-1. Select one of the companies. Based on the brief statement of its renewed strategy (or research the company for further details), think about how patterns of employee behavior will have to change.
2. Explore the challenges facing Stephen Elop at Nokia. What can he do to revitalize the company in the U.S. smartphone market?
3. What are the three approaches to organizational change? In what ways are they different, and in what ways do they overlap?
4. Identify the main external forces triggering the requirement for organizational change. Pick any three and discuss how they might necessitate behavioral change on the part of organizational employees.
5. Why is motivation important to behavioral change? How might leaders approach change differently if they are trying to motivate employees to change rather than forcing employees to change?

Case Discussion

Read "The ASDA Way of Working" and prepare answers to the following questions:

1. What are the types of changes that Archie Norman needs to undertake at ASDA?
2. Referring to Exhibit 1-3, what faces of change does ASDA need to engage?
3. What actions can Norman and his top management team take to build employee motivation to engage in change?

THE ASDA WAY OF WORKING

ASDA, the grocery store chain that Archie Norman had just been hired to lead, teetered on the edge on bankruptcy.[18] While ASDA had enjoyed a long run of success in the United Kingdom, upscale competitors and down-market deep discounters had sharply eroded its customer base. Norman, an outsider to ASDA who had never run any retailing operation, believed that ASDA could not afford the luxury of piecemeal or incremental improvement. Everything about the organization—from the way they purchased and displayed products to the way store managers interacted with shop floor employees—would have to change. *Everything.*

Company Background

With 65,000 employees in 205 ASDA stores and another 2,000 at corporate headquarters, ASDA was the fourth largest grocery store chain in the United Kingdom. ASDA enjoyed annual sales of $6 billion[†] and claimed 8 percent of the supermarket business, ranking fourth in market share.

Starting in the late 1960s, ASDA pioneered the concept of large supermarkets located outside of downtown areas with expansive parking lots and low prices. Flourishing particularly in working-class areas, ASDA became

[†]All figures are given in equivalent U.S. dollars.

known as a blue-collar store, specializing in low prices in a warehouse like atmosphere. ("Pile it high and sell it cheap" was a phrase commonly associated with this type of operation.) The demographic of their customer base was decidedly "down market." In that niche, ASDA was quite successful, operating without any real competition. The larger grocery store chains vied for more upscale (i.e., wealthy) customers and simply could not compete with ASDA on price.

ASDA's problems began when top management embarked on two equally disastrous paths. First, they diverted much of the profit from the grocery operations into nonfood acquisitions: retail operations such as furniture and carpeting. And second, management moved to change their customer base from blue-collar to more upscale shoppers. As part of that upscale strategy, ASDA moved out of their traditional blue-collar strongholds into wealthier suburban locations. That move had two negative effects:

1. In the wealthy suburbs, it placed them in competition with chains not burdened with the reputation of being blue-collar warehouse stores.
2. In their traditional working-class areas, they allowed competitors to steal market share from the very blue-collar base that ASDA seemed to be abandoning.

Top management exacerbated the problem by spending lavishly on themselves: corporate jets, high-style corporate offices, and the like. Soon ASDA products were pricier than its competitors' were. ASDA began to spiral downward. While the company borrowed money to expand into new markets and open new stores, same-store sales declined and overall growth slowed. In response, ASDA's board of directors fired its chief executive and brought in Archie Norman to turn ASDA around.

Enter Archie Norman

Thirty-seven-year-old Archie Norman had joined the McKinsey & Company consulting organization after receiving an MBA in the United States to work in the company's retail division. From McKinsey he moved to a large retail operation where he served as CFO. Norman arrived at ASDA with no specific experience in the grocery business and no general management experience aside from his graduate school training.

What Norman found when he arrived at ASDA was complete demoralization of the workforce; a highly politicized central headquarters; people caught up in their "chimneys"—operations—people did not talk to the trading people, and nobody listened to marketing. It was a place, noted one observer, completely bereft of any notion of where it was headed or how it might weather the crisis. And that crisis was deeper and more profound than Norman had expected:

> We had so much debt we thought we would be in breach of our loan covenants shortly. Our sales were running at 2 percent below the industry like for like, and the trend was heading south. We had, if anything, worse value than our competitors. And while everyone was very loyal about it, morale was actually quite poor.

Norman inaugurated his intervention by reaching an understanding with his board of directors. The turnaround would not happen overnight, they agreed. If the board would tolerate Norman's investments in renewing the chain, he would deliver significant return by the end of the third year:

> I told the stockholders and the market analysts, that I had a three-year plan that ASDA should be returned to profitability and growth within that time frame. The stockholders agreed to let me make short-term sacrifices for long-term profitability.

Building a Top Team

Norman immediately set out to attract other outsiders to the top management team. Over a six-month period, he replaced two of his three direct reports,[‡] creating a team that consisted of:

- Allen Leighton, vice president, marketing
- Phil Cox, chief financial officer
- Tony Campbell, vice president, trading

Of his three direct reports, only Campbell was a holdover from the previous ASDA regime. His past position had been vice president of operations. None of the new hires had any previous retail experience.

Among his direct reports, Allen Leighton emerged as the first among equals. He was friendly, outgoing, dynamic, expansive, bright, and creative—a complement to the generally more cerebral and contained Norman. Top managers suggested that nothing of significance occurred in the organization without the direct involvement and approval of Norman and/or Leighton.

The First Six Months

Norman's first task was to pull the organization back from disaster. "Archie had to convince people that there was a problem," said Phil Cox, "that our poor performance wasn't just a momentary hiccup." In speech after speech, to employees as well as investors, Norman laid out the details of what he referred to as ASDA's "dark moment." He ignored frequent advice that he soften his blunt message of "gloom and doom." A regional manager shook his head after one such speech, admitting:

> None of us understood how serious our financial difficulties were. When Archie brought all this out into the open, it finally dawned on people just how close to the edge we'd been. It became clear that we couldn't just wave a magic wand and make all things right.

In the first six months of Norman's tenure, all of the top management team took up residence in a local hotel. They were often joined by Chrispin Tweddle, a consultant hired by Norman with considerable retail experience. During the day,

[‡]Before walking in the door on his first day, Norman had decided to fire the current CFO and had already reached an agreement with Phil Cox to join the company.

Cox focused on ASDA's financial crisis,[§] while Norman toured the stores, talking to employees at all levels and taking copious notes. Then, the team would sit up together until past midnight talking about a vision for a new ASDA.

Every discussion was based on the shared assumption that the total organization was dysfunctional. Said Norman:

> We wouldn't survive if we simply created a little change. We had to revitalize the entire organization. We had to take the organization paradigm, which was over here, and move it over there. We assumed that however the organization worked when we got here was wrong.

In particular, the team believed that they needed to address ASDA's stovepiped functional culture, which made companywide collaboration a virtual impossibility. Observed Norman:

> The whole place was dysfunctional. The top management never met together except once a month at a board meeting. They never talked from week to week. And the whole organization ran down these functional pipelines.

Renewal

The process of change, which the top team came to refer to as "renewal," would occur within the 205 stores. But the team provided guidance to the renewal process in three forms: a statement of corporate strategy, an articulation of company values, and a blueprint for what came to be known as the ASDA Way of Working.

Strategic Renewal

Norman called on consultants from McKinsey to help him and his team formulate a new strategic position. Their deliberations started with gaining a thorough understanding of the grocery industry and ASDA's position in it. They then formulated a strategy statement: "We will supply the weekly shopping needs of ordinary working families."

Culture Change

The team realized early on that they would have to do more than change the old ASDA culture; they would have to shatter it and then rebuild it from the groundup. To set the parameters for that new culture, they drew up a statement of company values, plus a set of operational concepts that became known as the ASDA Way of Working. Store-based renewal would flow from a few key concepts: greater autonomy to store management in making operational decisions and, within the stores, self-managed autonomous teams focusing on particular product lines such as produce, bakery goods, and so forth.

[§]A number of steps were taken to raise money. Nonfood operations were either sold off or, failing that, shut down; head count at corporate headquarters was reduced by 30 percent; in-store middle-manager positions were cut by 10 percent; and an 18-month pay freeze was initiated for all employees.

In a speech laying out the ASDA Way of Working to store managers, Norman said, "I see a day when our stores consist of clusters of businesses, each with their own profit-and-loss responsibilities." A store manager, who had been with ASDA in the pre-Norman era, reflected on the message he heard concerning the ASDA Way of Working: "What they told me was to involve everybody in everything. As long as you're doing that, you're going to get the best out of people."

This sense of empowerment and responsiveness "will be a unique source of advantage," insisted Norman, "against the militarized and straight-jacketed competition."

Moving Renewal into the Stores

With his top management team in place to provide a general sense of direction, Norman turned his attention to the 205 stores. Renewal must become a reality within those stores, and Norman thought about how to proceed. As he considered his options for action, Norman analyzed several key issues.

1. Because ASDA's previous management had underinvested in the stores, physical plant had deteriorated precipitously. ASDA's new management estimated that each store required an average investment of $3.25 million to become a state-of-the-art facility, but they wondered about the connection between the required plant retooling and the cultural upheaval implied by the value statement and the ASDA Way of Working. Should the two processes be coupled or separated? If handled together, would physical revamping and cultural renewal simply be too much change for any one store to handle?
2. Norman wondered whether somebody—either an individual or a group—should be assigned responsibility for oversight and coordination of the renewal efforts within the stores. Or was ASDA likely to achieve greater innovation by allowing each store to finds its own way to define and apply renewal?
3. While Norman had shaken up his top management group, he knew that the functional stovepipes that had prevented collaboration in the past still existed. Could real innovation occur within a functional structure? How would he address the lingering constraints still being felt because of the company's past culture?
4. Ultimately, Norman knew everything about how the stores operated would have to change. But how much change should occur and how fast? Could he focus on all the stores at once, or should he concentrate on a small number of pilot stores?
5. Part of the concern over the pace of renewal had to do with the depth of managerial talent—or, more precisely, the lack of depth—at ASDA. At the corporate level, the 16 managers who reported directly to members of the top management team were all ASDA "veterans." The same could be said of the 205 store managers. Could individuals who had survived, or even thrived, under the old culture make the transition required of the new strategy, values, and way of working? Conversely, large-scale termination at the managerial level might prove disastrous: depriving ASDA of much needed grocery industry experience, undermining already shaky morale, fostering

risk-averse behavior, and stifling innovation. Plus, there was hardly a large queue of talented managers seeking employment at ASDA.

Finally, Norman wondered about his own role in the renewal effort. Already his colleagues on the top management team had reached consensus on his personal management style, and "controlling" was the most frequently applied label. Among the evaluations offered:

- He must have learned the lesson as a young boy that if you want to do anything right, you have to do it yourself.
- In truth, and I'm sure Archie would admit this, his preferred style is a controlling style. The issue of devolving power does not sit comfortably with him.
- The only thing you will never hear Archie say is, "I think you're wrong, but do it anyway."

Norman offered the following self-assessment:

> I do believe I give people the right to argue and challenge. But I still make decisions, and I don't want to delude people into thinking I don't. I simply won't tolerate any deviation around basic values and strategy.

While expressing his desire to avoid the "cult of personality" at ASDA, Norman realized that he would play a large role in determining the shape and direction of the renewal effort. The challenge going forward was to ensure that role be positive and productive.

Endnotes

1. Information for this case comes from Kevin J. O'Brien, "Nokia Dominates, but Rivals Insist that Could Change," *New York Times* (Feb. 13, 2008); Kevin J. O'Brien, "Nokia Plans to Slash 1,700 Jobs amid Sluggish Sales of Cellphones," *New York Times* (Mar. 18, 2009); Kevin J. O'Brien, "Nokia Tries to Undo Blunders in US," *New York Times* (Oct. 19, 2009); Nelson D. Schwartz, "Can Nokia Recapture Its Glory Days?" *New York Times* (Dec. 13, 2009); "The Curse of the Alien Boss," *The Economist* (Aug. 7, 2010); Kevin J. O'Brien, "Nokia Seeks to Reconnect with the US Market," *New York Times* (Aug. 15, 2010); Kevin J. O'Brien, "Nokia Executive to Leave; Hints of Chairman's Exit," *New York Times* (Sept. 13, 2010); Kevin J. O'Brien, "Nokia's New Chief Faces Culture of Complacency," *New York Times* (Sept. 26, 2010); and Kevin J. O'Brien, "Nokia to Cut Jobs as It Tries to Catch Up to Rivals," *New York Times* (Oct. 21, 2010).
2. The rise of Nokia as a world leader in cellphones is analyzed in Yves Doz, José Santos, and Peter Williamson, *From Global to Metanational: How Companies Win in the Knowledge Economy* (Boston, MA: Harvard Business School Publishing, 2001).
3. D. A. Nadler, *Discontinuous Change: Leading Organizational Transformation* (San Francisco, CA: Jossey-Bass, 1995).
4. Quoted in Tom Arango, "A Hot Social Networking Site Cools as Facebook Flourishes," *New York Times* (Jan. 12, 2011), p. A1.
5. M. Hughes, "The Tools and Techniques of Change Management," *Journal of Change Management* 7 (Mar. 2007), pp. 37–49.
6. D. Ulrich and D. Lake, *Organizational Capacity: Competing from the Inside Out* (New York: Wiley, 1990); J. Arthur, "The Link Between Business Strategy and Industrial Relations Systems in American Steel Minimills," *Industrial and Labor*

Relations Review 45 (1992), pp. 448–506; A. A. Lado and M. C. Wilson, "Human Resource Systems and Sustained Competitive Advantage: A Competency-Based Perspective," *Academy of Management Review* 19 (1994), pp. 699–727; M. A. Huselid, "The Impact of Human Resource Management Practices on Turnover, Productivity, and Corporate Financial Performance," *Academy of Management Journal* 38 (1995), pp. 635–677; J. J. Lawler, R. W. Anderson, and R. J. Buckles, "Human Resource Management and Organizational Effectiveness," in G. R. Ferris, S. D. Rosen, and D. T. Barnum, eds., *Handbook of Human Resource Management* (Cambridge: Blackwell, 1995), pp. 630–649; J. T. Delaney and M. A. Huselid, "The Impact of Human Resource Management Practices on Perceptions of Organizational Performance," *Academy of Management Journal* 39 (1996), pp. 949–969; S. A. Snell, M. A. Youndt, and P. M. Wright, "Establishing a Framework for Research in Strategic Human Resource Management: Merging Resource Theory and Organizational Learning," in G. R. Ferris, ed., *Research in Personnel and Human Resource Management*, Vol. 14 (Greenwich, CT: JAI Press, 1996), pp. 61–90; J. E. Delery and D. H. Doty, "Modes of Theorizing in Strategic Human Resource Management: Tests of Universalistic, Contingency, and Configurational Performance," *Academy of Management Journal* 39 (1996), pp. 802–835; M. A. Huselid, S. E. Jackson, and R. S. Schuler, "Technical and Strategic Human Resource Management Effectiveness As Determinants of Firm Performance," *Academy of Management Journal* 40 (1997), pp. 171–188; David Ulrich, "Intellectual Capital = Competence × Commitment," *Sloan Management Review* 39 (1998), pp. 15–26.

7. D. R. Denison, *Corporate Culture and Organizational Effectiveness* (New York: Wiley, 1990).
8. J. P. Kotter and J. L. Heskett, *Corporate Culture and Performance* (New York: Free Press, 1992); Jim Collins and Jerry I. Porras, *Built to Last: Successful Habits of Visionary Companies* (New York: HarperCollins, 2004).
9. This story is reported in Adam Lashinsky, "Chaos by Decision," *Fortune*, October 2, 2006, p. 88.
10. This definition of resistance is from Kurt Lewin, "Group Decision and Social Change," in G. E. Swanson, T. M. Newcombe, and E. L. Hartley, eds., *Readings in Social Psychology*, 2nd edn. (New York: Holt, 1952), pp. 459–473.
11. Several authors have argued for a reconsideration of the meaning of "change resistance," suggesting even that the term "resistance" should be dropped because of its pejorative implications. See, for example, Tony J. Watson, "Group Ideologies and Organizational Change," *Journal of Management Studies* 19 (1982), pp. 259–275; Sandy Kristin Piderit, "Rethinking Resistance and Recognizing Ambivalence: A Multidimensional View of Attitudes Toward an Organizational Change," *Academy of Management Review* 25 (2000), pp. 783–794.
12. That research was highlighted at a session, "Changing Individuals," at the 2007 Academy of Management meetings. See, in particular, Jane D. Parent and D. Anthony Butterfield, "A Model and Test of Individual and Organization Factors Influencing Individual Adaptation to Change."
13. Kenneth E. Hullman, "Scaling the Wall of Resistance," *Training and Development* (Oct. 1995), pp. 15–18.
14. See, for example, L. Coch and J. R. French, "Overcoming Resistance to Change," *Human Relations* 1 (1948), pp. 512–533; Lewin, *Field Theory in Social Science*; R. Likert, *The Human Organization* (New York: McGraw-Hill, 1967); Edwin A. Fleishman, "Attitude versus Skill Factors in Work Productivity," *Personnel Psychology* 18 (1965), pp. 253–266; C. Argyris, *Intervention Theory and Method* (Reading, MA: Addison-Wesley, 1970); W. W. Burke, *Organization Development: Principles and Practices* (Boston: Little, Brown, 1982); F. Heller, E. Pusic, G. Strauss, and B. Wilpert, *Organizational Participation: Myth and Reality* (New York: Oxford University Press, 1998).
15. The connection between employee participation and commitment to change has been demonstrated in Rune Lines, "Influence of Participation in Strategic Change: Resistance, Organizational Commitment and Change Goal Achievement," *Journal of Change Management* 4 (Sept. 2004), pp. 193–215.
16. L. A. Isabella, "Managing the Challenges of Trigger Events: The Mindsets Governing Adaptation to Change," *Business Horizons* 35 (Sept.–Oct. 1992), pp. 59–60.

17. J. Johanson and J. E. Vahlne, "The Internationalization Process of the Firm – A Model of Knowledge Development and Increasing Foreign Market Commitments," *Journal of International Business Studies*, 8 (1977), 22–32; J. Evans and F. T. Mavondo, "Psychic Distance and Organizational Performance: An Empirical Examination of International Retailing Operations," *Journal of International Business Studies*, 33 (2002), 515–532; C. M. P. Sousa and F. Bradley, "Cultural Distance and Psychic Distance: Two Peas in a Pod?" *Journal of International Marketing*, 14 (2006), 49–70.

18. The case is based on research conducted for Bert Spector, *Taking Charge and Letting Go: A Breakthrough Strategy for Creating and Managing the Horizontal Company* (New York: Free Press, 1995).

CHAPTER

2 Theories of Effective Change Implementation

A dynamic competitive environment prompts organizational leaders to alter or transform their strategies. That process of strategic renewal places new expectations on employees at all levels. Behaviors will be altered, some subtly, others fundamentally. Translating renewed strategies into new patterns of behavior—behavior that supports the new strategy and contributes to outstanding performance by the organization—that is, the change implementation challenge.

This chapter will explore theories of implementing change that can be called upon to help guide interventions. In particular, the chapter will:

- Present the three phases of the planned change theory of Kurt Lewin
- Delineate the key insights to effective implementation offered by the field of organizational development (OD)
- Differentiate between content-driven and process-driven change
- Explain an approach to change the management that emphasizes task requirements and performance results
- Offer a framework for change implementation that encompasses multiple theories

First, we will look at an attempt by the director of a university-based hospital to respond to a deep financial crisis. As you read this introductory case, ask yourself:

- What triggered the organizational transformation at Duke University's Children's Hospital?
- How did Jon Meliones build support among employees?
- What behaviors needed to be changed?
- Was it a good idea to start by focusing on a single unit?

TURNAROUND AND TRANSFORMATION AT DUKE UNIVERSITY CHILDREN'S HOSPITAL

In 1996, the 135-bed Duke University Children's Hospital faced a deep financial crisis.[1] Key administrators at the hospital provided the following dire assessment:

> A decrease in Medicaid allowances and an increase in patients with capitated reimbursement* were driving revenues down. Expenses were down as cost per case for children's services ballooned from $10,500 in fiscal year (FY) 93 to $14,889 in FY96. This caused a dramatic reduction in the net margin—from (−)$2 million in FY93 to (−)$11 million in FY96. Programs were slated to be eliminated and services were targeted for reduction. Sales productivity had fallen from the 80th to the 70th percentile range. In addition, patient and staff satisfaction was at an all time low.

Jon Meliones, the hospital's chief medical director, realized that he and fellow hospital executives faced a particular challenge. "No matter how effective the chief executive officer (CEO) and chief operating officer (COO) are," he observed, "they can control only a portion of the components that drive the organization's financial performance." Physicians determined length of stay, drug prescriptions, and tests, while accepting referrals that helped determine revenues. Nurses drove quality. Any effective change would require a united effort among administrators and clinicians.

Meliones led his staff through a diagnosis of the root causes of the hospital's financial crisis. They found a particularly troubling pattern of behavior. "The problem was that our hospital was a collection of fiefdoms," said Meliones. "Each group, from accountants to administrators to clinicians, was focusing on its own individual goal rather than on the organization as a whole." Creating a shared sense of responsibility for the hospital's performance and realigning patterns of behavior would be required.

A team consisting of Meliones, the chief nurse executive, and nurse managers agreed upon an approach that emphasized the interdependence between financial performance and excellence of health care. "We want patients to be happy ... and for them to have the best care," the team concluded. They also adopted a motto for their planned strategic renewal: "No margin, no mission." Excellent patient care *and* excellent financial performance would be the twin hallmarks of the hospital's strategic renewal.

Implementation next moved to a single unit: pediatric intensive care. Meliones and his team worked to operationalize new behaviors through a redesign of roles, responsibilities, and relationships. With the participation of doctors, nurses, the medical staff, and even accountants, the team redesigned how

*Under capitated reimbursement, insurance companies reimburse providers at a fixed amount, typically based on some calculation of the average cost of a procedure.

all members of the unit would undertake their responsibilities. The unit called on a popular measurement tool, the balanced scorecard that looks not just at financial outcomes but also customer perceptions, internal business processes, and the ability of an organization to learn and grow, to help reinforce desired new behaviors.[2] Meliones and his leadership team returned the hospital to profitability in three years.

THEORIES OF CHANGE IMPLEMENTATION

Organizational leaders, such as Jon Meliones at Duke Children's Hospital, have multiple tools and levers at their disposal that they can apply in pursuit of effective change implementation. The question that needs to be addressed to understand effective change implementation is not just *what* levers can be applied—diagnosis, cross-functional teams, and measurement systems, in Meliones' case—but also in what order or *sequence* should those levers be called upon.

Look carefully at the sequence of Meliones' interventions:

1. Involving his staff in a shared diagnosis of the root causes of the hospital's financial woes.
2. Putting together a cross-functional team—doctors, nurses, medical staff, and accountants—with the goal of figuring out how to provide both excellent patient care and excellent financial performance.
3. Piloting change within the pediatric intensive care unit.
4. Redesigning the roles, responsibilities, and relationships of all unit members.
5. Reinforcing the new behaviors with a new measurement system, the balanced scorecard.

That sequence, repeated in unit after unit, effectively transformed the hospital over a three-year period.

Would Meliones have been equally—or even more—effective if he had altered the sequence, say, by introducing a balanced scorecard earlier in the effort? To seek answers to the all-important sequencing question, we can turn to the body of theories that has been developed concerning organizational and behavioral change.

THEORY INTO PRACTICE

*Effective change involves both content—*what *is being changed—and process—*how *the changes are being implemented.*

Kurt Lewin's Field Theory in Social Science

The scientific study of change implementation can be traced back to the work of psychologist Kurt Lewin. In the aftermath of World War II, Lewin published two pathbreaking essays, "Behavior and Development as a Function of the Total Situation" (1946) and "Frontiers in Group Dynamics" (1947).[3]

It may be hard to think that a social scientist working over 60 years ago could have anything relevant and important to say about today's organizations. But Lewin offered two insights that, to this day, shape our understanding of how to alter patterns of behavior.

First, he highlighted the important, even decisive role that *context* plays in shaping individual behaviors. And second, he argued that the only way to motivate an individual to change her pattern of behavior is to create a sense of disequilibrium or *dissatisfaction with the status quo* within that individual. To fully appreciate Lewin's contribution, it is worth spending some time looking at each of these ideas.

CHANGING BEHAVIORS BY CHANGING CONTEXT We made the point in Chapter 1 that companies often call on organizational context to help shape employee behaviors. The leaders of Google, as we saw, attempted to create a context that encouraged risk-taking and tolerated failure in order to spur creativity.

Lewin made the same point about context. The behavior of an individual within a group setting—social groups were the context that Lewin was concerned with—is shaped both by that individual's psychology and the group setting or context in which she finds herself.

Lewin captured this duality in a simple formula: $B = f(P, E)$. Behavior (B) is a function of the person herself (P) and the environmental context (E) in which that person operates. Person and context are interdependent variables shaping behavior.

The question Lewin addressed was: How can that context be changed? To start, Lewin insisted that what does *not* work is telling people to change. Giving a speech about the need for change will not motivate new behaviors.

You might be able to imagine what such a speech about the need for change would sound like. An executive explains to employees that they need to be more responsive to customers, coordinate better with international operations, bring new products to market more quickly, work more effectively across functions, develop products that are eco-friendly, and so forth. That executive might be an extraordinarily effective communicator. Nonetheless, the likelihood that telling people about the need for behavioral change will lead to real and sustained change is quite small.

When leaders rely on "lectures" to drive change—in today's organizational context, that may mean speeches, small group meetings, PowerPoint presentations, video conferences, chat rooms, and so forth—they fail to take into account the power of context in reinforcing the status quo. In Lewin's view, getting group members to change their behaviors, and having those new behaviors become lasting rather than fleeting, involves breaking a "social habit."

To make matters more challenging, group members tend to assign *positive value* to those existing social habits. Those positive values become the norms that support behavioral habits. **Norms** are shared expectations of how group members ought to behave and come to be viewed by group members as good things: standards to be cherished and upheld.

Building a Vocabulary of Change
Norms shared expectations of how group members ought to behave.

Whatever an individual may glean from a speech, no matter how well delivered that speech may be, he is not likely to alter his behaviors. The positive value associated with the existing social arrangements continues to exert a powerful force on the individual, "keeping the individual in line with the standards of the group."[4] The old habits have not been broken; the positive value associated with past behaviors still exerts powerful pressure; so individual behavior returns to the status quo.

THEORY INTO PRACTICE

Telling employees why they need to change will not build motivation to change; it is necessary, but not sufficient.

The next important question, therefore, is how to exert a force that will alter not just the individual but also the social context of that individual.

CREATING DISSATISFACTION Leaders seeking to implement organizational change are often surprised by the degree of complacency they face. Why are employees clinging to the status quo—doing things the way they always have—even in the face of declining organizational performance? Isn't it *obvious* that we need to change?

When Carlos Ghosn took over leadership at Nissan Motors, he was puzzled by the apparent lack of urgency among company employees. At that moment, Nissan was $19.9 billion in debt with annual losses exceeding $250 million. Despite the obviously unacceptable level of performance, Ghosn encountered resigned acceptance among Nissan executives.

"For a company that has been losing money for seven years out of eight," he observed, "there is not enough of a sense of urgency. People should be banging their heads on the walls everywhere."[5] Instead, Ghosn observed a disturbing lack of dissatisfaction with the status quo.

THEORY INTO PRACTICE

Don't assume that poor organizational performance will create an urgent need to change within a company.

Potential change leaders are often stumped by the same situation that greeted Ghosn when he first arrived at Nissan: why, in the face of such apparently obvious distress, do employees remain attached to the status quo? Lewin had an explanation for that.

Group membership often confers a positive sense of belonging to members; they *like* being part of the group, accept the group's norms, and are pleased with what the group has been able to accomplish in the past. And the more they assign positive value to group membership and group norms, the greater the resistance will be on the part of individual group members to alter those norms.

Group membership creates a kind of inertia, or at least reluctance, to change what it is about that group that seems so positive. That is the phenomenon we often refer to as "complacency." The task of motivating individuals to alter their established behaviors, then, is a complex one. That is the challenge for leaders seeking change.

The act of announcing the need for change, of proclaiming new goals, of presenting a rational argument for how the changes will improve performance simply will not motivate behavioral change. What is needed, Lewin argued, is a kind of deliberate "emotional stir-up," a powerful intervention designed to "open the shell of complacency" and "unfreeze" the existent equilibrium.

THEORY INTO PRACTICE

To break the "social habits" that support existing patterns of behaviors, start with creating dissatisfaction, disequilibrium, and discomfort.

To be effective, then, a change leader's initial task is to create what Lewin called **unfreezing**. Look at the approach taken by Jon Meliones at the Children's Hospital. Rather than lecturing employees on why they needed to change, he involved them in a diagnostic process, allowing them to learn—just as he had—the financial situation of the hospital and to shape the appropriate response.

Building a Vocabulary of Change
Unfreezing the first stage in Lewin's change model in which group members become dissatisfied with the status quo.

Imagine if Meliones had, instead, given a talk about the dire need for change, supplemented with elaborate PowerPoints. Then, he would have told employees how they needed to alter their behaviors, and work together in different ways: doctors, nurses, medical technicians, even accountants pulling together to ensure outstanding performance. He would have then explained why he felt the balanced scorecard was an excellent tool for measuring their progress and reinforcing their new behaviors. Had he approached change implementation that way, he may well have faced a great deal of initial resistance, making the unfreezing stage extremely difficult to implement.

The second stage of Lewin's model involves **moving**, wherein members of the group move from one set of behaviors to another. Those new behaviors, in Lewin's view, must become permanent, for at least a desired period of time. It is the **refreezing** stage where a newly created equilibrium "is made relatively secure against change."[6] Refreezing is the stage where structures and systems align with and reinforce new behaviors. This is the stage at which measurement tools like the balanced scorecard—there are many others that we will discuss in Chapter 6—can be called upon to reinforce new behaviors.

Building a Vocabulary of Change
Moving the second stage in Lewin's change model in which group members alter their patterns of behavior.

Building a Vocabulary of Change
Refreezing the final stage in Lewin's change model in which group members institutionalize the new patterns of behavior into a new status quo.

LEWIN'S CONTRIBUTION TO CHANGE IMPLEMENTATION Lewin is best known for his three stages of change implementation: unfreezing, moving, and refreezing (summarized in Exhibit 2-1). Equally important is Lewin's recognition that the most effective way to manage behavioral change among individual members of a group is to work *first* on changing the group's norms, then focus on individual behaviors. If "one succeeds in changing group standards, this same force field will tend to facilitate changing the individual and will tend to stabilize the individual conduct on the new group level."[7] Context exerts a powerful shaping force on individual behaviors.

Lewin urged a kind of implementation sequence. To create sustainable behavioral change, organizational leaders need to work both at the individual

EXHIBIT 2-1 Implementation Implications of Lewin's Change Model.

State 1: Unfreezing	Stage 2: Moving	Stage 3: Refreezing
Create dissatisfaction with the status quo	Redesign organizational roles, responsibilities, and relationships	Align pay/reward systems
Benchmark operations against other companies	Train for newly required skill	Re-engineer measurement/ control systems
Diagnose internal barriers to improved performance	Promote supporters/ remove resisters	Create new organization structures

and contextual levels. There is a far greater leverage to be gained, however, from *first* working at the contextual level.

The positive social values created by the new equilibrium will motivate individuals to adapt to the new norms. If, instead, leaders first focus on the individual level, they risk undermining their best intentions. No matter how much impact they have on changing the expectations and behaviors of individuals, those new expectations and behaviors will not endure as long as the old equilibrium continues to exert a powerful and attractive force.

THEORY INTO PRACTICE

In order to implement change, target group norms first and then focus on individual behaviors.

Lewin's focus was on behavior within groups rather than on organizations in their totality. His approach does not transfer in its entirety to the current work of business organizations. For example, his linear approach—first unfreeze, then move, and finally refreeze—underestimates the potential for complex group dynamics to shift significantly during the intervention process. Additionally, his notion of refreezing assumes that a group will return to a stable state once the change intervention has passed. In fact, highly dynamic environments exert constant demand for adaptation and change.[8] Nonetheless, Lewin's attention to both the impact of context on behaviors and the requirement to create disequilibrium in order to motivate behavioral change continues to inform current theories of effective change implementation.

Building a Vocabulary of Change
Organizational development (OD) an approach to organizational effectiveness that calls on the fields of behavioral and social sciences to provide guidance to planned change efforts.

ORGANIZATION DEVELOPMENT AND CHANGE IMPLEMENTATION

Lewin's work represents an early foray by behavioral scientists in the world of organizational behavior and change management. The field of **organizational development (OD)** soon coalesced around emergent learnings from the behavioral and social sciences (mainly psychology, sociology, and systems dynamics) to inform approaches to planned organizational change. OD offers a complex and systemic perspective on how and why people behave and organizations operate. For that reason, OD provides particular insight into the process of changing people's behavior and organizations' operations.

Although different theorists and practitioners have offered their own insights into these matters, ten key perspectives and assumptions—summarized in Exhibit 2-2—underlie the field.[9] Three insights in particular help advance an understanding of effective change implementation.

EXHIBIT 2-2 Ten Defining Perspectives of Organizational Development.

Perspective	Underlying Assumptions
1. Systems perspective	Outstanding performance depends on interactions between and among the multiple elements of organization; between the people, processes, structure, and values of the organization; and between the organization and its external environment.
2. Alignment perceptive	The effectiveness of organizations will be determined by a state of congruence between people, process, structure, values, and environment.
3. Participation perspective	People will become more committed to implementing solutions if they have been involved in the problem-solving process.
4. Social capital perspective	To achieve outstanding performance, organizational leaders seek to create a network of interdependent relationships that provides the basis for trust, cooperation, and collective action.
5. Teamwork perspective	Accepting shared purpose and responsibility for interdependent tasks enhances coordination, commitment, and creativity and supports outstanding performance.
6. Multiple stakeholder perspective	Outstanding performance requires that organizational leaders balance the expectations of multiple stakeholders: shareholders, employees, customers, suppliers, host community, labor unions, trade associations, governments, etc.
7. Problem-solving perspective	Conflicts over task issues can increase the quality of decisions if they occur in an environment of collaboration and trust.
8. Open communications perspective	Open and candid communication, especially upward in the hierarchy, creates the opportunity for learning and development while building trust and collaboration.
9. Evolution/revolution perspective	Organizations must develop competencies to engage in both incremental (evolutionary) and fundamental (revolutionary) change.
10. Process facilitation perspective	Individuals who reside outside of the organizational hierarchy can become both facilitators and teachers of effective implementation processes in partnership with organizational members.

Building a Vocabulary of Change
Open system an organism or entity that exists in a constant interactive state with its external environment.

ORGANIZATIONS ARE OPEN SYSTEMS OD sees the organization as an **open system**: a unit that exists in constant interaction with its external environment and between its own internal elements. Effectiveness in an open system arises not just out of the actions of employees but also out of *inter*actions that occur at multiple levels:

- Between the personalities and activities of various employees
- Between employees and the requirements of their tasks
- Between the tasks and the culture of the organization
- Between the culture and the strategy of the organization
- Between the strategy of the organization and its external environment

Organizational effectiveness is best achieved when a state of fit or congruence exists between various elements of the open system (see Exhibit 2-3).

THEORY INTO ACTION

Performance problems often reside in the hand-offs between employees, between tasks, between functions, and between units; these are the problems to be targeted first for change.

EXHIBIT 2-3
A Congruence Model of Effectiveness.

Internal Context
- Organizational purpose
- Strategy
- Business model
- Organizational design

External Environment
- Customer, employee, and investor expectations
- Social/cultural forces
- Technological changes
- Labor market shifts
- Government regulation
- World events

Organizational Effectiveness

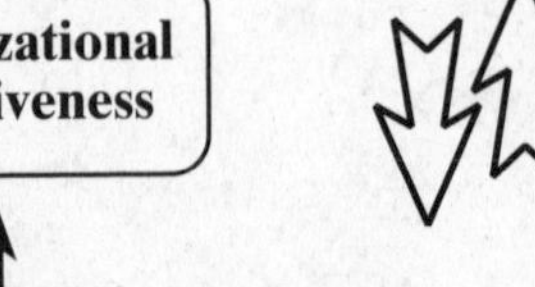

Patterns of Employee Behavior
- Enactment of roles and responsibilities
- Process of interaction among employees

A view of organizations as open systems emphasizes **alignment** of the internal dynamics of an organization (how employees act and interact) with the external marketplace in which the organization lives and competes. Alignment is a state of congruence between organizational sub-elements and their environment. Because the external environment changes, elements of the system must respond.

Building a Vocabulary of Change
Alignment the degree of congruence or compatibility between and among various elements of a system.

ORGANIZATIONS SERVE MULTIPLE STAKEHOLDERS OD assumes a multiple stakeholder perspective. **Stakeholders** are individuals or groups that have a *stake* in how the organization is doing. Those who have a financial investment in a company possess a legitimate interest in its performance, to be sure. So do employees, not to mention customers and suppliers. The host community, whose economy is impacted by the company's performance and who share an ecosystem with that company, also has a legitimate interest in how the company is performing.

Building a Vocabulary of Change
Stakeholders individuals or groups who lay legitimate claim to the performance of the organization.

The multiple-stakeholder perspective represents, in part, an ethical view of the role of business organizations in a community's life. Businesses, in that view, do not sit above or apart from other stakeholders; they must instead play a responsible citizenship role.

The multiple-stakeholder view also represents a perspective on effectiveness. A key source of outstanding performance lies in the willingness of organizational leaders to commit time, energy, and resources to tending to the interests of multiple stakeholders. That commitment translates into a responsive, adaptive organization capable of sustaining outstanding performance in a dynamic environment.

THEORY INTO PRACTICE

If leaders are successful at aligning the interests of multiple stakeholders—shareholders, employees, customers, suppliers, the host community, and so forth—they can contribute to outstanding performance.

DEAL WITH CONFLICT THROUGH PROBLEM SOLVING, OPENNESS, AND TRUST *Don't argue. Go along. Don't stir the pot. Get on board. Be a team player.* All of these expressions, and others you have surely heard, represent a particular view about conflict and its role in organizational life. Conflict is disruptive and dysfunction. Avoid it or soothe over it.

OD takes a fundamentally different view; it is that conflict, when managed properly, can improve effectiveness, increase innovation, and enhance adaptiveness. Not all conflict is desirable; interpersonal conflict based on personalities can be harmful. But conflict about how best to perform tasks can have a positive value on an organization.

Conflict can, for example, improve innovation by highlighting a diversity of viewpoints. Additionally, conflict can encourage individuals to articulate their personal points of view and assumptions while considering the viewpoints and assumptions of others. The potential benefits, therefore, involve both an enhanced grounding in reality and an increased opportunity for creativity.[10]

THEORY INTO PRACTICE

Don't shy away from conflict. As individuals articulate and analyze differences, they can improve organizational effectiveness.

Not all approaches to conflict produce equally desirable outcomes. Avoiding, accommodating, or even compromising when faced with conflicts around how best to perform the tasks of the organization will suboptimize the ability of organizational members to work together while achieving realistic and creative solutions. Collaboration, in which conflicting parties combine advocacy for a particular position while inquiring into the legitimate and conflicting views of others, leads to both superior solutions as well as commitment on the part of participants to implement that solution.[11]

ORGANIZATIONAL DEVELOPMENT'S CONTRIBUTION TO CHANGE IMPLEMENTATION The insights offered by OD can help leaders implement behavioral change in a manner that is both effective and sustainable. The major perspectives and assumptions of the field suggest that interventions that target just one aspect of an organization—say, its structures or its pay systems or its work processes—will likely fail to deliver the hoped-for performance improvements.

Because organizations are highly interactive systems, the keys to outstanding performance reside not in any one independent component of the organization but rather at the interface between many interdependent factors. Piecemeal approaches to change will likely fail, especially over the long run, because they target discrete units or issues rather than focusing on the "joints" of the organization, the places where organizational processes and activities come together.[12]

Additionally, OD points to the importance of an implementation process that builds a sense of ownership: trust, open communication, collaborative problem solving, and participation in the change process. Questions of both what needs to be changed and how the change should be implemented can be exclusive or inclusive.

In an *ex*clusive mode, top executives exclude all stakeholders except a small group of fellow senior executives who decide what behaviors need to be targeted and how the change process should proceed. In an *in*clusive process, representatives of multiple stakeholders are all included in the diagnostic, action planning, and implementation efforts. Employee motivation to adopt and sustain required new behaviors will be enhanced, making implementation more likely to be successful in the short run and sustainable in the long run.

THEORY INTO PRACTICE

Be sure to create an inclusive change process—one that builds ownership of and commitment to the desired improvements.

Process-Driven Change Interventions

Given the complexity and dynamism of the competitive environment, it is not surprising that change efforts have proliferated over the past several decades: employee involvement, customer relationship management, balanced scorecard, and lean enterprise, to name just a few. These efforts represent **content-driven change** that emphasizes programmatic responses to organizational requirements.

As an alternative methodology of implementation, **process-driven change** suggests that the manner in which change is conceived, introduced, and institutionalized will be more determinate of effectiveness than the specific content of any given change program.[13] While content-driven changes may serve as useful tools in reinforcing behavioral change, they can be ineffective as drivers and shapers of the transformation effort.

Building a Vocabulary of Change
Content-driven change programmatic change in which specific programs—customer relationship management, balanced scorecard, and lean enterprise, for example—are used as the driver and centerpiece of implementation.

Building a Vocabulary of Change
Process-driven change an approach to change implementation that emphasizes the methods of conceiving, introducing, and institutionalizing new behaviors and uses content as a reinforcer rather than a driver of new behaviors.

THEORY INTO PRACTICE

There are no one-size-fits-all solutions to performance problems in an organization.

To help understand and identify content-driven change, we can identify a set of characteristics that are common across different particular change efforts. Content-driven change:

- ***Serves as the initial centerpiece for launching and driving transformation throughout the company or unit.*** Company executives pick a single initiative—say, the balanced scorecard—in order to drive a whole range of changes across the organization.
- ***Is imposed by the top management.*** Top management selects the program, drives it through the organization, and makes decisions about whether to continue the initiative.
- ***Does not proceed from shared diagnosis.*** By virtue of their position atop the hierarchy, executives can simply impose change programs. Is there even dissatisfaction with the status quo? Content-driven change often flows from the assumption that if top management is dissatisfied, then everyone else is equally dissatisfied with the status quo.
- ***Relies on standardized, off-the-shelf solutions.*** Executives select a change program that has been used elsewhere. But is it apoprorpriate for all organizations? That question is often not asked.
- ***Is imposed uniformly across the organization.*** Perhaps one program is appropriate for some units, but does it fit all circumstances? Top management may not engage in such a diagnosis; instead, they applied the same program across the entire company.

The characteristics of content-driven change are summarized in Exhibit 2-4.

- Serve as the initial centerpiece for launching and driving transformation throughout the company or unit.
- Are imposed by top management.
- Do not proceed from shared diagnosis.
- Rely on standardized, off-the-shelf solutions.
- Are imposed uniformly across the organization.

EXHIBIT 2-4 Characteristics of Content-Driven Change Programs.

THE LIMITATIONS OF CONTENT-DRIVEN CHANGE The uniform nature of content-driven change creates its own set of problems. To decree that all managers in all divisions and units "should" undergo a training program or that all processes "should" use a particular methodology ignores the diversity extant in any complex organization, including differences in customer expectations, in competitive realities, in key task demands, and/or in workforce characteristics. Applied universally across organizational boundaries, change programs can drive out creativity and usually lack the specific relevancy needed to help managers in a given unit solve their real and immediate business problems.

The fact that change programs are imposed from above may reflect the commitment on the part of top management to the need for change. But the transformation effort often bogs down because that commitment is not widely distributed throughout and across the organization.[14] Only those individuals dissatisfied with the status quo—with the performance of their unit and the patterns of behavior supporting that performance—will be motivated to alter their patterns of behavior. Top-down change programs may *assume* the preexistence of such dissatisfaction, but they do little to actually *build* dissatisfaction and direct that dissatisfaction toward new patterns of behavior.

THEORY INTO PRACTICE

Just because top leaders believe in the need for change doesn't mean that all employees share that belief.

The cost of continued reliance on content-driven change as a way of transforming the organization is significant. In addition to the inefficient use of organizational resources, each unsuccessful and discarded program makes it much harder to effect successful transformation in the future. As one failed program leads to another, employees begin to discount and ignore all programs. Because employees have little commitment to these efforts, what they offer—at best—is compliance. They may tolerate the program, carry out procedures to the best of their ability, but fail to provide any lasting support for program continuation. They may complete the minimal requirements expected of them by filling out the proper forms or attending the expected conferences, but *disdain* and criticize all aspects of the effort. And to the extent that they can get away with it, they may avoid the effort entirely.

THEORY INTO PRACTICE

Content-driven change often fails because of inadequate attention to the process of change.

THE POPULARITY OF CONTENT-DRIVEN CHANGE Given the complexity and dynamism of the competitive environment, it is not surprising that content-driven change efforts have proliferated over the past several decades. Exhibit 1-2 in the previous chapter offered an overview of some of the most popular change efforts.

The popularity of content-driven change can be understood in terms of the dynamics in place in many organizations. Content-driven change efforts represent actions that can be put into place *quickly*. Faced with competitive crisis, top managers want to make change quickly. Pressures for quarterly earnings coupled with impatience and high task orientation lead managers to seek a lever that will demonstrate forward movement. Although simplistic and often ineffective, change programs are highly visible and provide tangible evidence of concerted effort.

THEORY INTO PRACTICE

Repeated failure to implement change effectively can build cynicism in an organization, "inoculating" it against future change efforts.

Furthermore, managers like to emulate well-known success stories, and they do so by importing programs. Best-selling management books present documented studies of the transformative impact of popular programs. Why shouldn't we do that, too? As one manager said of his support for a particularly trendy change program: "We were one of the *Fortune 500* companies and we were all into this buzzword kind of stuff, and so let's get with the program here. We don't want to be left behind."[15]

The tangibility of change programs offers another apparent advantage: they are easily measurable. Thus, they make it convenient for top managers to hold subordinates accountable. Executives can point to the number of teams or the number of managers who have attended a training program as a proxy—and not an especially useful or valid proxy at that—for accomplishment.

THEORY INTO PRACTICE

Content-driven change is both tangible and measurable—but that doesn't make it effective.

PROCESS-DRIVEN CHANGE AND ITS CONTRIBUTION TO CHANGE IMPLEMENTATION A process-driven approach to change works from the opposite direction of content-driven change. **Process-driven change** seeks to create a context and environment in which employees at all levels of the organization engage in a collaborative way to achieve the strategic goals of the organization. Collaborative, participative, and problem-solving approaches work to align behaviors with strategic requirements. Change programs including Six Sigma, business process reengineering, the balanced scorecard, lean enterprise, and Agile may then be used to reinforce rather than drive new behaviors. The leadership task becomes one of establishing purpose and strategic directions for the organization, then creating the fertile soil out of which new patterns of behavior may emerge.

THEORY INTO PRACTICE

Process-driven change seeks to create an organizational context in which employees will be motivated to adopt new behaviors consistent with the strategic direction of the organization.

THEORY INTO PRACTICE

Change programs—balanced scorecard, concurrent engineering, agile development, and so forth—are useful in reinforcing new behaviors; but avoid using them to drive change.

Building a Vocabulary of Change
Task alignment an approach to behavioral change that starts with the identification of the key strategic tasks of an organization or unit and then asks employees to redefine their roles, responsibilities, and relationships in order to perform those tasks.

Task Alignment as a Driver of Behavioral Change

Task alignment offers an approach to change intended to sharpen the connections between Lewin's requirement to alter the context and create a disequilibrium, OD-based interventions, process-driven change, and strategic renewal. Effective change implementation efforts display a common thread: management focused on the business' central competitive challenges as the means for motivating change and developing new behaviors and skills.[16]

Task alignment takes as a starting point for change, the work that needs to be undertaken in order for a unit to achieve its strategic goals and sustained outstanding performance. That was precisely the point at which Jon Meliones started his shared diagnosis at Children's Hospital. He did not ask, "How can we work together better?" Instead, he asked, "How can we achieve excellent patient care *and* excellent financial performance?"

In a dynamic environment, strategic renewal typically requires new behaviors in order to perform those tasks. Task alignment embeds the insights of OD in a drive to produce outstanding performance. Employees redefine their roles, responsibilities, and relationships in order to perform those tasks.

THEORY INTO PRACTICE

Task alignment combines the insights of organizational development with a bottom-line focus on performance.

TASK-ALIGNED CHANGE To understand task alignment as a performance-focused approach to change, let's look at a counter-example: a change process that was *not* task aligned.

At General Product's Technical Center, upper management focused on an "employee involvement" initiative aimed at white-collar, professional-level employees.[17] Intrigued by reports of improved performance due to increased employee involvement in manufacturing operations, management formed committees to address issues of urgent concern to employees. Because employees often mentioned their interest in career development, one committee discussed how to get employees more involved in their own career planning.

Top management at the center began holding regular meetings to discuss the meaning of employee involvement: Just how far should employee involvement go and over what issues should employees be involved? The head of the center, feeling that he could not be overly directive about an initiative heralding employee involvement, watched in frustration as two years of effort yielded few tangible results.

THEORY INTO PRACTICE

A task-aligned approach to change implementation can help create motivation to adopt new behaviors by focusing on real, immediate business problems, and producing tangible results.

Interestingly, a different change effort was occurring simultaneously further down the company. This one, however, followed more closely the framework of task alignment. Struggling with the requirement to speed up the new product development process, an implementation task force uncovered poor cross-functional coordination reinforced by strict functional lines and a lack of teamwork throughout the organization as the culprit. Several cross-functional product development teams were created as a result.

As teams began to produce results, relationships among functions improved, engineers and production specialists began to feel empowered, and demands for team skills were met with a training program.[18] Although the efforts of the employee involvement team spurred by upper management's desire to meet "urgent" employee concerns withered, employees' involvement increased on cross-functional teams designed to develop new products.

TASK ALIGNMENT'S CONTRIBUTION TO CHANGE IMPLEMENTATION The dramatic differences in the impact of these two interventions—one task aligned and one not—highlight a flaw of many change interventions. Look at the first non-task-aligned approach. Hearing "good things" about employee involvement and desirous of gaining the benefits that had apparently accrued to other companies, corporate management urged employee involvement initiatives. One employee involvement task force recommended placing artwork in the center's atrium as a way of enhancing the ambience of the facility. But what did employee involvement mean to managers and workers? And more importantly, how did it impact on the ability of the center to achieve and sustain outstanding performance?

The second task-aligned approach started with a different premise: not *we need to bring the idea of employee involvement into the organization* but *we need to improve new product development performance and involving employees will help us do that.* By following a task alignment approach to change implementation, employees at all levels of the organization are motivated to engage in behavioral change to the extent that they appreciate how that change is related to the performance of the core tasks of the organization.

Line managers have far greater ability to diagnose business and performance problems than to engage in psychological or therapeutic analysis of individuals. By focusing on solving real business problems, task alignment takes advantage of the knowledge and expertise in the organization. Tangible performance results that accrue from task-aligned change interventions reinforce the efficacy of such efforts, which in turn create momentum for renewed change intervention. Results build conviction.[19] Task alignment builds commitment by focusing on real and immediate performance drivers and producing tangible results.

PUTTING IT ALL TOGETHER: BUILDING A THEORY OF CHANGE IMPLEMENTATION

Each body of theory examined in this chapter offers critical insight into the effective implementation of change. Those theories and their implementation implications are summarized in Exhibit 2-5. The challenge for change implementation

EXHIBIT 2-5
Key Theoretical Approaches to Change Implementation.

Theoretical Approach	Main Theoretical Contribution	Help Explain How to Implement Change
Lewin's Field *Theory in Social* Science	Begin behavioral change by focusing on context and unfreezing existing social habits	• Build a pervasive sense of dissatisfaction with the status quo on the part of employees • Offer operational models for what new behavioral patterns will be • Reinforce new behavior with alterations to systems and structures
Organizational development	Organizations are dynamic, open systems	• Target entire organizational system for change • Create a climate of open discussion and upward feedback concerning the efficacy of change implementation • Call on process consultants to facilitate interventions
Process-driven change	Focus on organically developed and implemented efforts to improve organizational performance	• Do not use externally developed program as driver of change • Focus on the unique requirements of each organization and unit • Build support for change while implementing it
Task alignment	Link desired new behaviors to requirements of performing key tasks of the organization	• Analyze and identify key performance indicators and behavioral implications required for outstanding performance • Attach requirements for new behavioral to new strategic objectives of organization • Build line-management support for change effort

becomes: how can multiple theories of change be integrated into a common approach to effective change implementation?

The change implementation model presented in Exhibit 2-6 provides just such an integrated roadmap.[20] By melding theory and practice, the model suggests both what tools can be applied and the most effective sequence for that application. It suggests that once strategic renewal triggers a new requirement for transformation, effective implementation will start with **shared diagnosis**: a widely held and understood view of the barriers to strategic implementation and outstanding performance.

Building a Vocabulary of Change
shared diagnosis: a widely held and understood view of the barriers to strategic implementation and outstanding performance.

Starting Implementation with Shared Diagnosis

Trigger events often lead to strategic renewal. Driving change from strategic renewal assures that implementation aligns with the requirements of outstanding performance. However, in and of itself, the decision to alter or renew an organization's strategy does not create the disequilibrium that Lewin said is required to motivate changed behaviors.

For Duke University Children's Hospital, a trigger event—changes in insurance reimbursement that created a financial crisis—created a need for change. Jon Meliones did not impose a solution. Instead, he involved a cross section of administrators of health care providers in a diagnostic process that surfaced the interconnection between financial outcomes and patterns of behavior.

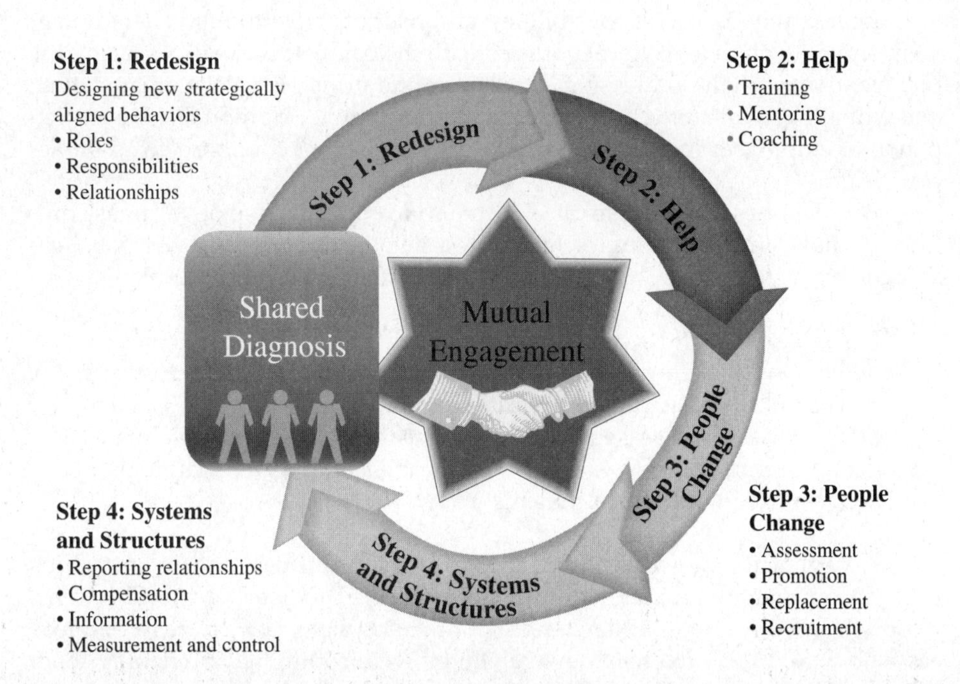

EXHIBIT 2-6
A Sequential Model of Effective Change Implementation.

THEORY INTO PRACTICE

Kicking off change implementation with shared diagnosis builds both dissatisfaction with the status quo and a commitment to enact new behaviors.

Change requires the commitment of a variety of employees. Meliones had to impact the behaviors of accountants and administrators no less than physicians and nurses. A participative and involving diagnostic process can be used to build that commitment. Broad-based participation helps overcome defensiveness and resistance to change. Dissatisfaction with the status quo is no longer a lecture from above; rather, it is an agreement among many employees concerning what needs to be changed and why.

Moving to Redesign

Building a Vocabulary of Change
Redesign an alteration in employee roles, responsibilities, and relationships.

Once diagnosis generates dissatisfaction with the status quo, employees can participate in redesigning behavioral patterns to support strategic renewal and outstanding performance. As part of that **redesign** effort, employees seek answers to these questions:

- What can employees do to contribute to the achievement of the company's strategy (roles)?
- What are the performance outcomes employees strive to achieve (responsibilities)?
- With whom must employees work in order to meet the expected outcomes, and what is the nature of those interactions (relationships)?

Redesigning roles, responsibilities, and relationships through shared diagnosis serves to align behavioral patterns with the competitive realities facing the organization; with the values, goals, purpose, and principles of the organization; and with the requirements of outstanding performance. Additionally, the participation of employees in the redesign process builds their commitment to implementation.

For Meliones and his team at Children's Hospital, the diagnostic phase produced a new understanding of how roles, responsibilities, and relationships should be enacted to support outstanding performance. Meliones explains:

> We moved from mission-bound departments in which people identified only with their particular jobs ("I am a manager," "I am a nurse," and so on) to goal-oriented multidisciplinary teams focused on a particular illness or disease ("We, the ICU team, consisting of the manager, the nurse, the physician, the pharmacist, and the radiologist, help children with heart problems").[21]

Note that the new definition of roles, responsibilities, and relationships flowed from a shared diagnosis of the performance problems facing Children's Hospital, and a common understanding of the hospital's new strategy, employees who would have to enact new behaviors were committed to making them work. Now the redesign of the unit—multidisciplinary teams focused on specific diseases—was not imposed by upper management. Rather, the new design represented an emergent consensus among employees concerning how to implement the hospital's "no margin, no mission" strategy.

Help

At the Children's Hospital, Jon Meliones asked employees who were used to working as individuals to join in a collaborative team effort. Not only that, but he was asking doctors and nurses to become familiar with the financial situation of the hospital, and accountants to develop an appreciation of excellent health care practices. It is typical, in fact, for change efforts to ask employees to develop new skills to match the required new behaviors.

It is in the help stage of change that organizations can offer employees assistance with enacting those new behaviors. Employees being asked, often for the first time, to work on a team will need to learn the skills of teamwork. Sales people being asked to demonstrate new products will need to learn the skills associated with that new functionality. Shop floor supervisors being asked to work as facilitators with work teams will have to learn a new set of skills.

In Chapter 5, we will look at specific tools for providing that help. The point to make for now is that training can be used most effectively in a change process when it follows a participative process of redesigning roles, responsibilities, and relationships. The commitment to enact new behavior drives a desire to learn the skills required of that behavior.

THEORY INTO PRACTICE

Asking employees to enact new behaviors—roles, responsibilities, and relationships—can be supported by organizational help in learning required new skills.

People Change

After a shared diagnostic process produces a shared understanding of the renewed strategy and a commitment to change, and *after* employees engage in a process of redesigning roles, responsibilities, and relationships, implementation calls upon **people change**: the process of matching the attributes of employees—their skills, motivation, attitudes, and behaviors—with the strategic requirements of the organization.

Building a Vocabulary of Change
People change the process of matching the attributes of employees with the strategic requirements of the organization.

The process is designed, to borrow a phrase from Jim Collins' book, *Good to Great,* to get the right people with the right competencies *on* the bus and the wrong people *off* the bus.[22]

The specific interventions that can be called upon in this stage of implementation include:

- ***Assessment of employees***—which can now reflect the new set of required competencies

- ***Recruitment***—which seeks to attract and select new employees based on the demand for new competencies and fit with the redesigned organization
- ***Promotion***—which identifies current employees whose skill makes them effective enablers of the change
- ***Removal and replacement***—which deals with individuals who cannot or will not alter their patterns of behavior in ways consistent with the newly defined roles, responsibilities, and relationships

Aligning human resource capabilities with the new strategic requirements of the organization—that is, the goal of the people change step.

THEORY INTO PRACTICE

Effective change implementation requires new skills and competencies on the part of the organization's employees.

Reinforcing New Behaviors

Now comes the point in the change implementation process when leaders reinforce altered patterns of behavior through new structures, systems, and technologies. Roles, responsibilities, and relationships have been redesigned, individuals have been offered the opportunity to learn and enact new behavioral patterns and competencies, and the right people are in place.

Making formal systems alterations early in the change process risks creating resistance. Meliones and his team at Children's Hospital decided *together* to call upon a performance measurement system—the balanced scorecard—to help institutionalize the new behaviors designed at early stages of the change. The measurement system became "an essential component of our culture and supports ongoing change."[23] "Hardwiring" changes, such as structures and systems that grow organically out of employees' experiences and are not imposed from above early in the change implementation process, have a far better chance of receiving the support of affected employees.

THEORY INTO PRACTICE

Altering formal organizational systems and structures can come at the back end of a change implementation in order to institutionalize new patterns of behavior.

Building a Vocabulary of Change
Mutual engagement the process of building a participatory dialogue among employees at all organizational levels to the requirements of and process for achieving change.

Mutual Engagement at the Core

At the center of the model and accompanying every stage is a process of **mutual engagement**.[24] Participation in decision making, as we noted in Chapter 1, helps build commitment to the outcomes of that decision-making process. The cycle of change implementation, then, needs to create opportunities for dialogue, discussion, communication, and participation as a way of building commitment to the changes. Those opportunities are what can be called mutual engagement. Mutual engagement rests on the assumption that multiple stakeholders—particularly the employees at all organizational levels whose behaviors have to change—will need to be committed to the change.

Beyond building commitment, mutual engagement provides another asset indispensable to effective change implementation. In all organizations, vital knowledge about the current state of the company's operations, shifting expectations of customers, required interface with suppliers, and emerging technological trends and developments in the industry are embedded deeply in and widely across the firm. Employees have a unique perspective on how well the organization is meeting its strategic goals and living up to its espoused values. Mutual engagement ensures that such critical knowledge is constantly considered in the change process.

THEORY INTO PRACTICE

Mutual engagement at every stage of the implementation process helps assure learning and builds commitment.

How does an organization gain access to such vital knowledge? By allowing employees to influence important change decisions at each step in the implementation process, organizations invite employees to share their knowledge and ensure that decision-making proceeds in full awareness of that knowledge, as well as the consequences of the decisions on the employees who will be impacted. We will address specific steps that can be taken to ensure mutual engagement in Chapter 3.

Avoiding Implementation Traps

Organizational leaders can maximize the likelihood that their implementation efforts will succeed if they orchestrate an intervention that moves sequentially through these required stages in a manner that integrates theoretical insights into specific interventions. The road map offered in the sequential implementation model provides both an analytic and planning tool. It also provides insights into **implementation traps:** the application of appropriate change tools at inappropriate points in the implementation process.

Building a Vocabulary of Change
Implementation trap applying the right tools at the wrong time in the implementation process.

Organizational leaders, for example, may call on Step 4 to initiate change. The difficulty with that, however, is that they are substituting "refreezing" for "unfreezing." When used to drive change, new structures have the effect of imposing new behavioral expectations on employees who are still attached to the "social habits." By leaping over the process of shared diagnosis and redesign, leaders who initiate change through Step 4 interventions have often failed to build commitment to new behaviors or to exploit the knowledge and insights embedded deeply and widely in their employees. Exhibit 2-7 presents different ways that change leaders can fall into the implementation trap by calling on interventions out of sequence.

EXHIBIT 2-7
Change Implementation Traps.

Trap	For Example	Why It Is a Trap
Starting at Step 4	Imposing new system or structure (e.g., global matrix, balanced scorecard measurement system)	Will be experienced as "change from above"; likely to be poorly understood and resisted.
Starting at Step 2	Driving change with training program	Because employees work in an unchanged organizational context, their learning is likely to be short-lived and will fade out.
Starting at Step 3	Recruiting new employees, removing and replacing, and replacing individuals seen to be resisters to change	Easy to make mistakes due to lack of understanding concerning what is required and who can adapt to new demands; can be viewed by employees as arbitrary, thus diminishing trust and commitment.
Starting implementation without shared diagnosis	Redesigning work (e.g., creating cross-functional teams)	New designs will be seen as unconnected to strategic reality and performance demands of organization; can lead to compliance or resistance on the part of line managers.
Ignoring mutual engagement	Driving change through top management	Leadership may be out of touch with realities of organization while employees may not understand strategic imperatives.

Conclusion

The sequential model of effective change implementation represents an integration of the key insights offered by previous theorists of organizational change. The diagnosis stage, as the model suggests, becomes the opening intervention in effective implementation. For an understanding of how that diagnostic stage can be the most helpful in propelling change implementation, we can turn to an analysis of organizational diagnosis.

Discussion Questions

1. According to Kurt Lewin, why is it so difficult to motivate employees to alter their patterns of behavior?
2. Discuss the various ways in which change theorists have attempted to introduce performance and results into the implementation process.

Case Discussion

Read "Blue Cloud Gets Agile," *and prepare answers to the following questions:*

1. What was the trigger event that led Shel Skinner to adopt Agile?
2. What is your evaluation of the change implementation steps followed by Skinner?
3. What behavioral changes, if any, does Agile require of employees?
4. How do you account for such widely varied responses to Agile among Blue Cloud employees?
5. What should Skinner do now?

BLUE CLOUD GETS AGILE

After attending a conference on a new methodology for software development known as Agile, Shel Skinner, CEO of Blue Cloud Development, a small software development company located in Mountain View, California, hired consultants to introduce the methodology.

At its core, Agile emphasized multiple iterations and short time frames. Created by a group of software developers, the Agile Manifesto (2001) declared:

We are uncovering better ways of developing software by doing it and helping others do it.

Through this work we have come to value:

- Individuals and interactions over processes and tools
- Working software over comprehensive documentation
- Customer collaboration over contract negotiation
- Responding to change over following a plan

That is, while there is value in the items on the right, we value the items on the left more

In addition, Agile held 12 principles:

1. Our highest priority is to satisfy the customer through early and continuous delivery of valuable software.
2. Welcome changing requirements, even late in development. Agile processes harness change for the customer's competitive advantage.
3. Deliver working software frequently, from a couple of weeks to a couple of months, with a preference to the shorter timescale.
4. Business people and developers must work together daily throughout the project.
5. Build projects around motivated individuals. Give them the environment and support they need, and trust them to get the job done.
6. The most efficient and effective method of conveying information to and within a development team is face-to-face conversation.
7. Working software is the primary measure of progress.
8. Agile processes promote sustainable development. The sponsors, developers, and users should be able to maintain a constant pace indefinitely.
9. Continuous attention to technical excellence and good design enhances agility.

10. Simplicity—the art of maximizing the amount of work not done—is essential.
11. The best architectures, requirements, and designs emerge from self-organizing teams.
12. At regular intervals, the team reflects on how to become more effective, then tunes and adjusts its behavior accordingly.

"These principles spoke to me on a very fundamental level," said Skinner. "These folks were saying out loud for what I'd been thinking most of my career."

Blue Cloud's traditional developmental cycle emphasized a deliberate sequence of development, with verification (testing and debugging) often occurring after a year's worth of work. "Why waste a year to find out whether our product is working," Skinner wondered. No more alpha and beta testing of new software: "Our new motto around here is, 'Release early, release often!' "

What appealed to Skinner was Agile's emphasis on teamwork, collaboration, and monthly releases. Cross-functional development teams held a daily "scrum" to ensure that all members were fully onboard with the progress and that all questions and concerns were raised in a timely manner. Skinner provided a description of the Scrum:[25]

> Scrum is an agile method for project management developed by Ken Schwaber. Its goal is to dramatically improve productivity in teams previously paralyzed by heavier, process-laden methodologies. Its intended use is for management of software development projects as well as a wrapper to other software development methodologies such as Extreme Programming.
>
> Scrum is characterized by:
>
> - A living backlog of prioritized work to be done.
> - Completion of a largely fixed set of backlog items in a series of short iterations or sprints.
> - A brief daily meeting (called a scrum), at which progress is explained, upcoming work is described, and obstacles are raised.
> - A brief planning session in which the backlog items for the sprint will be defined.
> - A brief heartbeat retrospective, at which all team members reflect about the past sprint.
>
> Scrum is facilitated by a scrum master, whose primary job is to remove impediments to the ability of the team to deliver the sprint goal. The scrum master is not the leader of the team (as they are self-organizing) but acts as a productivity buffer between the team and any destabilizing influences.
>
> Scrum enables the creation of self-organizing teams by encouraging verbal communication across all team members and across all disciplines that are involved in the project. A key principle of scrum is its recognition that fundamentally empirical challenges cannot be addressed successfully in a traditional "process control" manner. As such, scrum adopts an empirical approach—accepting that the problem cannot be fully understood or defined, focusing instead on maximizing the team's ability to respond in an agile manner to emerging challenges.

By bringing together business people, developers, customers' representatives, and other concerned parties in a disciplined, face-to-face encounter, Agile methodology was intended to simultaneously increase efficiency and improve quality.

After a year of applying Agile, Skinner asked his engineers to evaluate the effort. "Wonderful," said some, "what's new?" asked others, and "this is a definite step in the wrong direction," complained a few. Skinner remained unsure about whether to continue with the Agile methodology or look for a new approach to software development.

Endnotes

1. Information in this case is based on Jon N. Meliones, Richard Ballard, Richard Liekweg, and William Burton, "No Mission No Margin: It's That Simple," *Journal of Health Care Finance* 27 (Spring 2001); Jon Meliones, "Saving Money, Saving Lives," *Harvard Business Review* (Nov.–Dec. 2000); and *ITWeek.com* (Jan. 1, 2001).
2. Robert S. Kaplan and David P. Norton, "Transforming the Balanced Scorecard from Performance Measurement to Strategic Management: Part I," *Accounting Horizons* 15 (Mar. 2001), p. 87; Robert S. Kaplan and David P. Norton, "Using the Balanced Scorecard as a Strategic Management System," *Harvard Business Review* (Jan.–Feb. 1996), p. 3; Robert S. Kaplan and David P. Norton, *Integrating Shareholder Value and Activity-Based Costing with the Balanced Scorecard* In Context (Boston, MA: Harvard Business School Publishing, 2001), p. 4.
3. These essays and others are collected in Kurt Lewin, *Field Theory in Social Science: Selected Theoretical Papers* (New York: Harper & Row, 1951).
4. *Ibid*., p. 226.
5. Emily Thornton, "A New Order at Nissan," *Business Week* (Oct. 11, 1999), p. 54.
6. Lewin, *Field Theory in Social Science*, p. 229.
7. *Ibid*, p. 231.
8. Critiques of Lewin's theories can be found in Ralph Stacey, "Management and the Science of Complexity: If Organizational Life Is Non-linear, Can Business Strategies Prevail?" *Research and Technology Management* 39 (1996), pp. 2–5; Wanda J. Orlikowski and Debra Hofman, "An Improvisational Model for Change Management: The Case of Groupware Technologies," *Sloan Management Review* 38 (Winter 1997), pp. 11–21; Alexander Styhre, "Non-linear Change in Organizations: Organization Change Management Informed by Complexity Theory," *Leadership and Organization Development Journal* 23 (2002), pp. 343–351.
9. Based, in part, on Michael Beer and Bert Spector, "Human Resource Management: The Integration of Industrial Relations and Organization Development," in Kendrith M. Rowland and Gerald R. Ferris, eds., *Research in Personnel and Human Resources Management: A Research Annual*, Vol. 2 (Greenwich, CT: JAI Press, 1984), pp. 261–297.
10. That perspective on conflict is fully explored in Richard E. Walton, *Interpersonal Peacemaking: Confrontations and Third-Party Consultation* (Reading, MA: Addison-Wesley, 1969).
11. Kenneth W. Thomas, "Conflict and Conflict Management," in Marvin D. Dunnette, ed., *Handbook of Industrial and Organizational Psychology* (Chicago, IL: Rand McNally, 1976), pp. 889–935.
12. Michael Beer and Bert Spector, "Organizational Diagnosis: Its Role in Organizational Learning," *Journal of Counselling and Development* 71 (1993), pp. 642–650.
13. On the importance of process-driven change, see Beer, Eisenstat, and Spector, *The Critical Path to Corporate Renewal*; Richard P. Rumselt, "How Much Does Industry Matter?" *Strategic Management Journal* 12 (1991), pp. 167–185; Robert Macintosh and Donald MacLean, "Conditioned Emergence: A Dissipative Structures Approach to Transformation," *Strategic Management Journal* 20 (1999), pp. 297–316; Richard H. Axelrod, *Changing*

the Way We Change Organizations (San Francisco: Berrett-Koehler, 2000); L.C. Harris and E. Ogbonna, "The Unintended Consequences of Culture Interventions: A Study of Unexpected Outcomes," *British Journal of Management* 12 (2002), pp. 31–49.

14. Bert Spector, "From Bogged Down to Fired Up: Inspiring Organizational Change," *Sloan Management Review* 30 (Summer 1989), pp. 29–34.

15. Beer, Eisenstat, and Spector, *The Critical Path to Corporate Renewal*, p. 40.

16. *Ibid.*, pp. 45–46.

17. This case is detailed in Beer, Eisenstat, and Spector, *The Critical Path to Corporate Renewal*.

18. *Ibid.*, p. 52.

19. Robert H. Schaffer and Harvey A. Thomson, "Successful Change Programs Begin with Results," *Harvard Business Review* (Jan.–Feb. 1992), p. 83.

20. The framework presented here builds on one presented earlier, in Beer, Eisenstat, and Spector, *The Critical Path to Corporate Renewal*.

21. Meliones, *Saving Money, Saving Lives*, pp. 59–60.

22. James C. Collins, *Good to Great: Why Some Companies Make the Leap and Others Don't* (New York: Harper Business, 2001).

23. Meliones is quoted in *ITWeek.com* (Jan. 1, 2001), p. 1.

24. The concept of mutual engagement is developed in José Santos, Bert Spector, and Ludo van-der-Hayden, "Toward a Theory of Corporate Business Model Innovation," Northeastern University College of Business Administration Working Paper, (2008).

25. See *http://www.mariosalexandrou.com/methodologies/scrum.asp*.

CHAPTER

3 Mutual Engagement and Shared Diagnosis

Effective organizational change requires an alteration in patterns of employee behavior. At the outset of effective change implementation, leaders engage employees in a process of shared diagnosis. The goal of that diagnostic process is to unfreeze "social habits" and create a sense of dissatisfaction with the status quo. Mutual engagement helps build commitment to the change process among those who participate.

This chapter will describe and analyze mutual engagement and shared diagnosis. In particular, the chapter will:

- Describe the role of diagnosis in assessing behaviors and values and in creating dissatisfaction with the status quo
- Discuss the use of a systemic framework for guiding diagnosis
- Explore ways to overcome the "climate of silence" that blocks mutual engagement
- Provide the key ingredients of a diagnostic intervention
- Define the role played by after-action reviews (AARs) in creating quick learning and improvement

First, we will look at the initial days and weeks of a newly hired CEO intent on energizing transformational change. As you read the introductory case, ask yourself:

- How did Fiorina formulate her ideas for how to transform Hewlett-Packard (HP)?
- How did HP's top executives respond to Fiorina's direction of change?
- How would you evaluate her initial efforts to improve the HP's performance?

"A DEER CAUGHT IN THE HEADLIGHTS" AT HP

Plagued by poor performance in its computer and printer business, Hewlett-Packard's board hired Carleton (Carly) Fiorina from Lucent.[1] This represented the first time since its 1939 founding that HP had reached outside the company for a CEO. Appreciating the urgency of the situation, Fiorina hit the ground running. Her first public appearances were well staged and electric. What she had in mind was clear. She would reorganize HP in order to centralize decision making, revitalize the sales force, trim costs, and energize employees.

Based on her previous experience at Lucent, Fiorina had a clear idea of how she would achieve her goals, which she revealed at her first strategic meeting just a month after her arrival. To reverse the company's "sacred" emphasis on decentralization, she proposed a simpler, more centralized structure: two "back-end" divisions (each back-end division included design, manufacturing, and distribution—one for printers, the other for computers) and two "front-end" marketing and sales operations—one for consumers and the other for corporate customers. The company would also begin to focus on far fewer products. "This is a company that can do anything," she told executives, "it is not a company that can do everything." Finally, the culture would change dramatically and immediately to emphasize performance. "Let me make something very clear," Fiorina told executives. "You will make your numbers. There will be no excuses. And if you can't make your numbers, I will find someone who will."

Fiorina asked for the support of HP's top executives on her centralization and reorganization plan, and she got it. That is not to say, however, that they all *agreed* with her. "I don't know anyone who was in favor of it [her back-end/front-end reorganization plan] other than Carly," said one. "She came in with a recipe," said another, "and come hell or high water, she was going to use it." Carolyn Ticknor, head of laser printing, recalled, "I was a deer caught in the headlights when she [Fiorina] described the front and back end."

Six years after the announcement of the reorganization plan, the company's board demanded Fiorina's resignation. The board again looked outside of HP for a replacement; this time selecting Mark Hurd of NCR. When reporters asked Hurd about his plans to revitalize the company, he responded that it was too soon to tell. "We'll look at the entire enterprise," he said. "I can't give you any guarantees on anything," he added.[2]

DIAGNOSING THE ORGANIZATION

The desire on the part of executives such as Carly Fiorina to "hit the ground running" with solutions, particularly when their organizations are mired in poor performance, may be perfectly understandable. The tendency to believe that what has worked for them in the past can provide a kind of recipe for the future is also strong. Reorganization worked at Lucent; why not do the same at HP?

Taking that approach, however, fails to create mutual engagement and shared diagnosis that is so critical in shaping and guiding change. It can lead to solutions that are inappropriate to the target organization and are not supported—perhaps even actively resisted—by employees.

THEORY INTO PRACTICE

Effective change starts with action, not solutions.

The desire for quick solutions can lead executives to overlook the critical elements of learning and commitment that can be built through mutual engagement and shared diagnosis. The dynamics of every organization are unique. Additionally, an organization's external competitive forces are likely to be in a state of flux. Therefore, applying a recipe—what worked somewhere else in the past will work here now—can be overly simple, misleading, and even dysfunctional.

Lucent's best practices may not have been applicable to HP. The act of imposing those practices is likely to evoke resistance. Lack of mutual engagement—of holding an honest conversation among employees about what needed to change, why, and how—leads to low levels of employee commitment.

Diagnosis is meant to create learning about the real, current, and unique dynamics impacting the organization's performance. When combined with mutual engagement, it is designed to create deep and wide commitment to the desired outcome.

THEORY INTO PRACTICE

Don't expect formulas—solutions that have worked in the past and are imposed on the current situation—to work for your organization.

At its most fundamental level, diagnosis is about learning: learning *what* needs to be changed and *why*. **Learning** is the process by which individuals receive data from the external environment, analyze that data, and adjust their thinking and behaviors accordingly. The notion of *shared* diagnosis goes one step further. For effective change implementation to occur, many employees at multiple hierarchical levels and in varied units need to change in the same direction. A diagnostic process engaged in by an individual, no matter how insightful, highly placed, or influential that individual may be, will not lead to coordinated change. It is only when the same diagnosis is shared by multiple individuals that change implementation can move forward effectively.

Building a Vocabulary of Change

Learning the process by which individuals receive data from the external environment, analyze that data, and adjust their thinking and behaviors based on that analysis.

THEORY INTO PRACTICE

The most effective change implementation starts with a diagnosis that is shared by many employees at multiple organizational levels.

Altered and renewed strategies, new business models, and shifting external realities typically call for new skills, competencies, and patterns of behavior. The sequential implementation model depicted in Exhibit 2-6 starts with diagnosis in order to identify both the current state of skills, competencies, and behaviors and the requirements for future outstanding performance. Mutual engagement by employees generates awareness of the gap between the status quo and the desired future state. That awareness, in turn, provides the source of dissatisfaction and the drive for change.

Recall from Chapter 2 Lewin's warning that "lectures" about the status quo—speeches on the need for change or PowerPoint presentations on the new strategy, for instance—will *not* be sufficient to create the disequilibrium necessary to motivate change. Instead, effective change starts with a diagnostic process that engages employees in a learning process. Executives learn why the status quo is unsatisfactory; so, too, do employees at all levels and in all units.

In addition to generating learning, mutual engagement in shared diagnosis can create a consensus among employees not just about *what* needs to be changed but also *how* to bring about that change. Engaging employees in the process of collecting and learning from data and then using that learning to shape an intervention can help build real commitment to implementing change.

Building a Vocabulary of Change
Diagnosis the process of learning about the dynamics of the organization in order to take action intended to improve performance.

As an alternative to initiating change by announcing a solution, leaders can instead begin with diagnosis. **Diagnosis** is the process of learning about the dynamics of an organization's functioning. It is meant to engage employees in the process of identifying both the current state and the desired future state of the organization.[3] Employees collect data and engage in a dialogue concerning the meaning of the data. The diagnostic process provides a roadmap for change; mutual engagement in diagnosis helps build motivation on the part of employees to alter their behaviors.

THEORY INTO PRACTICE

Use diagnosis as the preliminary stage in implementing change.

Requirement for a Systemic Framework

Diagnosis should be guided by a broad, systemic view of the firm.

Organizations are composed of multiple units and functions and processes that link various activities. There are also design elements, both formal and informal, that organizations call upon to—they hope—align employee behavior with strategy. Additionally, organizations live in a dynamic world. New competitors, technologies, business models, customer expectations, changing government rules and regulations, shifting environmental imperatives, and ups and downs in the national and global economy all impact the organization.

Building a Vocabulary of Change
Diagnostic framework a roadmap to analyzing alignment that makes explicit both the key elements of an organization that need to be aligned and the interconnections and interdependencies among those elements.

A **diagnostic framework**—a roadmap for guiding mutual engagement in shared diagnosis—should help to identify all the key variables that impact the performance of an organization. But it must do more. None of these elements, after all, exist in a vacuum. Just think: employee behaviors are shaped by organizational design, which should serve the company's strategy. And all of the elements, in turn, must find success within an ever-shifting external environment.

Understanding that organizations exist in constant interaction with a dynamic external environment leads to an important insight: An organization whose internal processes are perfectly well suited for one kind of competitive environment may find those same processes becoming a burden in a new, shifting landscape.

THEORY INTO PRACTICE

In order to set the stage for effective implementation, diagnosis can do more than target-specific elements of the organization; it can focus on the entire organization.

Take the Federal Bureau of Investigation (FBI). The FBI built its reputation by battling crime and arresting criminals. The mission of the FBI—"G-men battling notorious criminals"—created a context and a set of structures and policies that gave absolute primacy to criminal investigations and special agents in the field. A highly decentralized structure allowed agents to focus their attentions locally. Additionally, the FBI preferred internally generated data, often distrusting and rejecting information supplied by external agencies and sources.

The attacks of 9/11 on New York and Washington triggered a change in the strategy of the FBI. Gathering information and *preventing* an attack—that was the new strategic task. Recognizing that the new mission would require altered patterns of thinking and behaving, FBI Director Robert Mueller took steps to transform the bureau.

When organizations such as the FBI attempt to undergo strategic renewal, leaders can call on a diagnostic framework to focus attention on the multiple elements that contribute to success. But an effective framework can do more; it can delineate and help make explicit the interactions and interconnects among the elements. If employee behaviors do not reflect strategy—let's say, in the case of the FBI, field agents concentrating most of their efforts on low-priority national threats, or, in other cases, salespeople spending most of their time selling products that are no longer core to the company's strategy, or functional employees continuing to work mainly within their functions rather than across functions when the company's strategy calls for rapid new product development—a framework can drive employees into analyzing the linkages that have created those misalignments.

THEORY INTO PRACTICE

Use a common organizational framework to shape mutual engagement and shared diagnosis.

No framework can, of course, explicate all the interconnects, causes and effects, and actions and reactions that occur within an organization and impact performance. That is why relying on a framework is only a preliminary step in the diagnosis. Mutual engagement and open, honest dialogue will build on the framework and enrich participants' understanding of organizational dynamics.

There are numerous frameworks available for judging alignment.[4] Exhibit 3-1 offers one such framework. The goal of any framework is to provide a common guide to participants as they seek to understand the interconnected linkages that affect organizational performance. Exhibit 3-1 summarizes the criteria that, according to David Nadler, any useful framework should adhere.[5] What makes a framework effective is that it leads people toward systemic thinking that

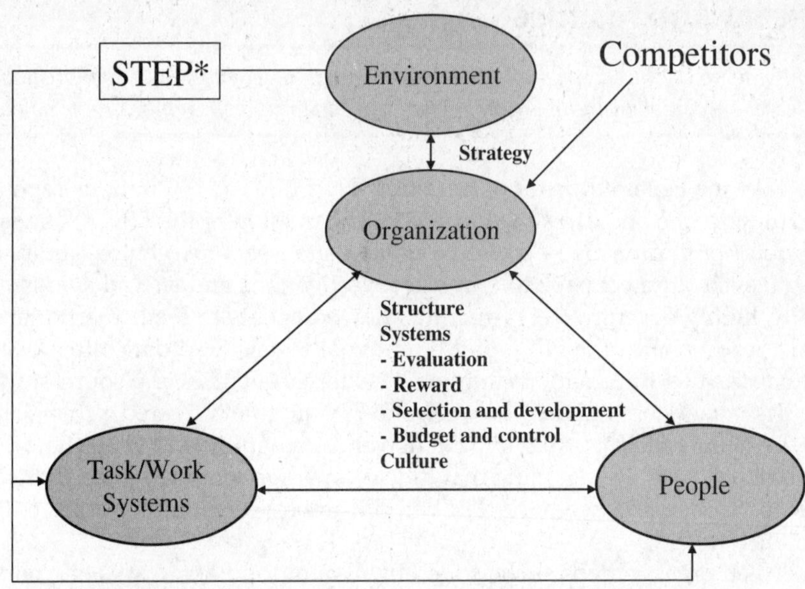

EXHIBIT 3-1 Diagnostic Framework†

can focus diagnosis on disjunctions that are impeding implementation of the renewed strategy and achievement of outstanding performance. A framework helps employees understand that outstanding performance can be achieved or sustained only with alignment between and among all the elements. It builds a common understanding and language that can form the basis of a shared diagnosis.

STARTING WITH MUTUAL ENGAGEMENT

The mutual engagement that forms the core of an effective change implementation effort starts at the diagnostic step. Employees can have the opportunity to engage in a dialogue that focuses on performance and the impediments and barriers to achieving an organization's strategic goals.

†This organizational design framework and analytic model has been adapted from a number of writers on the contingency theory of organizations: James D. Thompson, *Organizations in Action* (New York: McGraw-Hill, 1967); Paul R. Lawrence and J. W. Lorsch, *Organization and Environment* (Homewood, IL: Richard D. Irwin, 1969); Jay R. Galbraith, *Designing Complex Organizations* (Reading, MA: Addison-Wesley, 1973); Jay W. Lorsch and John J. Morse, *Organizations and Their Members: A Contingency Approach* (New York: Harper & Row, 1974); Jay R. Galbraith, Organization Design (Reading, MA: Addison-Wesley, 1977); Jay W. Lorsch, "Organization Design: A Situational Perspective," *Organizational Dynamics*, 5 (1977) American Management Association, 1977; Jay R. Galbraith and Daniel A. Nathanson, *Strategy Implementation: The Role of Structure and Process* (St. Paul, MN: West, 1978); John P. Kotter, Leonard A. Schlesinger, and Vijay Sathe, "Organization Design Tools," *Organization: Text, Cases and Readings on the Management of Organizational Design and Change* (Homewood, IL: Richard D. Irwin, 1979). See also H. W. Lane, "Systems, Values and Action: An Analytic Framework for Intercultural Management Research," *Management International Review* 20, no. 3 (1980), pp. 61–70.

Dialogue is a structured, collective discussion among two or more parties. Dialogue builds mutuality because the purpose of dialogue is to move beyond the understanding of any one individual and create an enriched and shared understanding and the multiple participants.

Building a Vocabulary of Change
Dialogue a structured, collective discussion among two or more parties with no predetermined conclusion.

Dialogue is meant to be more than one-way communication, more even than a simple conversation. Because the goal of dialogue is learning, it is a process that leads to unexpected conclusions. The process of participating in dialogue enriches both the understanding and the commitment of all parties to the implications and conclusions of that dialogue.

THEORY INTO PRACTICE

Creating a dialogue offers the opportunity for an open and honest conversation among employees.

Achieving an open, honest dialogue, especially in a hierarchical organization, can be difficult. Success in creating a dialogue depends on a number of factors. Because dialogue occurs in an organizational context, that context must be one that enables rather than impedes openness.

Organizational Enablers of Dialogue

Dialogue does not occur within a vacuum. It is up to organizational leaders to help create and maintain a context that allows, encourages, and enables an open and candid dialogue. Speaking openly and honestly can be a risky undertaking. Employees often feel inhibited when asked to speak up concerning organizational problems and barriers to outstanding performance.

The phenomenon that inhibits or even eliminates opportunities for the free and open exchange of ideas and views is known as organizational silence.[6] **Organizational silence** refers to the pervasive set of assumptions on the part of employees that candid feedback and open, shared dialogue is to be avoided. As we saw at HP, it is not just employees at lower hierarchical levels who can feel inhibited. Managers and executives can also hesitate to speak openly and honestly, even when they do not understand, agree, or both with the policies being promulgated from the top.[7]

Building a Vocabulary of Change
Organizational silence the lack of truthful dialogue in organizations caused by the widespread assumption on the part of employees that candid feedback and the open exchange of ideas will have either no positive impact or negative consequences to the individual, or both.

THEORY INTO PRACTICE

Don't confuse passive acceptance with agreement.

Organizational silence hinders mutual engagement. Silence, undermines an organization's ability to engage in learning. Learning requires engagement, participation, and openness. Silence—the unwillingness to engage, to participate, and to be open—inhibits learning and makes effective change implementation more difficult.

THEORY INTO PRACTICE

Leaders can take an active role in overcoming the "climate of silence."

Organizational silence—even in hierarchical organizations—is not inevitable. Leaders can help their organizations overcome silence by paying attention to particular dynamics that may block openness. Hierarchy, as we know, creates power distance: distinct differences in power based on hierarchical position. The problem is, large power distances—say, between a boss and a subordinate or a CEO and a division vice president—can encourage silence.

When one participant in the dialogue possesses significantly more organizational power than the other, both parties tend to filter their communication. The boss may be less than totally candid with her subordinates. Do they really need to know this information, she may ask herself? And what will they do with the information? The subordinate may think twice about what he says to the boss. What will my boss do with this information? Will it somehow be used against me? Both parties tend to withhold, or even distort, intending to protect and/or advance their self-interest.

THEORY INTO PRACTICE

A large power distance between parties in a dialogue inhibits openness and risk taking while distorting communications.

In a hierarchical organization, some power distance is inevitable. Filtering cannot be avoided entirely. Nevertheless, organizations have undertaken a number of approaches meant to lessen the distance and increase the effectiveness of the dialogue. One approach to reducing power distance involves *delayering*, that is, eliminating multiple levels of hierarchy. Many of today's business units have significantly reduced the number of supervisory and managerial levels existing in a unit. With fewer hierarchical levels, the distortion that arises from filtering is reduced significantly.

Decentralizing pushes decision making down to lower levels and can occur separately or be combined with delayering. By granting lower-level managers the autonomy to make decisions, those managers have the opportunity to involve their direct staff in diagnosis, thus eliminating hierarchical levels that more typically exist between workers and managers.

Many organizations have taken the symbolic step of creating an *egalitarian culture,* eliminating many of the perquisites often associated with hierarchical status:

- Doing away with executive parking and cafeterias is a now-common characteristic in new work facilities.
- Putting the entire workforce on salary erases the distinction between hourly and salaried employees.

- Informal attire and forms of address (calling everyone by his first name, for example), and an end to opulent executive offices removes obvious external signs of status.

These symbolic actions will mean very little if they are seen by employees as empty gestures or even as contradictions to an otherwise hierarchical, highly differentiated power structure. If, on the other hand, they are experienced as manifestations of a deeply embedded egalitarian culture, they can help reduce perceived power differentials and enable open dialogue.

Third-party facilitation can also be a powerful antidote to power differentials. In a structured dialogue where multiple hierarchical levels are involved, facilitators can suggest—and even enforce—communication rules meant to establish openness and trust. Third-party facilitators can create "situational" power equity.[8]

Most power equalization steps focus on power differences based on hierarchical position. Power distance can also exist *horizontally*. Horizontal power distance involves units that, in essence, compete for power within the organization. This will lead to power distances that can develop over time between functional units within an organization. "Engineering is king." "Marketing is everything." "We're completely numbers driven." All of these slogans are expressions of precisely this type of inequity among functions.

Horizontal power distance can be harmful to open dialogue. Communication can be filtered and ideas dismissed. A powerful research and development function can make it difficult for sales and marketing people to inject the customer perspective into the dialogue about product design decisions. An overly dominant finance function might block the voice of employers and customers. An isolated but influential research and development department might offer new products that business units feel are unattractive to their local markets.

A well-balanced top management team with shared purpose will help maintain mutual engagement, ensuring that all voices are respected and influential. In that circumstance, the voices of multiple functions and units are more likely to come through unfiltered in a diagnosis concerning barriers to outstanding performance.

Steps to equalize power help set the organizational context for dialogue. Organizations seeking to encourage mutual engagement will also need to create **psychological safety**—a belief on the part of employees that the organizational climate is conducive for taking personal risks, especially around dialogue. Leaders can look at all the elements that create or undermine trust between and among stakeholders. Creating a psychological safety zone in which all employees feel safe from threat and reprisal for both advocating and inquiring will help nurture a context in which mutual engagement can and will continue. Ultimately, in a change implementation process, leaders can help banish the barrier of silence by committing themselves to the desirability, even the necessity of entering into a dialogue with employees. Instead of announcing solutions, leaders can create a process of mutual engagement and learning, thus inviting employees at all levels to cross barriers of silence and participate in a dialogue.

Building a Vocabulary of Change

Psychological safety a belief on the part of employees that the organizational climate is conducive to taking personal risks, especially around dialogue.

EXHIBIT 3-2
Power Equalization Steps.

Steps	Lead to
Delayering	Removing hierarchical barriers that create distance and distort communications
Decentralizing	Pushing down decision making to close gap between decision makers and "doers"
Egalitarianism	Removing "artifacts" of status differentials
Third-party facilitation	Structuring effective "rules-of-engagement" around feedback and dialogue
Representation	Inserting voice from multiple levels, both vertical (managers, shop floor employees, etc.) and horizontal (union and management, various functions, etc.) into dialogue
Teamwork	Building shared purpose and mutual responsibility to ensure equal participation and influence by all members in dialogue

THE CONSULTANT ROLE

Mutual engagement in diagnosis requires more than just motivation, willingness, and psychological safety. It also requires skills. Those skills are different from the functional competencies—marketing, sales, technology, operations, and so forth—that are required in the typical workday of an employee.

Participating in an open dialogue where views—both positive and negative—are freely expressed and performance-focused might prove both unusual and uncomfortable. Participating in such a dialogue, not to mention facilitating the participation of others, might be alien to an employee's experience.

THEORY INTO PRACTICE

Leaders can call on a consultant to introduce and teach skills required of mutual engagement and diagnosis.

Building a Vocabulary of Change
Consultant an individual possessing a broad range of diagnostic and developmental skills who contracts with the organization's leaders to facilitate an intervention.

Employees *can* learn these skills. In fact, one of the goals of change can be to develop such skills and competencies among employees. But because diagnosis calls for new roles and skills that have yet to be developed, it often proceeds with the help of a consultant. A **consultant** is an individual possessing a broad range of diagnostic and developmental skills who facilitates a change intervention.

Consultants may arrive from outside the organization: professional consultants or academics with a specialization in organizational change and development. They may also come from within the firm: specially trained employees, often within the company's human resource or organization development staff. Whether internal or external, the task of the consultant is the same: to facilitate diagnosis and dialogue and to do so in a way that allows employees to develop those skills themselves.[9]

GETTING STARTED WITH ORGANIZATIONAL DIAGNOSIS

To increase the effectiveness of diagnosis as an opening stage of organizational change, the process can follow the principles outlined in Exhibit 3-3. It is now time to explore the specific steps that can be pursued based on these principles. These steps involve:

- *Collecting data* on the organization and its environment
- Entering into a *dialogue of discovery* that makes sense of and provides insight into the data that has been amassed
- Receiving and providing *feedback* on what has been learned
- *Institutionalizing dialogue and diagnosis* so that they become an organic and ongoing part of the organization's activities

Each step enhances mutual engagement and helps build commitment to change.

Data Collection

Effective diagnosis is data driven, that is, infused with and informed by valid information concerning the factors that impact the performance of the organization and its ability to implement its renewed strategy. A diagnostic framework will point to the target areas for data collection.

THEORY INTO PRACTICE

Make sure that diagnosis flows from valid data about the organization.

Data are more than a collection of cold, hard facts. Data amassed through the diagnostic process can have a powerful impact on the ensuing change by motivating employees to alter their behavior in ways that will support strategic

EXHIBIT 3-3
Principles for Organizational Diagnosis.

Systemic focus	Targets the entire organization and is guided by a framework that focuses on interactions
Consultant facilitated	Specially trained individual(s) bring external perspective and required skills
Participative	Employees participate in all stages as full partners in order to build commitment and competency
Data-based	Participants agree on the validity and strategic importance of data collected about performance
Honest conversation	Employees engage the requirements of shared dialogue: mutuality, reciprocity, advocacy, and inquiry
Psychological safety	Active steps taken to overcome climate of organizational silence

renewal. The motivational impact of data occurs as feelings are aroused and forces unleashed that bring about behavioral change. The act of collecting data potentially becomes a key way of mobilizing the considerable energy needed to abandon the status quo.

So the challenge of data collection becomes twofold:

1. To collect data on the key elements impacting an organization's capacity to support the new strategy and to achieve and maintain outstanding performance; and,
2. To do so in a way most likely to build motivation and commitment on the part of employees.

There are three basic forms of data collection: questionnaires, interviews, and observation. Each holds strengths and weaknesses, especially in light of that dual requirement.

THEORY INTO PRACTICE

The process of collecting data can help build motivation and commitment to altering patterns of behavior.

Building a Vocabulary of Change
Questionnaires self-administered paper-and-pencil data-collection forms, often stressing areas of behavioral interaction such as communications, goals, and coordination.

QUESTIONNAIRES The most popular form of collecting data involves written questionnaires. **Questionnaires** are self-administered paper-and-pencil or computer-based data-collection forms. Questionnaires often stress areas of behavioral interaction such as communications, goals, and coordination. Employees may be asked, for instance, to rate the clarity of the organization's strategy, the quality of information that is shared, or the nature of supervision. Although questionnaires can be developed internally, they are more typically packaged by an external consulting firm or an academic center. Exhibit 3-4 presents a sample from one such questionnaire developed by Robert C. Preziosi.[10]

Questionnaires have some tangible advantages as a source of data. They can be administered to a large number of employees and results compiled in a short time period. Because they are administered and returned anonymously, questionnaires can help overcome the climate of silence by allowing employees a greater sense of freedom and protection. They can provide a valuable benchmark for the organization to measure itself against. When administered to multiple units, they can offer comparisons and highlight units in the organization where results are especially positive or negative. When administered to the same unit over time, they can track progress or regression.

There is, however, a downside to the use of questionnaires in a change process. The preconceived categories represented in the questionnaires may measure theoretical constructs that are relevant to the developer of the questions, but they may not necessarily speak to the true needs of the organization. Questionnaires, write Jack Fordyce and Raymond Weil, "do not create the kind of personal involvement and dialogue that is so valuable in changing hearts and minds. The information generated by questionnaires tends to be canned, anonymous, ambiguous, and detached—i.e., cool data rather than hot."[11] Because of

EXHIBIT 3-4 Organizational Diagnostic Questionnaire.

A sampling of 10 questions is reproduced. The complete questionnaire along with an analysis by its author can be viewed at: http://www.g-rap.org/docs/icb/preziosi-organ_diagnosis_questionnaire_odq.pdf

From time to time, organizations consider it important to analyze themselves. It is necessary to find out from people who work in the organization what they think. This questionnaire will help the organization that you work for analyze itself.

Directions: DO NOT put your name anywhere on this questionnaire. Please answer all questions. For each of the statements, circle only one number to indicate your thinking.

Agree Strongly – 1, Agree – 2, Agree Slightly – 3, Neutral – 4, Disagree Slightly – 5, Disagree – 6, Disagree Strongly – 7

1. The goals of this organization are clearly stated.

   1 2 3 4 5 6 7

2. My immediate supervisor is supportive of my efforts.

   1 2 3 4 5 6 7

3. This organization is not resistant to change.

   1 2 3 4 5 6 7

4. The leadership norms of this organization help its progress.

   1 2 3 4 5 6 7

5. I have the information that I need to do a good job.

   1 2 3 4 5 6 7

6. The manner in which work tasks are divided is a logical one.

   1 2 3 4 5 6 7

7. The opportunity for promotion exists in this organization.

   1 2 3 4 5 6 7

8. The structure of my work unit is well designed.

   1 2 3 4 5 6 7

9. I have established the relationships that I need to do my job properly.

   1 2 3 4 5 6 7

10. All tasks to be accomplished are associated with incentives.

    1 2 3 4 5 6 7

Source: Excerpt from "Organizational Diagnosis Questionnaire," available at http://www.g-rap.org/docs/ICB/Preziosi%20-%20Organ.%20Diagnosis%20Questionnaire%20ODQ.pdf.

that lack of personal involvement and deep sentiment, managers may be more likely to respond with token reaction rather than significant response.

THEORY INTO PRACTICE

Be careful about the overuse of employee questionnaires in collecting data about organizational effectiveness. They can be useful for measurement purpose but do not create mutual engagement.

That is not to say that questionnaires have no important role to play. By providing a benchmark measurement against either other organizations or against best-practice units within the organization, questionnaires can help build dissatisfaction with the status quo and awareness of the need for change. When used for internal measurement, the results can serve as an early warning system for problems developing within a unit.

Building a Vocabulary of Change
Diagnostic interviews a form of data collection in which a trained diagnostician meets with an employee, or small groups of employees, to solicit information pertaining to the performance of the organization.

INTERVIEWS Other methods of data collection can provide far richer and more detailed insight into the dynamics of an organization. **Diagnostic interviews** involve a trained diagnostician—this may be an external expert, an employee with specific training, or a combination of the two—sitting down with an employee, or occasionally small groups of employees, and soliciting information. Interviews can provide far richer data than questionnaires.

Diagnostic interviews can be either structured or unstructured. In structured interviews, the interviewer prepares a set of questions to be asked of all respondents. In an unstructured interview, a small number of general questions—"What are the organizational barriers to achieving your strategic objectives?" or "What are the goals of your unit and what are the organizational barriers you perceive for achieving those goals?" for example—are intended to precipitate what Andrew Manzini calls "the respondent's own definition of relevant problems and issues."[12] What follows those broad questions is an open dialogue between the interviewer and the interviewee that helps determine the direction of the remainder of the interview.

THEORY INTO PRACTICE

Use diagnostic interviews and behavioral observation to collect rich and valid data about how employees behave and how the organization functions.

In addition to generating data, open-ended interviews offer the opportunity to clarify the data as they are being generated. The interviewer can ask questions of the respondent and probe more deeply: *What did you mean by that response?* Or, *can you tell me more about why you think that is true?* Because unstructured interviews can become a forum for personal issues that have little to do with improving organizational performance, interviewers will need to keep focus on pertinent, performance-related issues.

Professional consultants can conduct these interviews. There is also an advantage to training employees as interviewers. The involvement of employees in the data collection process enhances their commitment to the changes suggested by the process. Also, organizational members inevitably know more about the hidden but critical aspects of organizational life than would any outsider. They bring, in other words, their own expertise to the process. Finally, by participating in the data collection process, employees are gaining the skills necessary to engage in ongoing data collection and diagnosis in the future.[13]

OBSERVATIONS Apart from questionnaires and interviews, another source of data is **behavioral observation.**[14] The diagnostician can watch actual behaviors of employees: the meetings of top management teams, efforts of work groups to solve problems, interactions between boss and subordinate, and so forth. Behavioral observation has the advantage of eliminating self-reports by focusing directly on behaviors. The observer may remain apart from the behaviors themselves, acting as a sort of an unobtrusive fly-on-the-wall. Or, the observer may involve himself in the behaviors being observed. The participant–observer becomes immersed in the actual behaviors of employees as a way of reaching a deep understanding of their behaviors.

Building a Vocabulary of Change
Behavioral observation a form of data collection in which a trained diagnostician can watch actual behaviors of employees.

A broad literature in the social sciences exists on the strengths and weaknesses, validity and pitfalls, even the ethics of the participant–observer role.[15] For a well-trained observer, the interactions that result from participation in meetings, problem-solving groups, and the like can provide an indispensable source of data concerning the cognitive and emotional state of employees.

SUMMARIZING DATA COLLECTION METHODS The three types of data collection (summarized in Exhibit 3-5) do not have to be thought of as mutually exclusive. Used together—interviews and observations to collect rich data and questionnaires to validate data on a wider scale—the various methods of data collection provide invaluable input into the next stage of the diagnostic process: creating a dialogue about the organization's functioning.

Creating a Dialogue of Discovery

Data collection is only the preliminary step in diagnosis. The next step addresses the question: what does the data mean and what should the organization do about it?

In the **discovery** stage, employees engage in an analysis of the data, make sense of what they have learned, and consider the steps to take to act upon that learning. When diagnosis is the first step of a change process, the responsible leaders of the organizational unit being targeted—if it is the entire organization, then the responsible leaders are the top management team—can be engaged in that discovery.[16] The involvement of the individuals, groups, and teams required to take action enriches the understanding of the data while simultaneously building their commitment to the resulting change. Because their own behaviors will likely be part of the collected data, their mutual engagement in the discovery process and commitment to respond to their learnings become particularly valuable.

Building a Vocabulary of Change
Discovery the process of analyzing and making sense of data that has been collected as part of an organizational diagnosis.

EXHIBIT 3-5 Data Collection Methods for Organizational Diagnosis.

Methods	Advantages at Initial Stage of Change	Disadvantages at Initial Stage of Change
Questionnaires	• Can be administered to large number of employees • Can be processed quickly • Data is collected anonymously • Can be used to create benchmarks and make comparisons across organizations and over time	• Based on preconceived ideas about what issues and areas should be examined • Can over simplify vague and complex issues like culture • Do not expose root causes of problems • Do not create commitment to outcomes or motivation to change
Diagnostic interviews	• Collect rich data • Begin process of creating dialogue • Teach communication and active listening skills to employees	• Require up-front investment in training interviewers • Data may be hard to summarize and quantify • Lack anonymity
Behavioral observation	• Provides current work-based behavior as data • Offers deep and rich data on interactions among people • Can surface underlying emotions that impact behavior	• Act of observation will impact behaviors of those being observed • Time-consuming data collection process • Requires highly skilled observers

Determining *who* to engage is the first requirement of the discovery process. A blend of individuals representing a multitude of perspectives on the organization (say, representatives from various functions and units and from multiple hierarchical levels) will help ensure a broad, systemic view. The next vital question in designing the discovery process is *how*.

THEORY INTO PRACTICE

Mutual engagement in the discovery stage will help both to assure the validity of the conclusions and build commitment to corrective actions.

Mutual engagement in the discovery process can take place in face-to-face meetings: employees gathered in the same room when possible and connected via electronic means when necessary. Face-to-face interaction provides the richness required to help understand the complexity of the opportunities and problems to be addressed.

When employees themselves have been involved in the data collection process, they can deliver their data directly to the responsible individuals. The consultant can facilitate that exchange by setting ground rules for productive and open dialogue. The leadership group hearing the feedback, for example, can be allowed to ask clarifying questions but be stopped by the consultant if their responses represent defensiveness or denial.[17]

Mutual engagement in discovery is critical to determining the effectiveness of the change process. To ensure the systemic nature of the discovery process—that is, a focus on how the multiple elements of the organization do or do not align—the consultant can use a diagnostic framework. A discovery process guided by a systemic diagnostic framework will channel energy, in Michael Harrison and Arie Shirom's words, "toward decisions and actions likely to provide the broadest organizational benefits."[18] By creating disequilibrium with the status quo, discovery provides a vital staging for the upcoming change process.

Closing the Loop with Feedback

Employees who have engaged in the data collection and discovery phases will expect to learn how their efforts have been translated into action. There is an expectation, in other words, that feedback will be part of the diagnostic process. **Feedback** refers to the process of receiving information concerning the effectiveness of one's actions and performance.

Building a Vocabulary of Change
Feedback the process of receiving information focused on the effectiveness of one's actions and performance.

THEORY INTO PRACTICE

Mutual engagement can be enhanced when top management feeds back to employees what it has learned from the diagnostic process and uses that feedback as an opportunity to generate more learning.

The entire diagnostic process involves feedback, of course. By receiving data from the organization about performance and about the manner in which various organizational elements align, or do not align, in order to implement strategy, management benefits from rich and valuable feedback. In the discovery phase, management receives feedback not just about the particulars uncovered through data collection but also about the perceived meaning, importance, and performance implications of that data.

Feedback can also occur following discovery. Managers can report to employees on the conclusions reached as part of that process and on the plan of action intended to address what has been learned. When groups of employees participate directly in collecting data, the feedback loop can be closed directly if upper management communicates directly with those participants.

As top management reports its conclusions, mutual engagement can continue as employees react to the plan of action. The feedback loop can thus become continuous and ongoing. Two mechanisms advance the feedback process:[19]

1. The feedback from the top management group empowered to lead the change can occur in face-to-face sessions in order to increase the richness of

the process as well as to create responsibility and accountability for taking actions.[20]

2. The learning from the discovery process as well as the change plans that result can be presented as tentative rather than final, thus inviting additional dialogue and discovery.

Closing the feedback loop will work to keep mutual engagement continuous during the change process.

After-Action Reviews

Building a Vocabulary of Change
After-action review (AAR) an organized, disciplined approach to shared diagnosis and mutual dialogue in the immediate aftermath of a specific action or event.

A form of mutual engagement and diagnosis that has become popular in recent years involves a process of looking back. In an **after-action review (AAR)**, organizations take an "action" that has just occurred—some event of strategic import—and diagnose the dynamics of that action. The goal is to engage participants in a "just-in-time diagnosis" that leads to quick performance improvement.

An example of such an AAR occurred when Wall Street firm Wills & Somerset fumbled a potential contract with a large corporate client. Wills & Somerset CEO Carol Peters expressed frustration, of course, but also determination. The client was scheduled to ask for a new bid in six months. To make sure that Wills & Somerset would be better positioned to succeed this time around, she called on all the participants in the past effort to engage in an AAR. The cause of the problem emerged quickly. Sales and technical support had been unable to agree on either the scope of the product they were developing for a specific client. As a result, the price quoted to the client fluctuated wildly from week to week, meeting to meeting. Worse still, the lead salesperson had been unable to explain to the client just what the cost drivers were and why the price had been so difficult to fix. This insight was not a solution, of course. But the AAR helped point Wills & Somerset set a direction for needed change.

First developed by the U.S. Army at the Center for Army Lessons Learned, AARs are a structured effort to collect data, identify deficiencies, sustain positives, and improve performance.[21] The army's own definition is instructive, labeling the AAR "a professional discussion of an event, focused on performance standards, that enables soldiers to discover for themselves what happened, why it happened, and how to sustain strengths and improve on weaknesses."[22] In particular, the AAR offers an approach to shared diagnosis and mutual engagement that attempts to compress the elapsed time between action, learning, correction, and new action. For Wills & Somerset, the need to learn was pressing. For soldiers involved in military operations, that need is even more urgent.

The AAR is based on the premise that a lesson is not "learned" unless and until it leads to new behaviors. The review follows the principles of shared diagnosis and mutual engagement by involving those who participated directly in the "action"—in the case of Wall and Somerset, those individuals involved in putting together the proposal to the client—in gathering and interpreting data and then building an action plan for future success. Because those involved in the initial action are also engaged in the analysis and planning, their commitment to future improvements are enhanced.

The specifics of the army's AARs involved eight key components:

1. The review takes place either during or immediately after the event under study.
2. The review starts with a shared understanding of the objectives and aims of the event.
3. The review focuses on the overall performance of the targeted group.
4. The review is conducted by the participants in the event.
5. The review is governed by open-ended questions such as What occurred? Why? What can we do about it?
6. The review identifies strengths and weaknesses.
7. The review leads to new actions.
8. The lessons of the review become part of future training.[23]

In any organizational setting—whether it be the army or a business firm—the AAR approach to shared diagnosis and mutual dialogue offers an opportunity to learn, interpret, and act quickly. Wills & Somerset was able to overcome internal barriers to collaboration by forming a small cross-functional engagement task force and offer a successful rebid. Although AARs are, by definition, sharply focused on specific actions and activities, the resulting learning can be amassed by organizations as a way of sharing learning.

THEORY INTO PRACTICE

After-action reviews provided an opportunity for a sharply focused and timely mutual engagement that can lead to quick corrections.

Conclusion

If the need for change is urgent, executives may be tempted to rush toward a "solution." That instinct, while understandable, is likely to harm the effectiveness of the change implementation process. Mutual engagement in dialogue and diagnosis helps generate vital data. The process can also create commitment to learning and motivation to change on the part of participants, while building diagnostic competencies into the organization.

In order to target the performance of the entire organization and its ability to implement a renewed strategy, diagnosis can be shaped and guided by a systemic framework. With the facilitation of a consultant, employees can engage in data collection and a dialogue of discovery concerning those elements and their fit with each other, with the strategy, and with the external environment.

Creating a dialogue within the organization is hampered by many organizational factors. Power distance encourages participants to filter information rather than to be completely open. Organizational silence discourages honesty and must be overcome by organizational leaders. Only by creating a sense of psychological safety will employees willingly engage in a candid exchange of information and insight concerning the performance of the organization.

Once dialogue and diagnosis have been engaged, implementation can proceed. Dialogue and diagnosis likely will target patterns of behavior, asking if employees at all levels of the organization are enacting their roles and responsibilities in a way that is aligned with the demands of the strategy and the requirements of outstanding performance. The ability of an organization to create and sustain a climate of openness and honest conversation depends a great deal on the culture of the organization and the values of that organization's managers. Chapter 4 will focus explicitly on an understanding of values and culture.

Discussion Questions

1. How might Carly Fiorina have planned her early efforts at Hewlett-Packard? Pay particular attention to how she might have used the principles of mutual engagement and shared diagnosis.
2. What are the potential advantages of relying on a systemic framework for guiding diagnosis? Are there any potential disadvantages?
3. Why is open dialogue so difficult to achieve in many organizations?
4. In what specific ways can an executive actively promote a sense of psychological safety among employees to engage them in an honest conversation about performance?
5. How might the three forms of data collection be used together in the opening stages of a change process?
6. How can an organization make sure that diagnosis becomes a regular and ongoing element of the way it does business?

Case Discussion

Read "Managing Transformation at National Computer Operations" and prepare answers to the following questions:

1. Prepare an implementation plan for change that would enable Gar Finnvold to create a fully competitive computer service within two years.
2. How could Finnvold conduct an organizational diagnosis that would lead off his implementation? Be specific about how he could ensure mutual engagement.

MANAGING TRANSFORMATION AT NATIONAL COMPUTER OPERATIONS

Gar Finnvold knew his organization needed to change, to transform itself over the next two years. His 1,000 employees had enjoyed for their entire careers what amounted to monopoly status. They had been the exclusive provider of computer support services to the immense, global enterprises of the U.K.-based National Banking Group. All that was about to change. National Bank's newly appointed chairman had decreed that, starting in two years, all bank operations would be free to purchase their computer services from any vendor who could supply excellent value. Finnvold's operation would be competing against the best in Europe. At the same time, Finnvold would be free to market his computer operations on the outside, to build a customer base external to the bank.

Finnvold's excitement at the challenge of transforming his National Computer Operations (NCO) into a truly world-class competitor was matched by his anxiety (see Exhibit 3-6 for a partial organization chart). As the longtime manager of computer operations, he understood only too well that NCO was unprepared to compete, not internally and certainly not externally. Internal bank customers had complained for years of the high-cost/low-responsiveness culture

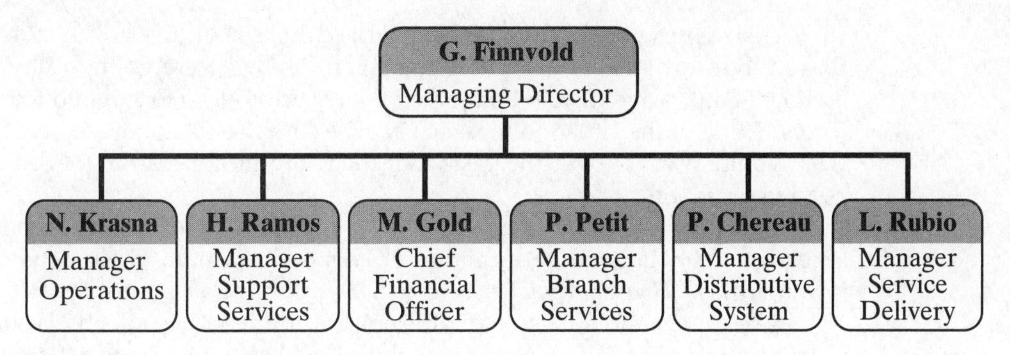

EXHIBIT 3-6 Partial Organization Chart—National Computer Operations.

of the NCO. Buffered by their monopoly status, NCO's computer technicians didn't worry much about whether the customer perceived them as providing value. We understand better than the customer both what that customer needs and how much they should be willing to pay for it. We'll define value.

In two years, Finnvold knew that equation would be reversed. Given a free-market choice to seek the best provider of computer services, would they re-up with NCO? Not likely, he thought.

At least inside the bank, NCO enjoyed a substantial cost advantage over potential external interlopers. National tax laws exempted bank operations from having to pay a nearly 20 percent tax on internally provided services. That tax advantage evaporated when NCO left the safety of the bank to hunt external customers.

What's more, no one at any level in NCO possessed real general management experience. No one, Finnvold included, had ever run a freestanding commercial enterprise with all that implied: managing costs, customers, and operations within a fiercely competitive environment. Was two years even close to enough time to undergo the radical transformation required to make such a venture successful?

NCO Operations

Listen to how Peter Kapok, a longtime NCO manager, described what his organization was like in the 1990s: "We weren't client oriented. We very much told our clients what they could and couldn't have. We came to work for ourselves and did pretty much what we wanted. We simply didn't consider ourselves working for a client." The notion that customers might define the ultimate value of their services was alien to NCO.

Henri Vieuxtemps, who entered the computer operations in 1988, recalled his amazement at how little the operation resembled a true business. "What surprised me," he said, "was that money was no object. Service was not a major consideration." What might be called the arrogance of technology permeated NCO's approach to the business. "We spent money on technology that really didn't matter," continues Vieuxtemps, "not to the customer anyway. It was just something that appealed to *us*. In fact, we didn't think of internal clients as customers at all. They were just other departments in the bank."

Vieuxtemps may have believed that the culture of NCO was fundamentally flawed, but to many of his fellow managers, things were going quite nicely. National Bank, after all, had eliminated the need for NCO to respond to market forces. Think of the situation in which NCO found itself: Guaranteed customers who would always cover the costs that the computer operation passed along, assured profitability.

It's little wonder that for most of NCO's managers, effectiveness was not measured by organizational performance or client satisfaction. Their focus turned inward instead. *How can* I *build up* my *functional domain? Enhance* my *personal career?*

"We were an organization of little empire builders," Kapok observed. "The more people you had working for you, the more likely you were to get promoted. There were few performance measures, and almost no coordination of our efforts." The functional silos of the organization were so powerful, said Kapok, that NCO's own staff "didn't quite consider ourselves working for the same operation. If someone from one unit went to someone from another to ask for help, they were considered a nuisance. We certainly never considered the impact of any of this on our costs."

NCO's high spending, "customer—what customer?" attitude could only lead to resentment on the part of client operations within the bank. That resentment finally boiled over into open rebellion. The bank's new chairman hired a consulting firm to evaluate internal computer operations. The findings were as disturbing as they were predictable. "They confirmed our worst fears," recalled an NCO manager. "We were moribund."

Until the consulting report provided irrefutable evidence to the contrary, computer operations managers felt they did an excellent job of providing these services to the bank. "If you had asked us how we were doing," admitted Gar Finnvold, "we would have said, 'We meet our customer service levels most of the time. We are improving our unit costs year-on-year. And *of course* we're adding value.'" It was only later that Finnvold came to recognize that customers held a view of NCO's effectiveness that stood in diametric opposition to the opinion of NCO's managers. "Our customers were saying, 'You're too expensive. Your damn system is always breaking down. And *what* added value?'"

At the time of the consulting report, computer operations were billing approximately $240* million annually (within an overall annual information technology expenditure of $1.5 billion), almost entirely to internal bank customers. Although NCO offered myriad services, including processing, project management, and technical support and consultancy, they pointed with pride to two distinct competencies. The first was facilities management. "NCO can take the responsibility for all or part of a company's Information Technology requirement," announced their official literature, "which can include every aspect from providing the workforce and premises to the systems and services." The second vital core competency was disaster recovery. "NCO provides planning and backup facilities for unforeseen crises or disasters such as fire and flood. Planning and backup facilities can be provided either separately or together and can be offered in either a 'hot start' or 'cold start' environment."

*Figures given in equivalent U.S. dollars.

The Challenge

The bank's new chairman quickly recognized that NCO customers and managers held completely different views of value. He knew that his first task was to force NCO managers to adopt the customer perspective. The way to do that, he reasoned, was to inject market forces into NCO's protected, monopoly-like world.

Using the consulting report as a driver, he first designated NCO as a profit center. He made clear that NCO would be expected to pare costs severely. Within a year, NCO dramatically downsized its workforce from 1,500 to 1,000. The chairman then called on Gar Finnvold to oversee more sweeping change, change that would be governed by two new ground rules:

1. NCO could actively and aggressively market its services to external customers.
2. In two years, all of the bank's internal units would be allowed to purchase computer services from outside vendors.

NCO, in other words, would have to become fully competitive in order to survive.

Finnvold said he welcomed the challenge, particularly the notion of becoming a true market competitor. "I had this gut feel that we should try to sell external from day one," he said. "If we didn't, we'd never learn the lesson of what being commercial is all about. It was the way out of our cocooned environment." He believed that there were external customers waiting to snatch up NCO's services. The facilities management business was expected to grow 50 percent annually worldwide. NCO planned on being part of that growth. "We thought we really had things to sell and that we were the best," said Finnvold.

Endnotes

1. Information on Hewlett-Packard is from Peter Burrows, *Backfire: Carly Fiorina's High-Stakes Battle for the Soul of Hewlett-Packard* (New York: Wiley, 2003) and George Anders, *Perfect Enough: Carly Fiorina and the Reinvention of Hewlett-Packard* (New York: Penguin Putnam, 2003).
2. Hurd quoted in Laurie J. Flynn, "Hewlett Chief Has No Plans but Says All Is on the Exhibit," *New York Times,* March 31, 2005, p. C11. In 2010, Hurd himself was asked to resign as the result of a sexual harassment probe. The board soon hired Leo Apotheke to replace Hurd. Apotheke had been CEO of SAP until he was asked to resign by the German software giant's board.
3. Many of the concepts in this chapter are based on Michael Beer and Bert Spector, "Organizational Diagnosis: Its Role in Organizational Learning," *Journal of Counseling and Development* 71 (July–August 1993), pp. 642–650.
4. See, for example, Paul E. Lawrence and Jay Lorsch, *Developing Organizations: Diagnosis and Action* (Reading, MA: Addison-Wesley, 1969); Jay R. Galbraith, *Designing Complex Organizations* (Reading, MA: Addison-Wesley, 1973); David A. Nadler and Michael L. Tushman, "A Diagnostic Model for Organizational Behavior," in Edward E. Lawler and Lyman W. Porter, eds., *Perspectives on Behavior in Organizations* (New York: McGraw-Hill, 1977); Michael B. McCaskey, "A Framework for Analyzing Work Groups," in Leonard A. Schlesinger, Robert G. Eccles, and John J. Gabarro, eds., *Managing Behavior in Organizations: Text, Cases, Readings* (New York: McGraw-Hill, 1983), pp. 4–24.

5. David A. Nadler, "Role of Models in Organizational Assessment," in Edward E. Lawler III, David A. Nadler, and Cortlandt Cammann, eds., *Organizational Assessment: Perspectives on the Measurement of Organizational Behavior and the Quality of Work Life* (New York: Wiley, 1980), pp. 125–126.
6. Elizabeth Wolfe Morrison and Frances J. Milliken, "Organizational Silence: A Barrier to Change and Development in a Pluralistic World," *Academy of Management Review* 25 (October 2000), pp. 706–725; James R. Detert, Ethan R. Burris, and David A. Harrison, "Debunking Four Myths about Employee Silence," *Harvard Business Review* (June 2010), p. 26.
7. Moskal, "Is Industry Ready for Adult Relations?"
8. Richard E. Walton, *Interpersonal Peacemaking; Confrontations and Third-party Consultation* (Reading, MA: Addision-Wesley, 1969).
9. Beer and Spector, "Organizational Diagnosis."
10. In a previous edition of the text, the source of this questionnaire was misidentified. Thanks to Professor Preziosi for calling our attention to the error and allowing us to use the properly attributed questionnaire.
11. Jack K. Fordyce and Raymond Weil, "Methods for Finding Out What Is Going On," in Wendell L. French, Cecil H. Bell, Jr., and Robert A. Zawacki, eds., *Organization Development: Theory, Practice, and Research* (Dallas, TX: Business Publications, Inc., 1978), p. 121.
12. Andrew O. Manzini, *Organizational Diagnosis: A Practical Approach to Company Problem Solving and Growth* (New York: AMACOM, 1988), p. 39.
13. Beer and Spector, "Organizational Diagnosis."
14. E. E. Lawler, D. A. Naddler, C. Cammann, *Organizational Assessment*, pp. 337–343.
15. See, for example, Severyn Bruyn, *The Human Perspective in Sociology: The Methodology of Participant Observation* (Englewood Cliffs, NJ: Prentice-Hall, 1966); Robert Bogdan, *Participant Observation in Organizational Settings* (Syracuse, NY: Syracuse University Press, 1972); Patricia A. Adler and Peter Adler, "Observation Techniques," in Norman Denzin and Yvonna S. Lincoln, eds., *Handbook of Qualitative Research* (Newbury Park, CA: Sage, 1994), pp. 377–392; James P. Spradley, *Participant Observation* (New York: Holt, 1997).
16. David A. Nadler, *Feedback and Organization Development: Using Data-Based Methods* (Reading, MA: Addison-Wesley, 1977).
17. Beer and Spector, "Organizational Diagnosis."
18. Michael I. Harrison and Arie Shirom, *Organizational Diagnosis and Assessment: Bridging Theory and Practice* (Thousand Oaks, CA: Sage, 1999), p. 25.
19. Beer and Spector, "Organizational Diagnosis," p. 648.
20. See also Nadler, *Feedback and Organization Development*.
21. The material on after-action reviews comes from Department of Army, *A Leader's Guide to After-Action Reviews*. (Training Circular 25-20) (Washington, D.C.: Headquarters, Department of Army, September 1993); Lloyd Baird, John C. Henderson, and Stephanie Watts, "Learning from Action: An Analysis of the Center for Army Lessons Learned (CALL)," *Human Resource Management* 36 (Winter 1997), pp. 385–395; Paul Wright, "Learn as You Go Through the After Action Review," *Knowledge Management Review* (March–April 1998), pp. 4–6; Lloyd Baird, Phil Holland, and Sandra Deacon, "Imbedding More Learning into the Performance Fast Enough to Make a Difference," *Organizational Dynamics* (Spring 1999), pp. 19–32; Marilyn J. Darling and Charles S. Parry, "After-Action Reviews: Linking Reflection and Planning in a Learning Practice," *Reflections* 3 (2001), pp. 64–72.
22. *A Leader's Guide to After-Action Reviews*, p. 1.
23. Based on Wright, "Learn as You Go," p. 4.
24. All names are disguised. This case is based on the research conducted for Bert Spector, *Taking Charge and Letting Go: A Breakthrough Strategy for Creating and Managing the Horizontal Company* (New York: Free Press, 1995).

CHAPTER

4 Organizational Redesign

Diagnosis exposes the current realities of organizational life, with particular attention to the fit between patterns of employee behavior and the strategic requirements of the firm, to discussion and analysis. Combined with mutual engagement, diagnosis provides both the motivation for and target of change. Now, employees can engage in a process of organizational redesign to help shape required new behaviors. Redesign provides a sense of direction for the change effort.

This chapter will analyze the complexities of design choices made to support change implementation. In particular, this chapter will:

- Define organizational design and differentiate between formal and informal design elements
- Explore the main challenges posed by organizational redesign
- Appreciate the special design challenges faced by multinational companies
- Analyze the requirements for building collaboration in an organization
- Discuss the dynamics of changing the design of an organization in order to impact patterns of behavior

First, we will look at the design challenges faced by the CEO of one of the world's oldest and largest humanitarian organizations. As you read this introductory case, ask yourself:

- Why was the original, decentralized design of CARE less effective in addressing 21st century issues than it had been in CARE's earlier years?
- What do you think the challenge will be in promoting collaboration across national units of CARE?
- What steps might Dr. Helene Gayle take to promote the improvements she hopes for?

DR. GAYLE BRINGS COLLABORATION TO CARE

CARE, one of the world's leading nongovernmental organizations, was created to provide aid to devastated European countries in the immediate aftermath of World War II. When Dr. Helene Gayle became CEO in 2006—after working at both the Center for Disease Control and the Bill and Melinda Gates Foundation—the mission had changed considerably. Under the broadly stated mandate of "Defending Dignity, Fighting Poverty," CARE expanded its reach. The organization described its new mission this way:

> CARE is a leading humanitarian organization fighting global poverty. We place special focus on working alongside poor women because, equipped with the proper resources, women have the power to help whole families and entire communities escape poverty. Women are at the heart of CARE's community-based efforts to improve basic education, prevent the spread of HIV, increase access to clean water and sanitation, expand economic opportunity and protect natural resources. CARE also delivers emergency aid to survivors of war and natural disasters, and helps people rebuild their lives.[1]

Dr. Gayle believed, however, that CARE was better designed to serve its past mission than its future opportunities.

The organization Dr. Gayle found when she became CEO was designed in a way that maximized the autonomy of country offices: France, Germany, Italy, and so forth. "The country officers raised most of their own funds and were used to being on their own," she explained, "having a lot of autonomy, and not thinking about the greater whole."[2] The managers in the organization were "comfortable" with that highly decentralized design, but Gayle believed the approach undermined CARE's effectiveness. Now, the organization had to learn how to collaborate across national borders. "To do that," she said, "we had to ask, 'How do we make the whole greater than the sum of its parts?'" The organizational change would require both improved information sharing across country units and more rigorous measurement of results to evaluate effectiveness.

One of CARE's first efforts at cross-country collaboration involved a project called Access Africa. That microfinance program (making small loans to encourage entrepreneurial efforts in poverty regions) was a 10-year investment commitment targeting 39 sub-Saharan African countries with a combined population of 150 million. "In 10 years," Gayle noted, "we'd like to be able to look back and say, 'Wow, this is very different than if we had continued to function as separate country units.'" Still, she could not deny the challenge of implementing this change.

Building a Vocabulary of Change
Organization design the arrangements, both formal and informal, that an organization calls upon in order to shape employee behavior.

ORGANIZATIONAL REDESIGN

In order to address the challenges of global poverty, Dr. Helene Gayle needed to encourage collaboration among formerly independent national units of CARE. To achieve that goal, she addressed organizational design. **Organization design** refers to the arrangements, both formal and informal, that an organization calls upon to help shape employee behavior (see Exhibit 4-1).

EXHIBIT 4-1
Design Elements.

Formal	• Compensation and measurement • Reporting structures
Informal	• Defining roles and responsibilities of employees • Defining relationships within the organization and between the organization and external stakeholders

Formal aspects of design include rewards and performance measurements as well as the reporting relationships depicted on an organization chart. Informal aspects of design relate to how people perform the required tasks of the organization and how they collaborate and work with others, both inside the organization (within their own groups as well as across groups and functions) and outside (with suppliers and customers, for instance). Informal design addresses questions of focus and coordination, of where decision-making authority will be located, and the necessary balance between the requirement for flexibility and the need for control.

Changing Informal Design First

Effective change implementation separates the two aspects of design, targeting informal design *before* seeking to alter formal design.[3]

THEORY INTO PRACTICE

Effective change implementation starts with informal rather than formal design changes.

That distinction between informal and formal designs can, at times, be confusing. Job design is informal, although job descriptions are formal. Expecting individuals to work collaboratively is informal, although paying them based on joint outcomes is formal.

To appreciate the distinction between formal and informal design elements, we can return to the case of ASDA from Chapter 1. Facing bankruptcy as the result of poor strategic decisions made by its leadership team, the chain's board brought in a new CEO with the goal of revitalization. The CEO and his top team elected to place their hopes for the revival of the chain in the hands of the 205 store managers, those responsible for making sure that the stores met the expectations of their customers while increasing revenues.

In the earliest stages of ASDA's transformation, store managers were asked to spend more of their time and energies looking outside of the store—at their customers and competitors—rather than inside. *Stop being supervisors and start being strategic leaders;* that was the direction provided by the company. In order to succeed, they would have to push more and more responsibility down to the individual department managers.

The roles and responsibilities of store managers changed dramatically. However—and here is the point—nothing in the formal design system changed, at least not at first. Job descriptions were not rewritten; pay systems were not changed; reporting relationships were not altered; measurement systems remained the same. Over time, those formal structures would all be altered, but *not* in the early stages of the process.

At the beginning, nobody in the company knew exactly what the store manager job would evolve into; they only knew it would be changed. Informal redesign—new definitions of how the store manager job would be played out—created a fluid, even experimental situation. Different roles were tried out as transformation moved from one store to the next.

Informal design fits more effectively at the early stages of change precisely because it is informal. No policies or procedures are altered. Nothing is written in stone or committed to formal documents. Instead, informal design involves experimentation, trying out new roles.

What will work? What will not work? Helene Gayle did not alter the organization chart at CARE. Reporting relationships remained unchanged. Instead, she focused on informal redesign—redefining roles, responsibilities, and relationships—in order to create greater cross-border collaboration. At a later stage, when new behaviors have been instilled, formal structures and systems can be changed, if required, to reinforce and institutionalize those behaviors.

Piloting Redesign

Design choices represent an attempt by organizational leaders to address the challenges inherent in managing in dynamic environments. Shifting customer expectations, disruptive technologies, new competitors, and renewed strategies provide the impetus for *re*design. If all those elements remained the same, then the design that worked effectively in the past would continue to prove useful in the future.

However, a truly static environment does not really exist. New competitors enter and exit the marketplace. New technologies replace existing processes. Customer expectations shift. Companies age; they expand and contract. Strategies change. No design solution, no matter how useful it may be at any one time, is impervious to the need for change.

Building a Vocabulary of Change
Organizational redesign the process of changing an organization's informal design in response to shifting dynamics in the organization's environment.

Changing an organization's design, a process known as **organizational redesign**, presents its own set of implementation challenges. Optimally, redesign occurs in a systemic and strategic way: aligning multiple design elements with the renewed strategy of the firm. Often, however, organizational leaders embark upon redesign in a much more haphazard, piecemeal manner.

THEORY INTO PRACTICE

The most effective way to change organizational design is to be systemic and strategic rather than piecemeal and haphazard.

Why is it that leaders often approach redesign in such a suboptimal way? For one thing, comprehensive redesign can be intimidating. Write Michael Goold and Andrew Campbell, "It's immensely complicated, involving an endless stream of trade-offs and variables."[4] In addition, organizational redesign can be divisive, often pitting individuals against each other and devolving into power plays.[5] Dr. Gayle admitted that country unit managers at CARE were "comfortable" with the current design. Organizational leaders may prefer to avoid the potential for discomfort and confrontation inherent in comprehensive redesign.

Given the potential for discomfort, it is not surprising that executives often stick with their existing designs long after shifting circumstances seem to demand change. They may tinker, making marginal design change, while leaving the core of the organization intact. *The status quo had worked well for us in the past,* they may conclude. *Why stir up all the potential conflicts in order to change?*[6]

In a dynamic environment, commitment to past design arrangements can undermine organizational effectiveness. CARE's broadened scope, for instance, required greater collaboration across national boundaries. When a diagnostic intervention reveals that existing design arrangements undermine performance, organizational leaders may wish to avoid that potential trap and decide that the negative performance consequences outweigh any perceived "advantage" of conflict avoidance.

The requirement for strategic change poses what seems to be a dilemma. Organizational redesign, to be effective, targets the entire organization. Targeting an entire organization is difficult, however. In a large, complex company, it is downright impossible. The way out of this apparent dilemma is through change pilots. Note that Dr. Gayle did not target all of CARE's activities for change. Rather, she focused attention on a single—albeit a bold—project: Access Africa. Likewise, Duke University's Children's Hospital (Chapter 2) focused its initial transformation on a single unit: pediatric intensive care.

In both cases, leaders utilized **change pilots:** individual units or processes that can provide the opportunity for change. They are, in essence, change laboratories: opportunities to try things out, experiment, and learn.

Building a Vocabulary of Change
Change pilots small units or specific processes that can be targeted at the early stage of change implementation to experiment and learn.

THEORY INTO PRACTICE

When implementing change, seek early "wins" through pilot projects.

Change pilots offer the opportunity to engage in systemic change within a small, contained unit. In selecting a target for early pilots, organizational leaders can consider the following characteristics:

- Select a self-contained unit with clear and measurable outcomes.
- Select a unit or process of strategic importance to the company.
- If the organization's strategy is changing, select a unit that exemplifies the desired future state.
- Most importantly, select a unit or process where success is most likely.

Early successes can build credibility and momentum, leading to more widespread transformation.

THEORY INTO PRACTICE

In selecting change pilots, select units where the change is most likely to be successful.

An understanding of the key issues involved in informal design will help focus the attention of leaders, so let us turn next to an analysis of those key informal design elements that will be addressed in a change process.

UNDERSTANDING DESIGN CHALLENGES

Although all organizations are unique in terms of purpose and strategic direction, they face some common design challenges:

- All organizations require some level of differentiated activities: focusing on different tasks and customers and operating in different competitive environments.
- At the same time, integrated activities will provide organizations with the benefits of efficiency and the ability to move knowledge and resources across and around their various activities and units.
- All organizations, regardless of their histories, strategies, and competitive environments, rely on some type of control mechanisms to help shape employee behaviors. They need to deploy control mechanisms, however, without losing requisite levels of creativity and innovative response from the employees whose behaviors they are attempting to influence.
- All organizations must decide how and where to allocate decision-making rights and responsibilities.

Before embarking on a change implementation effort, organizational leaders need to appreciate these three challenges: the challenge of integration and differentiation, of control and creativity, and of allocating decision-making rights.

The Challenge of Differentiation and Integration

To understand the challenge of differentiation and integration, we can turn to the shifting strategic choices made by management at SAP America.[7] SAP America is a subsidiary of Germany-based SAP AG, producer of the integrated software architecture that dominated the enterprise systems market.

The American division faced a number of organizational challenges. Its U.S.-based strategy supported growth through highly autonomous regional markets. Each region developed its own processes and procedures for selling and supporting SAP software. SAP's products, however, developed a reputation in the marketplace for being expensive, complex, slow to install, and confusing to maintain.

New SAP America president Jeremy Coote felt the need to focus on supporting customers. In particular, he was convinced that SAP's professional consultants, whose job it was to help clients plan, install, and support the systems, needed to share knowledge and coordinate their efforts across the regional markets. Customer service, in his view, was not a regional challenge; it was national.

Here is where past design decisions—especially the heavy emphasis on regional autonomy—provided a barrier. Regional autonomy offered flexibility in response to local customers. At the same time, it hampered coordinated national consulting support. SAP's consultants from different regions failed to share experiences and learning with each other. Consultants responded to the same customer issues in the Northeast and Southwest, for instance, without communicating with each other or sharing knowledge. It was like reinventing the wheel when a customer problem arose in, say, St. Louis. Even though the same problem had been dealt with effectively in Phoenix, that experience had remained local. The St. Louis folks had to address the problem as if they, and the company, had no experience with it.

In order to encourage sharing, Coote focused on his existing group of professional consultants. After collecting performance data from the regions and setting goals for the upcoming year, he worked with his newly hired national manager of professional consulting to redefine responsibilities while defining nationally agreed-upon consulting roles. SAP also involved consultants at an early stage of all new product development and implementation plans.

SAP America made a strategic choice early in its U.S. operation: to emphasize regional autonomy as a way of spurring rapid growth. The idea—an idea that, the evidence indicates, was perfectly valid—allowed regional managers to focus their resources and shape their responsiveness to match the particular needs of their regional customer base.

To pursue that strategy, SAP created a design high in **differentiation**, which refers to the degree to which different functions, departments, and units in an organization are allowed to develop their own approaches in response to their particular goals and unique competitive environments.

Building a Vocabulary of Change
Differentiation the degree to which different functions, departments, and units in an organization are allowed to develop their own approaches in response to their particular goals and unique competitive environments.

THEORY INTO PRACTICE

Use high differentiation to enable different functions, departments, and units in an organization to develop their own responses to their particular goals and unique competitive environments.

Paul Lawrence and Jay Lorsch's classic study, *Organization and Environment* (1967), defined the dynamics and challenges of differentiation and integration.[8] Highly differentiated designs, they found, become reinforced not just in terms of distinctive processes and procedures, but also in terms of cognitive and emotional orientation of employees. Comparing one highly differentiated unit to another, they found that individuals within those units not only *worked* differently but also *thought* and *behaved* differently. Individuals who work in functions such as manufacturing, engineering, marketing, and finance, for instance, think differently about how to approach problems and evaluate potential solutions. These differences should be embraced rather than avoided; they are part of what helps an organization think and act in a creative way.

EXHIBIT 4-2 Dimensions of Differentiation.

Goals	A sales function may have the goal of increasing revenues, while a manufacturing function may have the goal of reducing costs.
Time orientation	A research department will likely have a long-term orientation toward research and development, while a sales function will want new products that it can sell by the end of the quarter.
Interpersonal style	Research scientists might believe that they can maximize creativity and contribution by focusing all their individual attention on their task, while manufacturing managers might desire to create rich interpersonal relationships among key individuals to maximize quality.
Formality	An assembly operation is more likely to be governed by tight rules and strict procedures, while a research and development laboratory would find such rules stifling to creativity.

Because of the particular and differing nature of the tasks, each unit develops its own way of working, of thinking, and of behaving. Exhibit 4-2 presents the four distinct dimensions of differentiation. In complex organizations, differentiation relates not just to functional distinctions but also to product and/or geographic divisions. We saw that in SAP America, where consultants within each region developed their own patterns of thinking and behaving in response to local customers.

Differentiation is necessary, even helpful. It does raise its own challenges, however. After all, the differentiated parts must also work *together* if the overall organization is to perform at an exceptional level. Here's one example. With Christmas orders poured into a large retail toy business over the Internet, the traditional functions of logistics, warehousing, and distribution strained to the breaking point, causing a near disaster in customer relations. The manager of the e-business unit was stunned that the rest of the organization was surprised. "They acted as if they weren't expecting a Christmas surge," complained the e-business managers, while "they"—the managers of the more traditional functions—retorted, "It would have been helpful if *they* would have kept us in the loop."[9] High levels of differentiation had not been matched with requisite integration.

Building a Vocabulary of Change
Integration the required level of coordination across differentiated functions, units, and divisions.

Integration refers to the required level of coordination across differentiated functions, units, and divisions. Collaboration among differentiated units must occur, conflicts must be resolved, and unity of effort must be achieved. Within business units, differentiated functions can, and often do, fail to achieve the required level of integration. The same is true for multiple divisions in large corporations where poor coordination across business can hamper efficiencies.

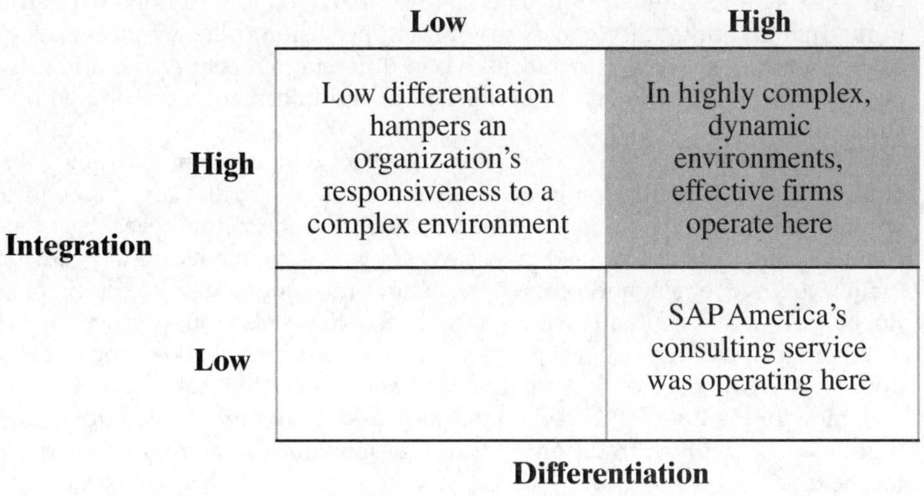

Integration	Differentiation: Low	Differentiation: High
High	Low differentiation hampers an organization's responsiveness to a complex environment	In highly complex, dynamic environments, effective firms operate here
Low		SAP America's consulting service was operating here

EXHIBIT 4-3 The Challenge of Differentiation and Integration.

THEORY INTO PRACTICE

Use integration to enable the organization to achieve efficient operations among different functions, departments, and units.

THEORY INTO PRACTICE

Levels of differentiation need to be matched by appropriate levels of integration.

Differentiation is a relatively easy achievement for organizational design: Most people respond positively to autonomy. But how is integration achieved? A number of possibilities present themselves:

- Cross-functional teams to achieve integration across differentiated functions. The challenge becomes even greater for complex, multiunit corporations
- Global teams to help with cross-national coordination
- A strong sense of common purpose and direction combined with a unified commitment to core values and business strategy
- Common, well-understood values applied across different business units

The particular challenges presented by multinational organizations will be explored later in this chapter.

Building a Vocabulary of Change
Control design choices called upon to shape employee behavior in alignment with the requirements of outstanding performance.

The Challenge of Control and Creativity

A second design challenge relates to the apparently paradoxical requirements for control and creativity. **Control** refers to design elements called upon to establish order, create predictability, and ensure efficiencies of operation. Traditional controls rely on a number of design features: fixed job descriptions with strict individual accountability; close, watchful supervision; a heavy emphasis on rules, procedures, and hierarchically based differences of status and authority; pay incentives tightly linked to performance; and information distributed on a strict "need-to-know" basis.[10]

Traditional controls are especially congruent with a business strategy that emphasizes predictability and standardization. Explicit rules and procedures will be useful when shaping consistent behaviors among employees. Fast-food chain McDonald's has achieved great success by proscribing in careful detail virtually every movement and action of its behind-the-counter employees. Stephen Robbins notes that United Parcel Service (UPS) drivers also follow strictly delineated procedures: "It's also no accident that all UPS drivers walk to a customer's door at the brisk pace of 3 feet per second and knock first lest seconds be lost searching for the doorbell."[11] When the core tasks of an organization are largely routine and repetitive, traditional control designs may be more than adequate for the task.

Building a Vocabulary of Change
Organic controls an approach to shaping employee behavior that emphasizes shared values, a common understanding of strategy, loosely defined roles and responsibilities, and overall organizational performance.

Traditional controls, on the other hand, may hamper an organization's ability to achieve high degrees of flexibility and creativity. But organizations seeking to enhance creativity and flexibility among employees cannot ignore controls. Instead, they can call on **organic controls:** controls that rely less on specific rules and procedures and more on shared values, clarity of organizational strategy, a common understanding about risks to be avoided, attention to performance outcomes, and expectations of interactive and open dialogue.

THEORY INTO PRACTICE

Traditional controls can create predictability and standardization but can undermine creativity, flexibility, and collaboration.

Sun Hydraulics is a Florida-based company that designs and manufactures screw-in hydraulic cartridge valves and manifolds for industrial and mobile markets. This may seem like an industry that would lend itself to traditional controls: lots of rules and procedures. Instead, since its founding in 1970, Sun has leaned heavily on organic controls. "Our workplace is as distinctive as our products," the company proclaims on its web page, "and provides just as many advantages. We have no job titles, no hierarchy, no formal job descriptions, organizational charts or departments. We have open offices, promoting open communication. Each member of our technologically skilled, cross-trained workforce is trusted to take the initiative and invent new ways to serve you better."[12]

Sun's reliance on organic rather than traditional controls provides it with both "a motivated work force" and a company "always on the lookout for emerging market needs and creating innovative ways to fill them."[13]

Companies that use organic controls expect employee behaviors to be shaped by company strategy and objectives as well as widely shared performance information. And it is not just small, hi-tech companies. A number of companies in a wide range of industries—Google, Southwest Airlines, Nordstrom, United Services Automotive Association, W.L. Gore, and Sun

Hydraulics among them—have decided that greater reliance on organic controls will increase the capability of employees at all organizational levels to serve customers, improve their satisfaction with their work, and reduce employee turnover—all of which will lead directly to improved customer satisfaction and enhanced competitiveness.

THEORY INTO PRACTICE

Organic controls, which are intended to increase employee flexibility and creativity, rely on shared values and clarity about overall strategy and performance expectations.

The Challenge of Allocating Decision-Making Rights

At what level of the organization are decisions made about how to allocate resources, what businesses to be in, when and how to enter new markets, or what strategies to pursue? How about deciding what discount to give to a favored customer, which supplier to use, or how to create work schedules in order to meet a pressing order?

All of these decisions must be made *somewhere* in the organization. However, because they represent different levels of decision making, they are likely to occur at different levels of the organization.

Building a Vocabulary of Change
Decision-making rights the determination of who should make what decisions in organizations.

Organizations have multiple points of decision making. The question of who makes what decision is therefore a key design challenge. **Decision-making rights** involve what Nitin Nohria describes as "the rights to initiate, approve, implement, and control various types of strategic or tactical decisions."[14] The ideal design, Nohria adds, is one that grants decision-making rights to those "who have the best information relevant to the decision."[15]

Just where does the "best information" reside? That is a judgment call for organizational leaders to make. That call can be based on a combination of company values and strategic intent. When Robert McDermott became CEO of United Services Automotive Association (an insurance company serving current and past U.S. armed forces officers and their families), he decided on a strategy that would convert customers into partners. That strategy would, he believed, take full advantage of the nature of his customer base.

In order to implement his planned strategic renewal, McDermott placed considerable discretionary decision-making rights in the hands of employees at the lower end of the traditional hierarchy. Telephone receptionists, for instance, had a great deal of liberty concerning how to deal with clients who phoned in their claims. Granting decision-making rights to individuals who dealt directly with customers, McDermott reasoned, would create a codependent bond with customers and improve performance.

Pushing down operational decision making to employees with the "best information" is intended to unleash motivation and creativity. At the same time, McDermott recognized that allocating decision making to frontline employees needed to occur within a controlled environment. The controls that McDermott designed were organic in nature, placing special emphasis on "the necessary education and training base" to support that allocation.[16] Clarity of purpose and strategy, and of values and performance expectations can support the allocation of decision-making rights to lower hierarchical levels.

THEORY INTO PRACTICE

Allowing frontline employees to make autonomous decisions is intended to unleash motivation and creativity among those organizational members with the "best information" to make decisions.

The Special Challenge of Multinational Organizations

When organizations move from operating in a single country to operating in multiple countries, they face special challenges regarding the allocation of decision-making rights. There are benefits, for example, in allowing the general managers of country operations high levels of autonomy. That way, they can respond to the particular and unique challenges and opportunities faced within their home country. These national managers possess greater understanding than do corporate personnel of their own operational, customer, and national issues. As a result, business units will be able to adapt in a speedy manner to shifts in their marketplace. Such autonomy promotes what Jay Lorsch called "entrepreneurial zeal" among country-based general managers.[17]

Too much autonomy, of course, comes with its own set of problems. For an example, we can look at Airbus, which suffered a very public humiliation with significant delays in the production of its A380 superjumbo jet. The double-deck, wide-bodied plane was designed to be the largest passenger jet ever built, boasting 50 percent more interior floor space than its nearest competitor. The goal of Airbus was to break the dominance of Seattle-based Boeing over the jumbo jet marketplace. Given the nature of that ambition, it would also be an intensely complex engineering and building feat. This is where too much autonomy created problems.

For the previous three decades, Airbus had divided itself into national "centers of excellence" that encouraged depth and focus on specific aspects of the aircraft manufacturing process. The avionics center was in France, cabin design and installation occurred in Germany, wings were manufactured in the United Kingdom, and tail sections were built in Spain. That system allowed for both multinational participation and technological focus.

For the multibillion dollar A380 project, however, the focus on technological excellence and national pride interfered with the company's ability to deliver a well-designed aircraft. "Rear-fuselage sections of the A380 built in Hamburg [Germany]," the *New York Times* reported, "arrived in Toulouse [France] in 2004 without the requisite electric wiring for the planes' in-flight entertainment system."[18] That hand-off glitch proved to be just the beginning. The computer modeling software used in Germany was incompatible with what was in use by the French center of excellence.

CEO Louis Gallois took a number of steps to enhance integration. He banned the use of national symbols in all PowerPoint presentations and formed transnational teams to redesign Airbus into an integrated organization. Finally, the A380 made its maiden commercial flight. Even then, the number of planes Airbus was able to deliver to commercial carriers fell far short of promises. In the end, delays cost Airbus an estimated $65 billion in profits.

THEORY INTO PRACTICE

The challenge for multinational organizations is to allocate a high level of autonomy to national units as a way of achieving marketplace responsiveness while simultaneously making corporate-level decisions that allow the exploitation of synergies across the divisions.

Working across country units allows the corporation to exploit opportunities for **synergies**—the advantages of efficiency and effectiveness conferred by the combined effect of interaction and collaboration among multiple units. For that reason, corporate executives will expect to make some decisions that apply to all divisions.

Building a Vocabulary of Change
Synergies the advantages of efficiency and effectiveness conferred by the combined effect of interaction and collaboration among multiple units.

The challenge for executives of multinational corporations is to seek synergies across country divisions while maintaining an adequate level of divisional autonomy. A number of integrative devices—planning and budgeting systems, regular interface meetings among divisional and corporate executives, task forces, and measurement and reward systems for divisional managers tied to corporate performance—can be used to exploit synergies.[19]

BUILDING COMMITMENT

Design choices represent attempts by organizational leaders to align employee behavior with renewed strategies and shifting realities. Helene Gayle needed to design high levels of collaboration across national organizations in order to address CARE's ambitious Access Africa project. Gayle, like all organizational leaders, seeks to increase effort, energy, creativity, and persistence among employees. That level of commitment to the achievement of organizational goals is also determined, in large part, by informal design.

High **employee commitment** exists when employees sense a strong overlap between individual goals and the shared goals of the organization. Highly committed employees find a sense of purpose within their organization's mission and actively seek out opportunities to fulfill that mission.[20]

Building a Vocabulary of Change
Employee commitment the internalized desire of employees to expend energy and discretionary effort on behalf of the goals of the organization.

Organizations able to achieve high commitment can gain a great many performance advantages:

- Highly committed employees are more likely to communicate with each other and to act in a collaborative manner.
- Productivity, quality, and creativity are all positively associated with high commitment.

- Additionally, from the change perspective, highly committed employees will be motivated to alter their own patterns of behavior based on the requirements of outstanding performance.[21]

From the perspective of organizational performance, the advantages of achieving high employee commitment are substantial.

THEORY INTO PRACTICE

High employee commitment can improve organizational performance by enhancing productivity, creativity, collaboration, and the willingness to change.

In recent years, a number of companies in widely diverse industries—manufacturing and assembly (Lincoln Electric, for example), food service (Stake n Shake, for example), retailing (Costco, for example), transportation (Southwest Airlines, for example), and software (SAS, for example)—have made design choices intended to increase employee commitment. In each case, the purpose is similar: improved productivity, increased quality, and greater flexibility and adaptation.

Organizations seeking to change to a high commitment approach have followed many paths, differing from company to company and industry to industry. However, some generalized approaches that can be adopted in the organizational redesign stage of change implementation include:

- Clarify organizational goals, strategy, and values
- Allow employees greater access to managers
- Create teams
- Share performance information widely
- Rely on organic rather than traditional controls
- Offer employees opportunities for individual development

Note that these changes are all informal, leaving the formal organization systems and structures untouched for the time being. These informal design mechanisms intended to build employee commitment are summarized in Exhibit 4-4.

Perhaps most fundamental to designing for high employee commitment is the manner in which work is performed. Organizational leaders seeking to engage in redesign as a way of building high commitment will benefit from a basic understanding of the options available for job design.

Building a Vocabulary of Change

Job design the amount of task identity, variety, significance, autonomy, and feedback built into the performance of a job.

Rethinking Job Design Choices

Step 2 of change implementation raises the question of how individuals perform the jobs to which they have been assigned. That question is addressed through **job design,** which refers to organizational expectations for how tasks will be performed in order to meet both individual task requirements and the overall performance requirements of the organization. At first glance, it may seem there are as many answers to that question as there are jobs in an organization. A closer

EXHIBIT 4-4 Informal Design Elements for Building High Commitment.

Clarity of organizational goals	Employees at all levels and in all units are provided with an understanding of the goals and values of the organization as well as its strategic choices.
Influence mechanisms	A variety of formal (elected board of representatives) and informal (open doors and accessible managers) mechanisms enable wide participation in the dialogue and decision making of the organization.
Teamwork	Teams designated to perform interdependent tasks.
Shared information	Employees kept informed about how the organization is performing, including the dissemination of data such as financial performance, costs, profitability, information on competitors, and feedback from customers.
Organic controls	Control exerted through peer pressure, organizational culture, and expectations of outstanding performance reinforced through performance feedback.
Individual developmental opportunities	Employees provided an opportunity through a combination of mechanisms—job mobility, task variety, facilitative supervision, and formal training—to develop competencies consistent with their own needs and those of the organization.

examination, however, reveals a set of underlying principles that shape job design choices and impact the commitment, adaptability, and performance of jobholders.

In search of high commitment, managers ask: how might they think about designing jobs in order to enhance their potential to evoke initiative and motivation? Richard Hackman and Greg Oldham offered a job characteristic model to suggest alternative job design options meant to enhance motivation and initiative.[22]

All jobs, they said, regardless of specific organizational levels or assigned responsibilities, can be understood as having the same core dimensions. By enhancing or enriching work on any or all of those dimensions, jobs will become more motivational. Exhibit 4-5 presents the five universal job dimensions as well as sample actions managers can take to enrich work and increase employee commitment.

THEORY INTO PRACTICE

By enriching jobs along any or all of five characteristics—skill variety, task identity, task significance, autonomy, and feedback—organizations can increase the motivation and commitment of employees performing those tasks.

Managers seeking to change job design as a way of enhancing employee commitment have something of a road map. Take *skill variety* as an example. Instead of having an employee perform a single job over and over again, the

EXHIBIT 4-5
Using Job Enrichment to Increase Commitment.

Job Dimension	Description	Enrichment Action
Skill variety	The degree to which job requires a variety of different activities in carrying out the work, involving the use of a number of different skills and talents	Enlarging task requirements to involve multiple and varied skills.
Task identity	The degree to which the job requires completion of a "whole" and identifiable piece of work; that is, doing job from beginning to end with a tangible outcome.	Combining individuals into a team with shared responsibility for the final product.
Task significance	The degree to which the performance of the task has a substantial impact on outcomes that are deemed to be important to employees, to the organization, and/or to society as a whole.	Communicating regularly and clearly how individual and group effort contributes to overall performance of the company.
Autonomy	The degree to which the job provides substantial discretion to the individual in scheduling work and determining procedures for carrying it out.	Allowing individuals or groups to schedule work and assign specific tasks consistent with achieving performance goal.
Feedback	The degree to which carrying out work activities required by the job results in the individual acquiring direct and clear information about the effectiveness of his or her performance.	Communicating frequently concerning progress toward work goals.

skills required of that worker in the performance of his job could be enlarged. A machine worker, for instance, might be asked to meet with suppliers or customers. By adding some measure of discretion to that employee's scheduling—say, providing that employee with a monthly production schedule but allowing the individual to make decisions concerning daily and weekly production schedules—managers could also enhance *autonomy*.

Providing regular information about the quality of work and the progress being made toward achieving the goal adds greater *feedback*. Communicating regularly to that employee about how her effort contributes both to the overall product or service being offered by the company and how that product or service helps advance the strategic purpose of the business enhances *task identity* and *significance*. The job characteristics model offered a systematic way of redesigning jobs in order to build employee commitment and achieve outstanding performance for the organization.

BUILDING COLLABORATION

As we saw in the opening case of this chapter, Dr. Helene Gayle sought to build collaboration at CARE so as to "make the whole greater than the sum of its parts." In his study of collaboration in business organizations, Morten T. Hansen notes how collaboration helped Apple leverage its capabilities to overcome Sony and gain dominance in the MP3 portable music players market.[23]

Sony had all but invented the portable music market with its Walkman, a devise originally built to meet Sony Chairman Akio Morita's passion for opera. Introduced to the public in 1979, the Walkman allowed the listener to play audiotapes (and later, CDs) using headphones. The devices were portable and easy to use. They held only one tape or CD at a time, of course, and required the owner to purchase the music independently of the listening device, with Sony capturing none of that revenue (except for music on the record labels owned by Sony).

In the late 1990s, several companies launched commercial versions of MP3 players with their own hard drives, eliminating the need to purchase separate tapes or CDs. Now, for the first time, music could be loaded directly on the listening devise. The MP3 market remained relatively unsettled until 2001, when Apple launched its revolutionary iPod. Coupled with iTunes, Apple quickly dominated not just the device market but also music sales and distribution, thereby capturing a much larger portion of the total revenues.

As revolutionary as it might have seemed, the iPod itself contained very little in the way of innovative technology. What made the iPod remarkable was not its components. Rather, the iPod represented a "design triumph."[24] And that triumph came about because of collaboration. What was especially vital was that Apple promoted a seamless interaction between its hardware and software units, as well as between its iTunes and industrial design units. After all, one of the factors that made the iPod so attractive was the ease of interacting with iTunes as a way of purchasing and downloading music from the Internet onto the player.

Building a Vocabulary of Change
Collaboration a process of willing cooperation among individuals and groups with a common goal.

Collaboration involves willing cooperation among individuals and groups with a common goal. Helene Gayle's notion that CARE needed collaboration across national units to make the whole greater than the sum of its parts lies behind an organization's desire to promote collaboration. It was collaboration among hardware and software units in particular that helped Apple triumph in the portable music business. But why couldn't Sony respond effectively to Apple? It was, says Hansen, the inability of the company to collaborate effectively.

Although still committed to its Walkman portable music player, Sony mounted a response to the iPod in 2003. Under the guidance of Howard Stringer and Phillip Wiser, head of Sony's U.S. operations and chief technology officer for Sony U.S., respectively, Sony attempted to take advantage of its considerable assets.[25] In terms of overall revenue, Sony was 10 times bigger than Apple. All the pieces seemed to be in place. The Walkman division could develop its own hard drive machine. In addition, Sony's various business units—VAIO personal computers, Sony Music, and Sony Electronics—could pull together to produce an iPod rival "in nine months" promised Wiser. Even the name of the product, the Connect, suggested Stringer and Wiser's faith that collaboration across Sony's business units could help the company respond to Apple.

In nine months, the Connect *was* launched, but it was a commercial flop. Stringer blamed the failure on the inability of the various Sony units to collaborate. "It's impossible to communicate with everyone," Stringer said, "when you have so many silos." Listen to this description provided by Morten Hansen:

> Each division had its own ideas about what to do. The PC and the Walkman groups introduced their own competing music players, and three other groups— Sony Music in Japan, Sony Music in the United States, and Sony Electronics in the United States—had their own music portals or download services. Stringer, who had no authority over Japanese operations, complained, to no avail, that the Connect software being developed in Japan was hard to use. Whereas the U.S. team wanted a hard disk for the music player, the Japanese team went with the arcane MiniDisc. And whereas the U.S. group pushed for using the MP3 format—the de facto U.S. standard—the Japanese PC division chose a proprietary standard called ATRAC.[26]

In 2007, Sony announced its intention to withdraw the Connect from the market. And in 2010, nine years after the introduction of the iPod, Sony discontinued Japanese manufacture of its once iconic Walkman.

Building a Vocabulary of Change
Team an interdependent group of individuals with shared responsibility for an outcome.

There are, as the iPod story suggests, compelling reasons for a business to build collaboration and integration across divisions. To promote collaboration, companies frequently turn to teams. **Teams,** which are interdependent groups with shared responsibility for an outcome, come in many forms: product development teams, project management teams, customer service teams, and process innovation teams. A summary of the main team prototypes is presented in Exhibit 4-6.

THEORY INTO PRACTICE

Collaboration will require effective teamwork across units and functions of an organization.

EXHIBIT 4-6
Team Types.

Work team	By sharing responsibilities, developing multiple skills, and performing varied tasks, motivation and quality are enhanced.
Product development team	Through concurrent rather than sequential development activities, speed to market and innovation are enhanced while costs associated with rework are diminished.
Problem-solving team	By bringing together individuals from multiple functions, problem associated with handoffs and cross-functional interactions can be creatively addressed.
Project management team	The multiple functions and tasks of the value chain are linked in order to enhance quality, coordination, and customer responsiveness.

Cross-Functional Teams

Traditional organizations are often made up of a collection of freestanding functional silos. Activities such as market research, design, engineering, manufacturing, quality checking, distribution, and sales all take place within discrete domains. Although those functional units provide required differentiation, organizations also need to achieve integration across functions in order to be effective.

Cross-functional teams, which are teams that span multiple organizational functions, provide a way of achieving that integration. Cross-functional teams address the difficulty of highly differentiated functions have in pulling together into seamless, well-integrated processes. By creating cross-functional teams, organizations seek to eliminate handoff problems that produce waste, high cost, quality problems, and sluggish response time. The teams are intended to create a seamless, interconnected web of activities.[27]

Building a Vocabulary of Change
Cross-functional teams teams made up of representatives from multiple organization functions typically intended to achieve required coordination along a chain of interrelated activities and processes.

THEORY INTO PRACTICE

Use cross-functional teams to help create seamless, well-integrated processes.

Creating Teamwork

The first requirement of effective teamwork is that team members transcend the individual or functional agendas each member brings to the effort and create a *shared purpose*. Team members agree both on what their goal is and why that goal is important.

Creating shared purpose can be a slow and difficult process. Individuals who have spent much of their professional lives within a function or unit adopt, often unconsciously, a particular lens through which they view all organizational problems. When they become members of a cross-functional team, their agenda—at least initially—is to optimize the interests of their own function or unit, often at the cost of others. Effective teamwork starts with the need to create a central purpose focused on companywide goals and equally accepted by all members.

THEORY INTO PRACTICE

Don't just place employees on teams and expect the performance benefits of teamwork; organizations need to create the context required for teamwork.

Effective teamwork is unlikely to flow from a group of individuals who do not feel equally and jointly accountable for an agreed-upon outcome. Therefore, effective teams develop *shared responsibility*. On effective teams, members evolve beyond seeing themselves as individuals with narrowly defined and measured outcomes. Instead, they take full responsibility for and joint ownership over every aspect, every contribution, every input, and every outcome of the team's task.

THEORY INTO PRACTICE

When members of a team feel equally responsible for the outcome of their efforts, teamwork is enhanced.

THEORY INTO PRACTICE

At least in the early stages of change, organizations need to make sure teams are buffered from traditional hierarchical power and are allowed to work across functions.

THEORY INTO PRACTICE

In order to encourage teamwork, organizations can take care to ensure that team members have the appropriate skills to perform the task effectively.

Effective teamwork also requires that team members possess a set of behavioral competencies, including critical thinking, brainstorming, problem solving, nondefensive communications, process facilitation, and conflict management. Many employees lack those skills. They have, after all, spent the better part of their lives learning how to work, think, and act as individuals. If an organization intends on enabling teams to operate effectively, then they have to provide individuals with the required competencies of teamwork.

Not surprisingly, as companies evolve toward reliance on teamwork, they increasingly require training for these required skills. Much of that training focuses on providing employees with multiple skills to enable them to understand all parts of the organization so they can operate more effectively in a cross-functional environment.[28] Training in specific teamwork skills also becomes vital. One of the most striking findings of a recent international study of high-performing companies (rated by profits, productivity, and quality of output) was that 100 percent of the high performers had trained their employees in problem-solving techniques compared to less than 20 percent of the low performers.[29]

Ultimately, no matter how successful an organization might be in creating teams, the success of teamwork depends on a culture and a context within the larger organization that supports coordinated efforts: recruiting and developing individuals with teamwork competencies; holding team members jointly accountable for joint efforts; removing barriers to effective cross-functional coordination.

All of these actions help create a context in which teams—and, more importantly, teamwork—are simply part of the way of operating. Most important of all, teamwork in the operations of the organization relies on teamwork at the top of the organization.

THEORY INTO PRACTICE

Teams succeed or fail in organizations based not just on the efforts of team members but on the overall design and context of the organization, which must support and reinforce joint efforts.

Conclusion

Organizational design refers to the ways an organization defines roles that employees enact and relationships among employees both within their own functions, units, and divisions as well as across those boundaries. No matter how well designed an organization may be at any one time, a dynamic competitive environment is likely to demand that the design be reconsidered.

Poor coordination, high levels of dysfunctional conflict, slow decision making, and low responsiveness to shifts in the external environment are all symptomatic of an organization whose design has outlived its functionality. When a diagnostic intervention reveals that these types of issues hinder the implementation of an organization's strategy or the achievement of outstanding performance, leaders will need to consider addressing the redesign challenge as the next sequential step in the change process.

That does not mean, however, that *all* design issues need to be addressed at an early stage of change implementation. Organizational design has two interrelated but separate components. Formal aspects of design relate mainly to reporting relationships as depicted on the "official" organization chart and systems such as pay and performance measurement. Informal elements of design relate to how an organization meets the challenges of differentiation and integration, of controls and creativity, and of decision-making allocation. Informal design also encompasses how an organization seeks to build employee commitment and coordination.

Both elements of design—formal and informal—need to be addressed in a change implementation process. It is useful, however, to separate the two sequentially: addressing informal design challenges first and formal design challenges later. Effective change implementation requires experimentation and learning. No leader knows precisely what solutions will be needed. Even if she did, the impositions of solutions from above would engender resistance.

When design changes are informal, employees at multiple levels and from numerous units and divisions can try things out. Ideas on how to approach the challenges posed of differentiation and integration, the tension between control and creativity, and the allocation of decision-making rights can be tested: maintained if they succeed, discarded otherwise. As experimentation and learning unfold, employees can seek to "refreeze" (Lewin's term—see Chapter 2) desired behaviors by calling on more formal design mechanisms.

The next step in the change implementation process involves addressing an organization's human resource policies and practices, both as a way of helping to develop required new behaviors and of reinforcing those behaviors among the organization's employees.

Discussion Questions

1. Why do organizations find it so difficult to address the requirements of differentiation and integration simultaneously?
2. What are the advantages and disadvantages of allowing for high levels of autonomy within divisions of multidivisional organizations? What are some effective means of coordinating efforts among divisions?
3. Why is it so difficult to achieve high levels of employee commitment within today's business organizations? List the factors that are working against commitment and the potential benefits to be achieved through high commitment.
4. Some people have argued that there is far too much emphasis on "teamwork" in today's business world and that the danger is that individual creativity and initiative is being sacrificed. Do you agree or disagree? Explain.
5. The chapter argues that change efforts should address informal design before addressing formal design. Do you agree with that theory? Explain your thinking.

Case Discussion

Read "Transferring Innovation across National Borders" and prepare answers to the following questions:

1. What triggered the new product strategy at Minnesota Biolabs (MB)?
2. What prediction would you make for the success of getting the country general managers in Europe and Japan to adopt the new product? Explain your prediction.
3. What changes might MB make in its design in order to better promote the transfer of new products across national borders?

TRANSFERRING INNOVATION ACROSS NATIONAL BOUNDARIES

Imagine entering a hospital for treatment of a medical condition only to come down with a far more serious, perhaps even life-threatening disease caused by that very treatment.[30] That, unfortunately, is an increasingly common experience in hospitals located in the United States and elsewhere. The culprit is often an infection transferred to the patient through a tainted "injectable": that is, a needle, an IV drip, and so forth. This is known as a sepsis infection: an overwhelming infection of the blood stream resulting from toxin-producing bacteria (endotoxins). National health regulatory agencies seek to limit such negative outcomes by requiring that products intended for injection be tested.

Minnesota Biolabs

Traditionally, tests for sepsis infection were performed on live animals—rabbits, for the most part—lead to the animal's death. Minnesota Biolabs (MB) was one of the companies that supplied rabbits to the producers of injectable devices. Headquartered in suburban Minneapolis, MB served customers—mainly pharmaceuticals but also university and private laboratories—in over 20 countries. Europe was divided into three MB national units, MB-France, MB-Germany, and MB-United Kingdom. A fourth country unit, MB-Japan, served Asian markets.

Each of those four units—France, Germany, the United Kingdom, and Japan—was managed by a country general manager. That general manager was typically left alone to operate his or her unit autonomously. Corporate headquarters set annual growth goals for the units and measured their profit and loss. As long as the units performed according to those goals, the managers were paid a bonus and mostly left alone. Strategies, product decisions, and acquisitions were determined by corporate executives in the States and communicated to these country managers.

MB's CEO frequently said that he liked this approach to management because it delineated clear lines of authority and responsibility. Country managers also preferred this autonomy. They were allowed, they believed, to decide on local strategies that best served their customers while maintaining good relationships with the national regulatory agencies to which they needed to respond. MB's exceptional history of sustained, profitable growth reinforced the belief of managers that this was a well-designed organization.

The Search for an Alternative Test

In the early years of the 21st century, MB began to look for an alternative method of testing for sepsis infection in injectable products. As animal rights became increasingly important,MB sought a methodology that would leave the animals alive. Because most of MB's growth over its history had come from acquiring other businesses and integrating their products into the company's offering, that is what MB executives sought to do now.

An opportunity arose when a small, Rhode Island-based company received government approval for a test known as Sepsis Detection Test (SDT). Instead of conducting tests in live rabbits, SDT used blood extracted from horseshoe crabs for the tests. After extraction, the crabs were returned to the ocean where they were able to regenerate lost blood. MB purchased the company, and horseshoe crab-based testing quickly became the standard for the United States. In addition to leaving test animals alive, SDT was both less costly and more profitable for MB than the previous rabbit tests.

After several years of rapid growth in its home market, MB executives urged country general managers in Europe and Japan to move from rabbit-based tests to SDT. At the annual strategy meeting in Minneapolis, corporate executives presented the business case for SDT and urged the country general managers of MB-France, MB-German, MB-United Kingdom, and MB-Japan to switch over their product line. The country general managers agreed to move forward as quickly as possible.

Endnotes

1. Quoted on the CARE website: CARE.org © Cooperative for Assistance and Relief Everywhere, Inc. (CARE).
2. Quoted in Rasika Welankiwar, "Conversation," *Harvard Business Review* (Apr. 2009), p. 22.
3. Michael Beer, Russell A. Eisenstat, and Bert Spector, *The Critical Path to Corporate Renewal* (Boston, MA: Harvard Business School Press, 1990).
4. Michael Goold and Andrew Campbell, "Do You Have a Well-Designed Organization?" *Harvard Business Review* (Mar. 2002), p. 5.
5. *Ibid.*
6. Danny Miller has documented the tendency of once-successful companies to avoid design change. See *The Icarus Paradox: How Exceptional Companies Bring About Their Own Downfall* (New York: Harper Business, 1990).
7. Information on SAP America is from "ASAP's a Wrap," *Managing Automation* (February 1998); Colleen Frye, "SAP Soothes Implementation Worries," *Software Magazine* (1997); and David A. Garvin, *SAP America* (Boston, MA: Harvard Business School Publishing, 1996).
8. Paul R. Lawrence and Jay W. Lorsch, *Organization and Environment: Managing Differentiation and Integration* (Boston, MA: Harvard Graduate School of Business Administration Division of Research, 1967).
9. These quotes come from a consulting engagement by the author.
10. Richard E. Walton, "From Control to Commitment in the Workplace," *Harvard Business Review* (Mar.–Apr. 1985), pp. 5–12.
11. Stephen P. Robbins, *Essentials of Organizational Behavior* (Upper Saddle River, NJ: Prentice-Hall, 2005), p. A-3.
12. www. sunhydraulics.com.
13. *Ibid.*
14. Nitin Nohria, *Note on Organization Structure* (Boston, MA: Harvard Case Services, 1991), p. 2.
15. *Ibid.*, p. 3.
16. McDermott is quoted in Thomas Teal, "Service Comes First: An Interview with USAA's Robert

F. McDermott," *Harvard Business Review* (Sept.–Oct. 1991), p. 119.

17. Jay W. Lorsch, *Note on Organization Design* (Boston, MA: Harvard Business School Publishing, 1975), p. 15.
18. Nicola Clark, "Turnaround Effort Is Challenging at Airbus, a Stew of European Cultures," *New York Times* (May 18, 2007), p. C1.
19. Jay W. Lorsch and Stephen A. Allen III, *Managing Diversity and Interdependence: An Organizational Study of Multidivisional Firms* (Boston, MA: Harvard University Graduate School of Business Administration Division of Research, 1973), pp. 53–79.
20. Daniel Goleman, *Working with Emotional Intelligence* (New York: Bantam Books, 1998), p. 118.
21. Robert M. Marsh and Hiroshi Mannari, "Organizational Commitment and Turnover: A Prediction Study," *Administrative Science Quarterly* 22 (Mar. 1977), pp. 57–72; Walton, "From Control to Commitment in the Workplace"; Gary J. Blau and Kimberly B. Boal, "Conceptualizing How Job Involvement and Organizational Commitment Affect Turnover and Absenteeism," *Academy of Management Review* 12 (1987), pp. 288–300; Stephen L. Fink, *High Commitment Workplaces* (New York: Quorum Books, 1992); Mark A. Huselid, "The Impact of Human Resource Management Practices on Turnover, Productivity, and Corporate Financial Performance," *Academy of Management Journal* 38 (1995), pp. 635–661; Julian Gould-Williams, "The Effects of 'High Commitment' HRM Practices on Employee Attitude: The Views of Public Sector Workers," *Public Administration* 82 (2004), pp. 63–81.
22. J. Richard Hackman and Greg R. Oldham, *Work Redesign* (Reading, MA: Addison-Wesley, 1980).
23. Morten T. Hansen, *Collaboration: How Leaders Avoid Traps, Create Unity, and Reap Big Results* (Boston, MA: Harvard Business School Press, 2009).
24. Erik Sherman, "Inside the Apple iPod Design Triumph," *Electronics Design Chain*, accessed Oct. 27, 2010.
25. This account from Hansen, *Collaboration*, is based in large measure on the *Wall Street Journal* reporting of Phred Dvorak. See particularly "Out of Tune: At Sony, Rivalries were Encouraged, Then Came the iPod" (June 29, 2005), p. A1.
26. Hansen, *Collaboration*, p. 8.
27. The notion that coordination across functions, units, and divisions lies at the core of organizational effectiveness has received a great deal of attention in recent years. See, for instance, Edwad E. Lawler, III, "Substitutes for Hierarchy," *Organizational Dynamics* 17 (1988), pp. 5–15; Christopher A. Bartlett and Sumantra Gloshal, *Managing Across Borders: The Transnational Solution* (Boston, MA: Harvard Business School Press, 1989); D. Keith Denton, *Horizontal Management: Beyond Total Customer Satisfaction* (New York: Lexington Books. 1991); John A. Byrne, "The Horizontal Corporation," *Business Week* (Dec. 20, 1993), pp. 76–81; Jay R. Galbraith, *Competing with Flexible Lateral Organizations* (Reading, MA: Addison-Wesley, 1994).
28. David Nadler, "Ten Years After: Learning About Total Quality Management." A paper delivered at the Total Quality Management conference sponsored by the Management Centre Europe, Brussels, Oct. 1993.
29. International Quality Study, *Best Practices Report: An Analysis of Management Practices That Impact Performance* (Cleveland, OH: American Quality Foundation and Ernst & Young, 1992).
30. This case study is adopted from the research conducted by the author and his colleagues under a grant from the National Science Foundation. See Bert Spector, Henry W. Lane, and Dennis Shaughnessy, "Developing Innovation Transfer Capacity in a Cross-National Firm," *Journal of Applied Behavioral Science* 45 (June 2009), pp. 261–279.

CHAPTER

5 People Alignment

The need to implement behavioral change in response to a new strategy places new demands on employees. Redesigned roles, responsibilities, and relationships may require the following: formerly individualistic employees become team players; formerly internally focused employees become responsive to customers; formerly functionally oriented employees become collaborative with people from other functions; formerly technically oriented employees adopt a general management perspective; formerly autocratic managers become facilitators and coaches; and formerly parochial employees become global. Each and every one of these changes calls for new skills to support those behaviors.

This chapter looks at two steps of effective change implementation, both focused on people. People alignment involves two distinct and sequential steps. First, in Step 2, the organization seeks to *help* develop in employees the necessary skills and competencies. Then, in Step 3, the company engages in *people change* in order to meet its strategic requirements. Step 2 involves training and developing current employees; Step 3 involves attracting new employees and, potentially, removing and replacing existing ones.

Both steps deal with people alignment. They are treated as separate steps, however, to make a key point about sequencing. Step 2—*help*—involves informal changes and processes. It proceeds to Step 3—*people change*—which deals with formal human resource systems. In particular, this chapter will:

- Define people alignment and its role in implementing strategic renewal and organizational change
- Understand how to match selection and recruitment with the shifting requirements of behavioral change
- Analyze how an organization can help employees gain the new skills required of the change effort
- Present the particular choices available to organizations as they seek align employee competencies with the requirements of the organization as part of their change effort
- Analyze the role of removal and replacement in implementing change

First, we will look at an attempt by a national electronics retail chain to expand its market, and to align its people with that strategy. As you read this introductory case, ask yourself:

- What triggered the drive for change at Best Buy?
- In what ways did Best Buy need to align its people with the goal of expanding its market?
- What steps did Julie Gilbert take and how effective were they?

EXPANDING THE MARKET FOR BEST BUY

Julie Gilbert, senior vice president at Best Buy, recognized an opportunity.[1] Women were showing a growing interest in shopping for electronics. That shift was due in part to the introduction of entertainment systems and flat screen televisions that attracted the attention of women shoppers. According to the Consumer Electronics Association, women now influenced 57 percent of the $140 billion annual electronics purchases made in the United States.

Best Buy stores were often seen as unappealing, even hostile, to women. Noted one female shopper, "I avoid Best Buy like the plague. I find it difficult to get the attention of an employee, and then they seem to be somewhat terse. They rarely have offered options or helpful advice. If I really need something from there and I can't find it elsewhere, I send my husband." Other women reported a preference for shopping on the Internet for electronics.

Given Best Buy's origins, its appeal to male shoppers was hardly surprising. The company began in St. Paul, Minnesota in 1966 and catered to young male consumers. As the business expanded, that focus remained unchanged. "Our stores used to have one primary customer in mind," agreed current CEO Brad Anderson. "That was the young, techno-savvy male."

It was Julie Gilbert who noticed both the problem and the opportunity. In 2005, she calculated that of the $90 billion annual purchases in the U.S. market influenced by women, Best Buy accounted for $10 billion. Not bad, she thought, but Best Buy could do much better. Gilbert also knew that return and exchange rates were 60 percent lower on purchases when couples were involved in a purchase than when they were made by men alone. Furthermore, couples tended to buy higher end (and higher margin) products than did men when shopping alone. Gilbert saw an opportunity to expand Best Buy's market dominance by claiming a larger share of women-influenced purchases.

But how?

Some of the changes were relatively simple. "We were a boy's toy store designed for boys by boys," noted Gilbert. Stores were to be retooled. Out went the loud music and stacks of electronic components. Personal shopping assistants were added, living rooms were set up to display home entertainment systems, and aisles were widened to accommodate children and baby strollers. Although it would take time and money to implement these changes in the chain's 700 plus stores, there was little resistance to the ideas.

The more difficult challenges involved people alignment. The first step required identifying new behaviors for the sales people, known in the company as "blue shirts": greeting and making eye contact with women shoppers, asking her about her favorite movies, demonstrating those movies on systems. But simply identifying helpful new behaviors would be insufficient. Gilbert felt that for Best Buy to take full advantage of this under served market, the company would have to place more women employees on the store floors and more women in executive positions.

Blue shirts had typically been recruited from the electronics departments of rival chains such as Wal-Mart and Target. Now, Gilbert began looking at a broader spectrum of retail outlets including Victoria's Secret (women's lingerie) and Origins (make-up). "We're working with the Girl Scouts, with private female colleges, and others to recruit amazing women so we can delight our women customers," said Gilbert. The goal was for 50 percent of Best Buy's workforce to be women, with a disproportionate number working in the home theater departments.

Gilbert's 50 percent goal applied to more than just the Blue Shirts. Aiming to change the role of women in the entire organization, she focused on the management and executive level as well. She created and led "WoLF" packs, for Women's Leadership Forum. Women from all levels of the organization came together to share ideas and generate innovations designed to expand the customer base. The WoLF packs also made it easier for Best Buy to recruit and retain women employees. When Gilbert left Best Buy in 2009 to promote WoLF pacts in other organizations (through a private consulting firm, WOLF Means Business), Best Buy had grown its women's influenced purchases by 30 percent.

PEOPLE ALIGNMENT AND CHANGE

Best Buy had identified a new product marketing strategy:

- New products—increasing emphasis on high-end home entertainment systems rather than components.
- New market—increasing emphasis on women shoppers.

Julie Gilbert's initial insight was that Best Buy would need to change the behaviors of its Blue Shirt employees. Greetings, eye contact, and demonstrating systems for women would all be required behaviors.

Identifying new behaviors required of a strategic renewal is one thing; developing those behaviors among current employees is another. Best Buy was fully staffed with employees, overwhelmingly male, recruited and trained to implement the company's past strategy: selling components to tech-savvy male customers. And they had been remarkably successful. But the new strategy required change, and Gilbert knew there was no "before" and "after" switch. She looked to make sweeping changes in the firm's human resource practices.

Building a Vocabulary of Change
People alignment organizational efforts taken to match the skills and behaviors of employees within the organization with the business' strategy.

People alignment involves assuring that the skills and behaviors of employees within the organization will enable the effective implementation of the organization's strategy. Effective change requires alignment between employees—the selection, training, evaluation, promotion, even removal of employees—and the shifting strategic goals of the organization.

In seeking people alignment, leaders can select a "make" or "buy" approach. *Make* implies developing the needed new set of competencies and

EXHIBIT 5-1 Make/Buy Options for Changing Human Resources.

Option	Steps	Advantages	Disadvantages
Make	Training Altered incentives	Takes advantage of existing knowledge/ skill base	May be slow. Not all current employees willing or able
Buy	Recruitment selection	Can quickly add required knowledge/ skills	May undercut morale/ commitment of existing employees

behaviors in current employees. *Making* assumes that employees are both capable of and motivated to acquire and utilize new skills and engage in new behaviors.

Not all employees can or will make that shift, of course. Additionally, the time required may be too long. Leaders, therefore, will also have to consider a buy approach. *Buy* involves injecting the organization with new employees who possess the desired set of competencies.

The choice between making and buying (summarized in Exhibit 5-1) is not either/or. Best Buy's change effort involved both. Getting the make/buy mix "right" means doing them both appropriately and in the appropriate sequence. That matter of sequencing will be addressed later in the chapter.

THEORY INTO PRACTICE

In order to develop required human resource competencies, organizational leaders need to align the selection, training, development, and removal of employees with the behavioral requirements of the desired change.

HELP

When organizations seek to redefine their strategy—Best Buy altering its product—market mix, for instance—they face the requirement of developing new competencies among their employees. Thus, once the required new behaviors and their supporting competencies are defined in Step 1, effective change implementation seeks to help employees gain the new competencies and skills. That is why training and development provides the key intervention in Step 2.

Training

Quite a lot of training occurs in organizations. U.S. companies alone spend more than $60 billion a year on training, plus another $180 billion on informal day-to-day instruction. Not all of that training, of course, is designed to be a part of strategic renewal and change. Training is often called upon to teach basic literacy, update technical skills, as well as to develop management skills in individuals

EXHIBIT 5-2
The Two Components of Training for Change.

This component:	Focuses on:	By:
Knowledge development	Developing understanding within employees of new strategy and requirements for change	Classrooms, lectures, discussion groups, etc.
Skill development	Developing capability within employees to enact required new behaviors	Role-playing, experimentation, real-time feedback, etc.

leaving functional areas and assuming management responsibilities. In these cases, training programs are intended to improve individual performance within current organizational arrangements rather than changing the organization.

To be part of a change effort, training programs need to contain two components, as summarized in Exhibit 5-2. The first is a *knowledge component*: an awareness of the forces demanding strategic renewal and change and the options available to the organization in response to those forces. What are the relevant changes in the external environment? What are the design choices available to the organization? And what are the strengths and weaknesses of those choices? Understanding both the reasons for abandoning the status quo and the options available to the organization in the future helps motivate employees to change.

THEORY INTO PRACTICE

Training can help convey to employees how their competitive environment is changing and why their own behaviors need to be altered.

The second component of training involves *skill development*. As the organization moves toward greater collaboration and teamwork, for example, people will have to acquire a set of skills associated with teamwork: effective communications, conflict management, trust building, norm setting, diversity awareness, negotiations, and so on.[2] Traditional training approaches such as classrooms, lectures, and discussion groups are more effective at achieving the knowledge component than at skill development.

THEORY INTO PRACTICE

Training can, under the right circumstances, help employees gain new behavioral competencies.

Building a Vocabulary of Change
Experiential training training programs that focus on behaviors and typically include role-playing and feedback.

As a way of impacting behavior, organizations can supplement traditional knowledge-based training with **experiential training**. Traditional training programs emphasize the delivery of knowledge from the instructor to the learner.

Experiential learning, on the other hand, focuses on behaviors while allowing participants to try out the new behaviors required of the change effort.

Companies attempting to promote teamwork and collaboration, for instance, can engage employees in experiential training. Trained facilitators are made available to provide real-time feedback to participants and to model the very behaviors the organization is now seeking. Experiential learning occurs in a protected environment, allowing participants to experiment with new behaviors.

The problem with experiential learning is that new behaviors acquired in a training program often disappear quickly once the participants return to their jobs. That phenomenon is known as **training fade-out**. The extent to which the learning gained from a training opportunity is transferred back into the work environment is impacted by three factors:

Building a Vocabulary of Change
Training fade-out the failure of behaviors learned as part of a training exercise to transfer to on-the-job experience or behaviors that disappear over time.

1. Supervisory/managerial support—Does the employee's supervisor/manager endorse, encourage, provide feedback, and reward new behaviors, or does that supervisor/manager discourage or oppose the application of new skills and behaviors?
2. Peer support—Do the employee's peers support the application of new skills and behaviors, inquire about that learning, provide feedback, and encourage, or do they ignore, discourage, and even attempt to prevent the application of new skills and behaviors?
3. Work conditions—Does the employee have the opportunity to use new skills and behaviors when back on the job, or are new skills and behaviors overtly or covertly discouraged by time pressures, inadequate resources, and/or unchanged responsibilities?[3]

An organizational context that encourages, even demands, the use of new behaviors will lead to greater peer and supervisory support and help to prevent fade-out. Most importantly, to avoid the fade-out problem, participants need to understand and believe that the competencies transferred as part of the training process are useful in order to enact behaviors required of the new strategy.

THEORY INTO PRACTICE

Watch out for fade-out—whatever is learned in training opportunity can lose its impact over time.

Feedback

One of the most important opportunities for developing new competencies and skills among existing employees arises from a simple but powerful mechanism: feedback. The challenge in using feedback in order to develop new competencies is twofold:

1. To make sure that the feedback is offered in a way to maximize its impact on behaviors.
2. To make sure that the feedback moves employees toward new behaviors rather than reinforcing old behaviors.

Organizations can, under the right circumstances, use the traditional tools of performance feedback and appraisal to help support change implementation.

In a change implementation process, expectations and definitions of outstanding performance are in flux. It becomes valuable, then, for employees to evaluate the performance of employees for four reasons:

1. It allows an assessment of the current state of the firm's human asset.
2. It helps identify the gap between what skills and organization currently possess and what gaps need to be filled.
3. It identifies poor performers and potential future leaders.
4. It identifies needed development and training efforts.

From the data generated by the performance evaluation process, organizations can construct developmental tools—training, career pathing, mentoring, etc.—as well as guide future recruitment and selection.

Individual employees also gain value from performance feedback. An assessment of their effectiveness can offer employees invaluable answers to a number of questions:

- How is my effort being perceived and received by the organization?
- What is my future with the company?
- What gaps do I need to address between my efforts and the organization's expectations?
- What set of experiences do I need to construct for myself in order to advance my own aspirations?

The desired goal of the process is alignment between the future needs of the organization and the desires and motivations of employees.

Much of the feedback on performance occurs informally. Informal feedback can occur in both obvious and obscure ways. Regular, real-time feedback discussions between superiors and subordinates or among peers can occur spontaneously and/or as part of the culture of the organization which creates expectations that evaluation and performance dialogue will occur regularly and routinely.

Organizations typically seek to supplement such informal feedback with a more formal approach to evaluation: the **performance appraisal**. Although firms implement performance appraisals quite differently, there are some generalizations that can be made. Performance appraisals tend to:

Building a Vocabulary of Change
Performance appraisal a formal, regularly scheduled mechanism designed to provide employees with performance feedback, typically resulting in a performance rating.

- Be regularly scheduled events, occurring annually, semi annually, or even quarterly
- Be individual, one-on-one sessions between a supervisor and a subordinate
- Be guided by a form designed by the organization's human resource department
- Involve some sort of grading system, covering both specific performance elements and an overall evaluation of effectiveness
- Be designed for both administrative purposes—documentation of poor performance, distribution of performance-based rewards, etc.—and developmental purposes

Formal evaluation such as performance appraisal often fail to enhance desired behavior. Extensive research has demonstrated that both appraisers and appraisees are highly dissatisfied with their performance appraisal experience.[4] Appraisers fear that, except in the case of a "superior" performance rating, they will be doing more harm than good, leaving the employee demoralized, demotivated, even alienated.

Apparently, those fears are justified. Managers often report that subordinate performance actually *deteriorates* as a result of conducting a performance appraisal, and indicate that the only reason they conduct such interviews is to comply with company mandates. Employees report greater uncertainty *after* the performance appraisal than before. Most likely, that confusion results from a mismatch between the informal feedback described earlier and the formal feedback offered as part of the performance appraisal.

When performance appraisals become exercises in compliance, as they apparently do with great regularity, they are unlikely to generate commitment on the part of employees to increased effectiveness.

Employee commitment is also impacted by issues of validity and accuracy. Is the performance appraisal actually assessing what it claims to be assessing, and is it doing so accurately? Employees often leave an interview doubting whether either validity or accuracy has been achieved. Empirical evidence suggests that their suspicion is well founded. Supervisory ratings are regularly and significantly distorted by subjectivity, personal bias, deliberate distortion, and unintended but common rating errors.[5]

To increase employees' perceptions that the feedback they are receiving from the appraisal process is valid—and thus increasing their commitment to enhancing their own high performance behaviors—organizations have tried a number of innovations.

Building a Vocabulary of Change
360° feedback
performance feedback gathered from peers, subordinates, supervisors, and customers.

One—the **360° feedback**—attempts to expand the data and bring multiple points of view into the effectiveness appraisal process. Peers, subordinates, and even customers are invited to contribute data on an employee's effectiveness relating to both dimensions: task performance and behavioral patterns consistent with the organization's culture.

Approximately 90 percent of Fortune 500 companies use some form of 360° feedback for purposes of employment evaluation, development of needed competencies, or both.[6] The effectiveness of 360° feedback will be enhanced if the organization's culture emphasizes openness and learning, deemphasizes strict power distinctions based on hierarchy, and places a high value on customer responsiveness.

Another innovation relies heavily on *self-appraisal,* where the appraisal discussion is based on the subordinate's view of himself or herself. When employees perceive themselves to be active participants in the appraisal process, they are more likely to alter their behavior in ways desired by the organization.[7] Both self-appraisal and 360° performance appraisals represent attempts by organizations to increase employee acceptance of the feedback, thus leading to improved behavior and performance.

THEORY INTO PRACTICE

Self-appraisal and data from multiple sources can help increase the validity and effectiveness of performance feedback.

Top Management Development

Concentrating on the development of new competencies at lower and middle levels of the organization is a necessary component of effective change implementation; it is not, however, sufficient. Effective change will also demand new behaviors from executives at the top of the organization.

THEORY INTO PRACTICE

Behavioral change requires attention to the behavioral pattern of those at the top of the organization as well as lower level employees.

Greater coordination, higher levels of innovation, speedier response to a dynamic marketplace—all these outcomes are associated with the behaviors and interactions of top managers. Both behavioral and cognitive training interventions are useful in developing new skills among executives, but Richard Boyatzis has suggested that on-the-job experience is far more effective in developing required competencies.[8]

At the CEO level, corporate boards often pursue a "buy" rather than "make" strategy in search of change. Insiders, especially those who have stayed with the company long enough to rise to the top, are products of the culture that have been targeted for change. A change in business fortunes requires a change in top leadership, which means, in turn, injecting the top of the organization with "new blood."[9] Outsiders such as Meg Whitman at eBay and Archie Norman at ASDA have been effective at implementing significant and successful change.

Experience suggests, however, that outsiders are *not* a requirement for out-of-the-box thinking and organizational change. Three longtime insiders who rose to the top of their organizations—Vineet Nayar at HCL, Judy McGrath at MTV Networks Group, and Sam Palmisano at IBM—demonstrated that understanding the existing culture and connecting to the founding mission of the company enabled them to transform business strategies and organizational performance.

No organization can rely entirely on outsiders, of course. To meet the challenge of developing internal leaders capable of transforming their organization, companies can systematically manage the careers and experiences of executives. Those experiences can provide individuals with the opportunity to learn new knowledge, attitudes, and behavior within the unique and special environment of the firm.

Within organizations, career experiences are typically managed through a **succession planning** process in which top executives regularly review all managers at or above a certain hierarchical level, looking at both performance and potential, and devise developmental plans for their most promising individuals.

Building a Vocabulary of Change
Succession planning a formal process in which top executives regularly review all managers at or above a certain hierarchical level, looking at both performance and potential, and devise developmental plans for their most promising individuals.

The implementation of succession planning is often flawed by inadequate—even nonexistent—follow-up. Said one executive of her company's succession planning system, "Our procedures are as good as any... The only problem is that people don't pay any attention to them."[10]

Lack of follow-up is not the only limitation. Succession planning can pay a great deal of attention to so-called fast-trackers, while ignoring the potential of others. The problem here is twofold. First, it is possible that those identified as

EXHIBIT 5-3 Practices for Developing Executives Capable of Adaptation and Leading Change.

Structural and design changes	Delayering, increased span of control, matrix, or horizontal structures—all of these work to develop generalists far earlier in their careers and place a greater premium on interpersonal competencies.
Explicit international movement	Assigning managers to work in a non native culture for a significant period of time develops cross-cultural awareness and skills that can be vital in a culturally diverse environment.
Career mazes	Explicit lateral movements replace rapid upward functional mobility with a far broader set of experiences. Functional blinders are removed, general management skills are enhanced, and commitment to the organization as a whole is enlarged.
Slower velocity to allow greater learning	So-called fast-track managers often fail to stay in one position long enough to deal with the consequences of their actions (and the reactions of employees). Learning about and dealing with the consequence of actions requires greater length of tenure in a position.

non-fast-trackers have been held back less by their lack of potential than by contextual constraints imposed by the organization. Second, fast-trackers may be individuals who possess skills more associated with past successes than the future demands of change.[11]

THEORY INTO PRACTICE

Companies can manage the careers of executives in order to create a continuous stream of leaders from inside the organization capable of overseeing and leading effective change.

Career development can also help develop executives capable of adaptation and change. Effective change requires individuals who have learned, through a set of on-the-job activities, to be flexible and adaptive. Exhibit 5-3 offers a number of career development practices that can help organizations develop managers capable of moving out of their comfort zones, taking risks, and leading change.

PEOPLE CHANGE

In his study of companies that moved from "good" to "great"—companies such as Walgreens and Kimberly-Clark—Jim Collins noted that these successful transformations were built on getting "the right people on the bus"—that is, attracting, selecting, and retaining individuals whose skills and behavioral patterns aligned with the transformed requirement of outstanding performance—and getting "the wrong people off the bus."[12]

The challenge of getting the right people on the bus and the wrong people off the bus lies at the core of Step 3. At this stage of implementation, leaders will have to ask and answer two key questions:

1. What does the organization mean by the "right" and "wrong" employee?
2. What are the most effective ways to manage this stage of the change process?

Let's start with the question of identifying and selecting the "right" employee in a situation of change.

THEORY INTO PRACTICE

People alignment—getting the right people on the bus and the wrong people off the bus—is a key to effective change implementation.

Selecting the "Right" Employees

Individuals are attracted to organizations for a number of reasons: money, to be sure, as well as location, opportunity for advancement, prestige, and so on. There is also an attraction that derives from a perception of personal alignment. Potential employees may believe that the "personality" of an organization—its goals, structures, ways of working, and so on—matches well with their own. Conversely, they may feel that there is too much of a discrepancy between them and the organization.[13]

"We're looking for personality," noted a recruiter for Disney World (known in the company as a "director of casting"). "We can train for skills."[14] Undoubtedly, organizations, especially those with strong corporate cultures such as Disney, take on personalities shaped by a combination of values and goals. Individuals, of course, have their own personalities with personal values and goals. During the joining-up process, individuals tend to seek out and organizations tend to select for a match between organizational values and individual personalities. Individuals attracted to Disney, for instance, are likely to be quite different from people interested in working for General Electric.

THEORY INTO PRACTICE

Employees attracted to and selected by the organization in an earlier phase are not necessarily the right employees for the newly defined strategies and goals of the changing organization.

The idea of attracting the right employees is important to any organization. When an organization is attempting to implement change, the matter becomes even more complex. The personality of the organization is changing. Individuals attracted to and selected by the organization in an earlier phase are not necessarily the right employees for the newly defined strategies and goals of the changing organization. In redefining the personality of their organizations, change leaders are, in essence, overturning the sense of personal alignment that existed in the past. They are changing what they are looking for in the "right" employee.

But what, exactly, is meant by the right employee? It is useful to introduce the concept of *fit*. The right employee means an employee who fits certain needs or requirements. Even that explanation does not tell us enough, because the question still remains: *what* needs or requirements? The requirements may be technical, behavioral, attitudinal, or some combination of all the three.

CRITERIA FOR SELECTION To help clarify the choices an organization faces in the selection process, it is useful to approach fit in two ways. The first involves fit with a specific job, and the second involves fit with the larger organizational culture and values.

Building a Vocabulary of Change
Person-task fit screening and selecting individual employees based on their ability to perform certain tasks and fulfill specific jobs.

Person-task fit is the most common approach taken to hiring employees. The organization has specific tasks that need to be done, so it hires individuals with the skills required of those tasks. Need an electrical engineer? Hire the most skilled electrical engineer available (keeping costs in mind, of course).

To help ensure that the organization hires people with the requisite skills, human resource specialists work in a structured way to define the key knowledge, skills, and abilities required in the performance of core organizational tasks. Individuals are sought, and often tested, to determine their competency levels to perform. The best-qualified individuals are then selected to fill the organization's job vacancies.

Building a Vocabulary of Change
Person-organization fit screening and selecting employees based on congruence between patterns of organizational values and patterns of individual values.

The second approach to selection involves what can be thought of as **person-organization fit**. Unlike the person-task approach, person-organization fit looks beyond the specific skill demands of a task, focusing instead of the values of an individual. Now, the organization asks: how do the values of potential hires fit with the values we are trying to promote?

Person-organization fit looks beyond specific jobs to the desired future state of the organization. What are the mind-set, the personality, and the competencies that the organization seeks through its change? What newly defined roles, responsibilities, and relationships are sought? Most importantly at this stage, what new competencies—both technical how-to competencies and interpersonal (creative problem solving, decision making, collaboration, communication, and so on) competencies—are required of this desired future state?

THEORY INTO PRACTICE

Talent is important but fit with where the organization is headed is vital.

Determining who fits with the organization is a complex, even tricky business. Supervisors often make decisions about which employees fit or do not fit, implicitly, perhaps even subconsciously, based on the goal of reproducing themselves. Instead of asking whether the employee behaves in ways consistent with the values and culture of the organization, the supervisor may ask whether the employee thinks and acts like the evaluating supervisor.

When supervisors seek—consciously or otherwise—to clone themselves, the effect can be damaging both to employees and to the organization. Employees may rightly wonder just how valid supervisory decisions are. Additionally, if organizations become homogeneous, they are in danger of weakening both diversity and creativity.[15]

That approach can be particularly harmful in periods of change. The supervisors' past successes may be the result of behaviors that no longer fit with the desired future state of the company. Additionally, the reproduction phenomenon risks eliminating diversity and promoting conformity within the organization. When change efforts are designed to enhance creativity and innovation, actions that drive out diversity, however inadvertently, will be detrimental. Finally, employees themselves may experience replacement less as a valid measure of ability to adopt new behaviors and more as a self-serving device that enhances supervisors' views of themselves.

An explicit and shared understanding of the new behaviors required of strategic renewal and outstanding performance can help to overcome the dangers of selective perception and reproduction. That understanding is developed in the diagnostic and redesign phase of transformation. Once the requirements have been made explicit, managers are better able to make valid assumptions about whether individuals are displaying the required behaviors. Simultaneously, employees are more likely to accept the validity of those decisions.

SCREENING FOR FIT Particularly when an organization is attempting to implement change, there is an urgent need to attract employees whose behavior exemplifies the desired *future* state rather than the organization as it had been in the *past*, even if that past had been successful. But just how can organizations screen for person-organization fit?

Microsoft prides itself in screening potential hires for intelligence and creativity as much as—if not more than—depth of technical expertise. Even "technical" interviews for potential software developers focus more on "thought processes, problem-solving abilities, and work habits than on specific knowledge or experience." *How many times does the average person use the word "the" in a day?* an interviewer might ask. The manner in which the individual organizes his thought processes and attacks the problem is the key, not providing any technically "right" answer.[16]

Microsoft considers creative problem solving to be a cornerstone of the company's culture and uses the screening process to find individuals who will fit with that desired culture.

Paying attention to the selection of new employees is a key to change implementation. Attracting and hiring employees who already possess both the motivation and competencies to enact the new culture will enhance the effectiveness of the desired change.

This is not to say that *all* issues of person–organization fit must be resolved in the selection process. Behaviorally focused training can help, while removing employees who cannot or will not adopt new behavioral patterns may be necessary. Getting it as right as possible in the selection phase certainly will reduce both the cost and time associated with training and minimize the difficulties—both emotional and financial—associated with removal and replacement.

THEORY INTO PRACTICE

Selecting the "right" employees—that is, employees who possess the values and competencies required of the change—will reduce time, cost, and other revenues required in later developmental interventions.

Building a Vocabulary of Change
Standardized tests self-administered and quantifiable tests used as part of a screening, selection, or assessment process.

SELECTION TECHNIQUES Companies can use any number of techniques to screen for the "right" employee, starting with **standardized tests** which are typically self-administered and quantifiable. These tests assess any number of attributes, ranging from general intelligence and mental ability to mechanical aptitude and technical and industry-based knowledge.

When strategic renewal requires an alteration in the culture of the company, the most obvious standardized instruments to call upon involve personality and psychological tests. These tests offer insight into whether an individual is open or defensive, extroverted or introverted, individualistic or team-oriented, easy-going or reserved, suspicious or trusting, and so forth.

Using standardized tests in the screening process offers some obvious advantages to a company in transition. The tests are relatively easy to administer and score. Quantifiable results are simple to compare. Most importantly, there is validity to the tests as predictors of on-the-job success as long as multiple tests are used in combination.

Standardized tests are not without flaws. Opportunity for abuse and misuse of data are significant. Additionally, their use tends to produce a less diverse workforce in terms of race.[17] Differences in early cultural experiences and unfamiliarity with test-taking techniques on the part of applicants, especially when combined with unintended biases in the formulation of test questions, can produce undesired outcomes.[18] Minority job seekers often express deep suspicion of these tests and their use. Organizations desirous of seeking greater diversity within their workforce may find standardized tests working against that goal.

Building a Vocabulary of Change
Behaviorally anchored interviews potential hires are asked to recount specific examples from their past experience to illustrate how they have responded to challenges and opportunities.

There are alternatives to standardized tests. **Behaviorally anchored interviews** ask potential hires to recount specific examples from their past experience to illustrate how they have responded to challenges and opportunities:

- Give me an example of a work-related problem that you had to deal with, and how you responded.
- Talk about a recent group experience you had at work and the role that you played.

When a group of employees participates in the interview, each asking questions and rating responses, the validity of the assessment increases. The goal is to increase the likelihood of achieving fit between new hires and the behavioral goals of the change without driving out diversity. Exhibit 5-4 offers examples of behaviorally anchored interview questions.

EXHIBIT 5-4 Behaviorally Anchored Interview Questions.

- Describe a time when you were placed on an ineffective work team and how you dealt with it.
- Tell me about a specific employee with whom you had difficulty managing and how you dealt with it.
- Describe how you handled going into a new work situation.
- Describe how you went about learning what was going on in a unit to which you were just moved.
- Tell me about a change process you were involved in and what role you played.
- Tell me about the best performing team you ever worked on and what your contribution was.

Building a Vocabulary of Change
Behavioral simulation potential hires are asked to demonstrate behaviors, usually in a structured role-play exercise with external observers.

A selection process keen on exploring fit between a potential hire and the new behavioral demands might go beyond asking potential hires to recount past actions. A technique known as **behavioral simulation** asks applicants to *demonstrate* behaviors. An illustration of behavioral simulation in screening occurred at Cummins Engine Company's Jamestown, New York, plant.

Collaboration and teamwork were among the core values of plant management as they sought to create high employee commitment. As the diesel-engine plant grew beyond its original start-up levels, the management team realized that they would have to pay close attention to person-organization fit in the recruitment and selection process. The plant's high wage structure assured an abundant supply of applicants, but not just any employee would do. The management team focused the selection process on behaviors that matched the plant's culture and values.

Human resource specialists performed the initial screening. Soon, shop floor workers—team members in the parlance of the plant—entered the process. Teams did their own hiring in order to ensure fit with their particular orientation and set of expectations. In addition to conducting interviews, team members observed applicants in role-play situations—typically, team exercises (see Exhibit 5-5 for a

EXHIBIT 5-5 Components of Behavioral Stimulation.

A group of individuals are assigned a complex problem to solve.

- Solving the problem requires multiple skills.
- The problem's solution is such that effective performance can be rated objectively.

Individuals are placed in teams and asked to solve the problem jointly.

- A facilitator is on hand to offer behavioral observations.
- The joint problem-solving phase may be videotaped to allow participants to observe their behaviors.

A trained facilitator leads the team through a discussion of behaviors.

The solutions of the teams are measured, providing an effectiveness metric for each group.

Team members engage in a further discussion of behaviors based on their performance.

EXHIBIT 5-6
Techniques for Person-Organization Fit Screening.

Mechanism	Description	Strengths	Weaknesses
Paper-and-pencil tests	Standardized, quantifiable, self-administered instruments	• Easy to administer and score • Inexpensive to use on large scales • Simple to compare • Valid job success predictors when used in combination with other mechanisms	• Produce homogeneous workforce • May be resisted/resented by applicants
Behaviorally anchored interviews	Applicants recount specific examples of past experiences	• Can focus on specific behaviors • Valid supplement to other screening mechanisms • Validity increases when multiple interviewers score results	• Deal with recounted rather than actual behaviors • Can be slow and expensive to administer
Behavioral simulation	Applicants engage in role-playing exercise while observed by screeners	• Focus on actual rather than recounted behaviors	• Can be slow and expensive to administer

description of a typical behavioral simulation). After conducting this kind of informal assessment, team members worked together to select future colleagues.

The techniques for person-organization fit screening (summarized in Exhibit 5-6) focus on personality and interpersonal behavior. Screening cannot ignore technical skills, although it is useful to remember that many technical skills can be learned relatively quickly. Interpersonal skills are often more difficult to develop. Organizations would do well to screen for traits that are both critical to performance success and the *most difficult to develop*. Attitude, values, and cultural fit are attributes that are difficult to develop within the context of organizational life yet vital to the sustained outstanding performance of a company.[19]

Patagonia, an outdoor clothing and gear company, bases its personnel selection decisions more on who the applicants are than on what specific skills they possess. "This is a unique culture, extremely unique," said founder/owner Yvon Chouinard. "Not everyone fits in here." That is why the company places its greatest effort into looking for creative and committed "dirt bags," its term for outdoor types. "I've found that rather than bring in businessmen and teach them to be dirt bags," Chouinard observed, "it's easier to teach dirt bags to do business."[20]

Learning business skills, Chouinard insisted, is far easier than learning how to be a true dirt bag. Hiring individuals with the desired personality traits and behavioral competencies and then teaching required skills (rather than hiring for skills and attempting to teach personality and behavior) is far more likely to be successful.

THEORY INTO PRACTICE

It is often easier to teach new skills than to develop new values.

Removal and Replacement

In support of strategic renewal and change, a company may attempt to improve its mix of competencies rapidly by increasing the outflow of personnel through early retirement programs and/or layoffs. Early retirement increases the percentage of recently hired employees who may bring with them new skills, new values, or both. At the same time, personnel reductions allow for a rapid lowering of payroll costs, which will, it is hoped, improve profitability in the short term.

Although a workforce reduction approach (turnaround) may be popular, it has not been terribly effective in helping an organization transform itself into an outstanding performer. Given the short-term severance costs of large-scale reductions (a cost that is considerably higher in Europe than in the United States), the savings in compensation to the organization and subsequent impact on the bottom line are often minor.

THEORY INTO PRACTICE

Don't count on workforce reductions and employee layoffs to produce the competencies required to support strategic renewal and sustain outstanding performance.

Layoffs represent large-scale interventions designed mainly to improve short-term financial performance. **Removal and replacement** is a more specific, targeted people alignment tool. Removal and replacement deals with individuals who cannot or will not develop new competencies and behaviors.

Building a Vocabulary of Change
Removal and replacement a change tool that targets individuals who cannot or will not adopt behaviors required for the redesigned organization.

Although well-designed training programs can indeed be helpful in supporting new patterns of behavior, success will not be universal. Not all employees, after all, are capable of developing the new skills or enacting the new behaviors. Others might simply prefer not to alter their past behaviors.

IMPLEMENTING REMOVAL AND REPLACEMENT When ASDA, a large U.K.-based grocery store chain, sought to transform its failing business in the 1990s (see

Chapter 1), removal and replacement became a vital part of the effort. A cross-functional renewal team started ASDA's store-based change by designing a new set of roles and responsibilities for store employees at all levels. Team members realized that the targeted new behaviors would require store managers who were both willing and able to support the desired new culture.

After selecting three stores to pilot the "new" ASDA—a store culture focused on value, offering customer responsiveness, with high levels of autonomy for individual department managers and strategic planning on behalf of store managers—the renewal team called on the corporate human resources department to evaluate current managers. In the terms Collins used, the team wanted to make sure they had "the right people on the bus" within the targeted stores. That review revealed that much of the challenge of change would focus on getting "the wrong people off the bus."

A sense of urgency required that the early change build on a store management team that displayed the potential for being able to make the required changes. Within the first three stores, about 40 percent of the existing managers were removed and replaced. Some were fired, others moved to other stores not immediately targeted for change. The renewal team brought in managers to the selected pilot stores who had been identified by the human resources staff as more likely to be effective in the new environment.

Removal and replacement does not necessarily involve firing individuals. When the general manager of Rubbermaid's Commercial Products division decided to redesign his operation around cross-functional business teams, it became clear that many employees were uncomfortable with the new approach. The vice president of marketing used a sports analogy to characterize the differences among employees in their reactions to the requirement for teamwork:

> When we first formed the business teams, we had a lot of tennis players and golfers on the team, not team players. They had good functional expertise, but because they weren't team players we were getting into trouble. They didn't try to understand how and what they were doing on their piece of the product was affecting other functions.[21]

Having the wrong people on the bus at Rubbermaid Commercial Products hurt team performance. A member of the upper-management operating team responsible for creating and supporting the various business teams in the division acknowledged the requirement to engage removal and replacement as a human resource development tool:

> When we have seen teams fail, the majority of the time, it was not due to lack of technical expertise. It was because there was a person on the team who was not a team player. We, as an operating team, have to recognize this, and insure that non–team players are relocated from the business team to another position which best complements their personality.[22]

Individuals who could not make the change were replaced and then carefully located in positions where their behaviors would not block or slow down the sought-after change to a team-based operation.

There will be situations in which replacement and removal is not an immediate option to change leaders. Collins described the change at a medical school where the institution of tenure—essentially, guaranteed employment for professors—constrained the actions of the school's academic director. Because he could not remove tenured professors, the director of academic medicine waited for openings to hire "the right people." By doing so, he created "an environment where the wrong people felt increasingly uncomfortable and eventually retired or decided to go elsewhere."[23] When leaders are clear about the behavioral implications of the desired new strategy, and employees are clear that behavioral change is required, individuals may elect to remove themselves.

GETTING THE SEQUENCE RIGHT: FAIR PROCESS

The change implementation model presented in Exhibit 2-6 separates sequentially the Help (Step 2) interventions from People Change (Step 3). In that sequence, organizations offer employees training in the new required skills and behaviors (Step 2) before decisions are made about moving employees (Step 3).

That sequence—first Help and *then* People Change—raises an interesting question. Why invest in training an employee if, in the very next step of the sequence, the organization may have to remove the same employee? The answer lies in the concept of fair process.

Building a Vocabulary of Change
Fair process a widely shared perception that decisions are being made on the basis of valid criteria.

Fair process is a widely shared perception that decisions are being made based on valid criteria. Perceptions of unfair process lead to declining morale, increased turnover, and deteriorating commitment. Conversely, perceptions of fair process lead to higher levels of individual motivation and commitment to the organization and its changing goals.[24]

W. Chan Kim and Renée Mauborgne suggest that a fair process derives from three factors:

1. ***Engagement*** —involving individuals in decisions that impact them, both at the front end (collecting valid data) and the back end (allowing individuals to refute ideas and assumptions).
2. ***Explanation*** —making transparent the thinking that underlies decisions.
3. ***Expectation clarity*** —making clear the criteria that have been and will be used for decision making.[25]

Employee commitment will remain high even if employees disagree with the decision, Kim and Mauborgne conclude, "If they believe that the process the manager used to make the decision was fair."[26]

In terms of Step 3 people change decisions, fair process is, in large part, a function of validity. Are people change decisions based on selective perception or on the requirements of the new strategy?

Perceptions of fairness can also be impacted by the degree to which an organization provides employees with due process and appeal mechanisms. What avenues are available to employees who believe that they have been treated by people change decisions such as evaluation, promotion, or even firing?

Union contracts typically offer grievance and appeal avenues with union officials advocating for members. In nonunion settings, employers may provide their own grievance and appeal mechanisms—panels of managers and employees; trained fact finders, mediators, or arbitrators—that can either make suggestions or overturn decisions if they find an employee has been treated unfairly.

THEORY INTO PRACTICE

Unless people change decisions are viewed by employees as being fair in process, valid in content, and appropriate in sequence, the decisions can undermine commitment to change implementation.

Finally, perceptions of fairness will be based on the timing of people changes. Perceived fairness will be enhanced by a sequence of actions that has already been included:

- A shared diagnosis that has surfaced the relationship between past behavioral patterns and current performance shortcomings
- A redesign process that has identified new patterns of behavior required for sustained outstanding performance
- Training and development has offered current employees an opportunity to gain and demonstrate required new behaviors

At this stage, individuals who cannot or will not make the required changes have been identified. People change decisions—promotion, removal and replacement—can be seen as conforming to the imperatives of outstanding performance rather than to the selective perception of individual supervisors.

Conclusion

Transformational change demands new behaviors from employees. Patterns of behavior that have sustained a company in the past will need to be altered in response to the dynamics of the competitive environment. The diagnostic stage of change has surfaced a misfit between current behaviors and competitive realities. Global customers, for example, may be expecting greater coordination between a company's various units, local customers may be expecting greater employee responsiveness to their specific and special needs, and increasing competition may be demanding faster innovation and greater speed to market with new products and offerings.

In the redesign stage (Step 1), employees create a behavioral model for how the business will respond to those shifts in order to achieve and maintain outstanding performance. At this stage, leaders face a new challenge. Employees who have succeeded in the past may not possess the skills required to excel in the future. Companies may do an assessment to analyze "old" and "new" patterns of behavior and identify the gap that exists within their current human resource.

Now is the time in the change implementation process for leaders to turn their attention to people alignment. Organizations first seek to help (Step 2) employees acquire the necessary competencies and skills. Then, in Step 3, change implementation looks at ways to change the people in the organization. When Step 3 involves removal and replacement, those decisions are viewed by employees as being both fair and valid, those decisions will support the change effort.

Now at the final stage (Step 4), organizational leaders can seek to reinforce behavioral patterns. For that purpose, they turn to new structures and systems. That will be the subject of Chapter 6.

Discussion Questions

1. What are the important differences between Step 2 (Help) and Step 3 (People Change)?
2. What are the main differences between hiring for task and hiring for organizational fit? When is each one most appropriate?
3. What specific recommendations would you make to an organization seeking to avoid training fade-out?
4. The author sees removal and replacement as a key element of aligning people with the requirement of a new strategy. Do you agree or disagree? Why?

Case Discussion

Read "'*Employee First, Customer Second': Vineet Nayar Transforms HCL Technologies*," and prepare answers to the following questions:

1. Explain how—or *if*—Vineet Nayar's new strategy for the company and his approach to people alignment reinforce each other.
2. Do you see potential problems implementing Nayar's people alignment initiatives within India?
3. Are Nayar's ideas about people alignment transferable to other industries and other countries?

"EMPLOYEE FIRST, CUSTOMER SECOND": VINEET NAYAR TRANSFORMS HCL TECHNOLOGIES

Headquartered in Noida, a suburb of New Delhi, HCL Technologies competed in India's hyperdynamic information technology (IT) sector.[27] Founded in 1976, HCL defined itself as "one of India's original IT garage startups." For its first 25 years, HCL found success offering IT hardware. However, as the global IT industry shifted from hardware to software and to offering infrastructure services, HCL proved to be less than nimble.

In April 2005, the company looked within and promoted Vineet Nayar to the position of president. Nayar immediately set his goal for HCL: transformational change within the company in order to position HCL as a global leader in transformational outsourcing services "working with clients in areas that impact and redefine the core of their business."

Strategic Renewal

Strategic renewal at HCL would involve, Nayar announced, a movement away from "small time engagements" and toward high value-added integrated service consulting and outsourcing. In order to turn that vision into reality, Nayar would oversee transformational change at his $1.5 billion, 46,600-employee company. (HCL had operations in 11 countries including the United States, France, Germany, China, and Japan, with 96 percent of its employees worldwide being Indians.)

His first strategic goal was to pay a great deal more attention to internal operating efficiencies than HCL had in the past, while simultaneously emphasizing innovative offerings. Nayar would, he promised, "put our house in order by rejuvenating employees and improving operating efficiencies."

From his past management experience, Nayar (who had spent seven years as an HCL engineer before taking the assignment of running an internally developed start-up company) had come to believe that employees rather than leaders would be the source of improvement and innovation.

India's traditional hierarchical culture led executives to take a "dictatorial" approach to management. Studies of national culture have found that India ranks high on two dimensions: power distance and long-term orientation. High-power distance suggests greater acceptance of hierarchical authority and a greater capacity to follow than lead. A high score on the long-term orientation index suggests a preference for thrift, perseverance, and predictability. If HCL was to compete successfully against larger Indian competitors such as Infosys, Nayar wanted to "invert the pyramid," he said, explaining his meaning in blunt terms. For most companies, "it's the employee who sucks up to the boss." Nayar's goal for HCL was to create a culture where "as much as possible, [we] get the manager to suck up to the employee."

Rejuvenating Employees

Three months after assuming the president's position, Nayar announced two initiatives designed to rejuvenate employees and unleash their creative potential. Both initiatives, he also admitted, were intended to be "shocks" to the system and signal a shaking up of the old culture.

"Employee First, Customer Second"

In July 2005, Nayar introduced his "Employee First, Customer Second" initiative in order to "invert the pyramid." That initiative, explained Dilip Kumar Srivastava, head of corporate human resources, had four strategic objectives:

1. To provide a unique employee environment
2. To drive an inverted organizational structure
3. To create transparency and accountability in the organization
4. To encourage a value-driven culture

Added Nayar, "I wanted value focused employees that were willing and able to drive an innovative, sophisticated experience for customers. From the start, though, I was clear: Employee First was not about free lunch, free buses, and subsidies. It was about setting clear priorities, investing in employees' development, and unleashing their potential to produce bottom-line results."

360° Performance Evaluations

Along with announcing the Employee First, Customer Second philosophy, Nayar introduced 360° performance evaluations. Initially, the evaluations were performed on Nayar and his top 20 managers. That was not the shock however; rather, it was Nayar's directive that the results of that evaluation be posted online for any employee to see.

Executives report to feelings of unease at the airing of those results. Said R. Srikrishna, head of the U.S. infrastructure services division, "There was this whole picture of me that [emerged] as a heavy taskmaster. It was very unsettling the first time."

For Nayar, the publication of 360° results signaled that HCL was serious about his Employee First philosophy. Nayar expanded the system so that employees can see the results for their managers as well as their peers. Nayar assured them that the ratings would *not* be used to determine bonuses or promotions. Instead, they would allow the individuals to work with the company's human resources department to create developmental programs for them.

Nayar appreciated that the idea of posting results would be shocking, at first, to employees. He referred to this as disruptive thinking. "When I put my 360° evaluation in the Intranet within my first 90 days of taking charge at HCL Technologies, it showed that the CEO was willing to put his neck on the line. It is a simple gesture that galvanizes others into thinking on similar lines. We [India] claim to be the world's largest democracy, but while running our businesses we are dictatorial toward our employees."

Additional People Alignment Initiatives

Some additional initiatives started by Nayar include the following:

- HCL's training program was renamed "Talent Transformation and Intrapreneurship Development." "We did not just want to have swanky off-site development programs, then have employees return to work and go back to status quo," explained Anand Pillai, who headed the program. Instead, HCL rotated employees through multiple projects and jobs and then helped them "understand the work of their operation at both the tactical and strategic level."
- HCL abandoned performance-based bonuses and adopted, instead, what was called "trust pay." Aimed most especially at junior engineers, pay would be fixed at the beginning of the year. That represented a dramatic break from the industry standard of having variable pay account for up to 30 percent of total compensation. "It increased our cost base," admitted Nayar, but the idea was, we'd pay you fully, but we trusted that you would deliver. It was intended to reduce transaction volume and increase trust."

Further Challenges

By 2007, Nayar could point to some impressive improvements. Under his leadership, HCL has achieved the highest level of organic growth—defined as growth achieved through internal development rather than by acquisitions and mergers—among India's IT sector. Employee retention had been a particular problem for HCL. In 2005, the company's attrition rate—the percentage of total employees who leave a company in a year—was 20.4 percent, among the highest in the industry. In 2007, that figure dropped to 17.2 percent (still higher than many competitors). At the same time, competition remained unrelenting and was becoming more global. IBM announced plans to invest $6 billion in India in the upcoming three years, up from $2 billion in the previous three years.

Endnotes

1. I first became aware of this story from reading Ronald Heifetz, Alexander Grashow, and Marty Linsky, "Leadership in a (Permanent) Crisis," *Harvard Business Review* (July—Aug. 2009), pp. 62–69. Additional material comes from "Best Buy Gets in Touch with its Feminine Side," *USA Today* (Dec. 20, 2006); Jackie Crosby, "Women's Warrior at Best Buy," *Star Tribune* (Dec. 18, 2007); Bala Chakravarthy and Peter Lorrange, "Continuous Renewal and How Best Buy Did It," *Strategy and Leadership* 35 (2007), pp. 4–11.
2. George Bohlander and Kathy McCarty, "How to Get the Most from Team Training," *National Productivity Review* (Autumn 1996), pp. 25–35.
3. Raymond A. Noe, *Employee Training and Development* (Boston, MA: McGraw-Hill Irwin, 2002), pp. 150–175. These conclusions were confirmed empirically in Dian L. Seyler, Elwood F. Holton III, Reid A. Bates, Michael F. Burnett, and Manuel A. S. Carvalho, "Factors Affecting Motivation to Transfer Training," *International Journal of Training and Development* 2 (1998), pp. 2–16.
4. This research is reviewed in Herbert M. Meyer, "A Solution to the Performance Appraisal Feedback Enigma," *Academy of Management Executive* 5 (1991), pp. 68–76.
5. Gary P. Latham and Kenneth N. Wexley, *Increasing Productivity Through Performance Appraisal* (Reading, MA: Addison-Wesley, 1981); David B. Balkin and Luis Gomez-Mejia, *New Perspectives on Compensation* (Englewood Cliffs, NJ: PrenticeHall, 1987); C. Longenecker, H. Sims, and D. Gioia, "Behind the Mask: The Politics of Employee Appraisal," *Academy of Management Executive* 1 (1987), pp. 183–191; George T. Milkovich and John W. Bourdeau, *Human Resource Management* (Homewood, IL: Irwin, 1991); Donald J. Campbell, Kathleen M. Campbell, and Ho-Beng Chia, "Merit Pay, Performance Appraisal, and Individual Motivation: An Analysis and Alternative," *Human Resource Management* 37 (Summer 1998), pp. 131–146.
6. Tracy Maylett and Juan Riboldi, "Using 360° Feedback to Predict Performance," *Training and Development* (Sept. 2007), pp. 48–52.
7. M. M. Greller, "Subordinate Participation and Reactions to the Appraisal Interview," *Journal of Applied Psychology* 6 (1975), pp. 544–549; R. J. Burke, W. Weitzel, and T. Weir, "Characteristics of Effective Employee Performance Review and Development Interviews: Replication and Extension," *Personnel Psychology* 31 (1978), pp. 903–919; Charles C. Manz and Henry P. Sims, Jr., "Self-Management as a Substitute for Leadership: A Social Learning Perspective," *Academy of Management Review* (1980), pp. 361–367; R. L. Dipboye and R. de Pontbriand, "Correlates of Employee Reactions to Performance Appraisal and Appraisal Systems," *Journal of Applied Psychology* (1981), pp. 248–251; J. M. Ivancevich and J. T. McMahon, "The Effects of Goal Setting, External Feedback, and Self-Generated Feedback on Outcome Variables: A Field Experiment," *Academy of Management Journal* (1982), pp. 359–372; D. M. Herold, R. C. Liden, and M. L. Leatherwood, "Using Multiple Attributes to Assess Sources of Performance Feedback," *Academy of Management Journal* (1987), pp. 826–835.
8. Richard E. Boyatzis, *The Competent Manager: A Model for Effective Performance* (New York: Wiley, 1992); Richard E. Boyatzis, Scott S.

Cowen, David A. Kold, and associates, *Innovation in Professional Education: Steps on a Journey from Teaching to Learning* (San Francisco, CA: Jossey-Bass, 1995).

9. Research has demonstrated that lagging organizational performance is one of the key reasons for turning to outside leadership. See Donald C. Hambrick and Phyllis A. Mason, "Upper Echelons: The Organization As a Reflection of Top Managers," *Academy of Management Review* 9 (1984), pp. 193–206; Rajeswararao Chaganti and Rakesh Sambharya, "Strategic Orientation and Characteristics of Upper Management," *Strategic Management Journal* 8 (1987), pp. 393–401; James P. Guthrie and Judy D. Olian, "Does Context Affect Staffing Decisions? The Case of General Managers," *Personnel Psychology* 44 (1991), pp. 263–292.
10. Quoted in Douglas T. Hall, "Dilemmas in Linking Succession Planning to Individual Learning," *Human Resource Management* 25 (Summer 1986), p. 237.
11. Anil K. Gupta, "Matching Managers to Strategies: Point and Counterpoint," *Human Resource Management* 25 (Summer 1986), pp. 215–234.
12. Jim Collins, *Good to Great: Why Some Companies Make the Leap and Others Don't* (New York: Harper Business, 2001).
13. The notion of "personality fit" between individuals and organizations is explored in Benjamin Schneider, Harold W. Goldstein, and D. Brent Smith, "The ASA Framework: An Update," *Personnel Psychology* 48 (1995), p. 749.
14. Disney recruiter quoted in Ronald Henkoff, "Finding, Training, and Keeping the Best Service Workers," *Fortune* (Oct. 3, 1994), p. 114. For research on personalities and the attraction/selection process, see Chris Argyris, "Some Problems in Conceptualizing Organizational Climate: A Case Study of a Bank," *Administrative Science Quarterly* 2 (1957), pp. 501–520; Benjamin Schneider, "The People Make the Place," *Personnel Psychology* 40 (1987), pp. 437–454; Benjamin Schneider, Harold W. Goldstein, and D. Brent Smith, "The ASA Framework: An Update," *Personnel Psychology* 48 (1995), pp. 747–773.
15. Benjamin Schneider, D. Brent Smith, Sylvester Taylor, and John Flannor, "Personality and Organizations: A Test of Homogeneity of Personality Hypothesis," *Journal of Applied Psychology* 83 (June 1998), pp. 462–470.
16. Quotes from Christopher A. Bartlett and Meg Wozny, *Microsoft: Competing on Talent* (Boston, MA: Harvard Business School Publishing, 2000), p. 2.
17. Neal Schmitt, "Employee Selection: How Simulations Change the Picture for Minority Groups," *Cornell Hotel and Restaurant Administration Quarterly* 44 (Feb. 2003), pp. 25–33.
18. William C. Byham, "Recruitment, Screening, and Selection," in William R. Tracey, ed., *Human Resources Management and Development Handbook* (New York: AMACOM, 1994), p. 197.
19. Donald Bowen, Gerald E. Ledford, Jr., and B. Nathan, "Hiring for the Organization, Not the Job," *Academy of Management Executive* 5 (1991), pp. 35–51; Randy W. Boxx and Randall Odom, "Organizational Values and Value Congruency and their Impact on Satisfaction, Commitment, and Cohesion," *Public Personnel Management* 20 (1991), pp. 195–205; Jennifer Chatman, "Matching People and Organizations: Selection and Socialization in Public Accounting Firms," *Administrative Science Quarterly* 36 (1991), pp. 459–484; Charles A. O'Reilly, Jennifer Chatman, and David F. Caldwell, "People and Organizational Culture: A Profile Comparison Approach to Assessing Person-Organization Fit," *Academy of Management Journal* 34 (1991), pp. 487–516; Elizabeth F. Cabrera and Jaime Bonache, "An Expert HR System for Aligning Organizational Culture and Strategy," *Human Resource Planning* 22 (1999), pp. 51–60.
20. Chouinard quoted in Edward O. Wells, "Lost in Patagonia," *Inc.* (Aug. 1992), p. 54.
21. Teresa Amabile and Dean Whitney, *Business Teams at Rubbermaid Inc.* (Boston, MA: Harvard Business School Publishing, 1997), p. 14.
22. *Ibid.*
23. Collins, *Good to Great*, p. 41.
24. The topic of fair process—and the related subject, organizational justice—has received a great deal of attention of late. See, for example, Kees Van Den Bos, Henk Wilke, Lind E. Allen, and Riël Vermunt, "Evaluating Outcomes by Means of the Fair Process Effect: Evidence for Different Processes in Fairness and Satisfaction Judgments," *Journal of Personality and Social*

Psychology 74 (June 1998), pp. 1493–1503; Kees Van Den Bos, "Assimilation and Contrast in Organizational Justice: The Role of Primed Mindsets in the Psychology of the Fair Process Effect," *Organizational Behavior and Human Decision Processes* 89 (Sept. 2002), pp. 866–881; W. Chan Kim and Renée Mauborgne, "Fair Process: Managing in the Knowledge Economy," *Harvard Business Review* 81 (Jan. 2003), pp. 127–136; Kwok Leung, Kwok-Kit Tong, and Lind E. Allan, "Realpolitik Versus Fair Process: Moderating Effects of Group Identification on Acceptance of Political Decisions," *Journal of Personality and Social Psychology* 92 (Mar. 2007), pp. 476–489.

25. Kim and Mauborgne, "Fair Process," p. 132.

26. *Ibid.*, p. 127.

27. This case is based on information from the following sources: www.hcltech.com; "Wanted: Employees Ready for a Challenge," *Business India Intelligence* (June 21, 2006), p. 8; Linda A. Hill, Farun Khanna, and Emily A. Stecker, *HCL Technologies (A-B) Abridged* (Boston, MA: Harvard Business School Publishing, 2007); "Hungry Tiger, Dancing Elephant," *The Economist* (Apr. 7, 2007), pp. 67–69; "Vineet Nayar's Inverted Pyramid," *CNN Money* (July 12, 2007); "How Vineet Nayar Transformed HCL Tech," *Rediff India Abroad: India as It Happens* (Nov. 7, 2007); Jena McGregor, "The Employee Is Always Right," *Business Week* (Nov. 19, 2007), pp. 80–82; Peter Cappelli, Harbir Singh, Jitendra V. Singh, and Michael Useem, "Leadership Lessons from India," Harvard Business Review 88 (Mar. 2010), pp. 90–97; Vineet Nayar, "A Maverick CEO Explains How He Persuaded His Team to Leap into the Future," Harvard Business Review 88 (June 2010), pp. 110–113.

CHAPTER 6 Reinforcing New Behaviors

As we have seen, effective change implementation proceeds in a logical sequence of interventions. A dynamic competitive environment triggers the requirement for change.

Diagnosis sets the stage for effective change implementation by surfacing any misalignment that may exist between patterns of internal behavior and a desired new strategy.

In Step 1, redesign considers alternative patterns of behavior that will help the organization create and sustain outstanding performance. Out of the diagnostic process comes a shared understanding of the roles and responsibilities that employees must enact and the relationships that employees must create both among themselves and with key external stakeholders.

In Step 2, training and development helps employees acquire the required new skills and behaviors.

In Step 3, people change decisions ensure that the organization has employees with the needed competencies and behaviors.

Now, at Step 4, organizational leaders reinforce the new behaviors through what might be thought of as the "hardwiring" of the organization: structures, systems, and technologies. This chapter will explore the choices available in terms of hardwiring and analyze the importance of placing structural, system, and technology changes at the back end of a change process rather than leading with those interventions.

In particular, this chapter will:

- Identify the major structural choices faced by organizational leaders and the behavioral implications of those choices
- Consider the role of compensation in shaping desired behaviors
- Analyze the role of information technology (IT) in impacting employee behaviors

Before doing so, we will examine an attempt by a large national retail chain to restructure in order to revive their market during a recession. As you read this short case, ask yourself:

- How would you evaluate Macy's response to the recession?
- Is it really feasible to do both turnaround (layoffs) and transformation (restructuring) simultaneously?
- What and whose behaviors is Macy's attempting to change?

LOCALIZING A RETAIL GIANT CHAIN

Macy's is the largest division of the retail giant Macy's Inc. (which also operates macys.com, Bloomingdale's, and bloomingdales.com). The department store chain sells clothing and accessories for men, women, and children, as well as a wide assortment of home furnishings. The chain operates in 45 states and, until the 2009 construction of Shinsegae Centum City in Busan, South Korea, boasted the largest single department store in the world (in New York City).

In the 1990s, the department store industry in the United States experienced considerable restructuring. Federated Department Stores purchased the Macy's chain and soon consolidated many of the other brands it had recently acquired—Jordon Marsh, Filene's, Rich's, Marshall Field's, Famous-Barr among them—under the Macy's banner. In 2007, Federated itself changed its corporate name to Macy's.*

Like other retailers, Macy's executives understood that while all of these consolidations offered many advantages associated with the economies of scale and scope, they also tended to deprive the stores of local focus or flavor.† Decisions about what merchandise to carry and how to market and display that merchandise were made in corporate headquarters. Macy's relied on sophisticated market research, of course. But still, each store tended to resemble every other one. They had all become more or less generic.

The recession of 2008 led to cost cutting—4 percent of Macy's jobs were eliminated—but Macy's executives also wanted to increase revenues. Their strategy for doing that, labeled My Macy's, would move away from the cookie-cutter image of the chain by emphasizing local appeal and regional differentiation. The company experimented with six stores, allowing local managers greater say over what merchandise to carry and how to market it. Product mix could vary by region. Even the same products could be packaged and marketed according to local tastes. Decisions would now be made by local managers. This was an advantage over corporate market research, explained CEO Terry Lundgren. "It is much more accurate to have people living in the marketplace tell you, 'This is who is shopping in my store.'"

With the success of these half-dozen pilots, Lundgren decided to roll out My Macy's to the chain's 800-plus stores. To do that, he knew that he would have

*So, Macy's is the name of both the corporate umbrella and its largest single business unit. This case focuses on the Macy's business unit.

†Economies of scale allow an organization to become more efficient by increasing the number of times it performs a single activity, while economies of scope allow a company to gain efficiencies by performing more than one activity with spare capacity.

to change the company's highly centralized structure. The businesses would now be subdivided into 69 "geographic districts" (approximately 12 stores per district). Results proved promising, helping Macy's recover from the recession. "We see the power in the local input from our experience over the past year," said vice chairman Tom Cody. "We know that the critical piece comes from the intelligence of the local market."

SELECTING THE APPROPRIATE ORGANIZATIONAL FOCUS

Macy's new strategy called for regional differentiation, while its formal structure made such differentiation difficult, if not impossible. So, in order to achieve that strategy, Macy's changed its structure. After running six pilots, the company moved to a focus on regional markets.

In all organizations, the activities of employees need to be focused on two separate issues:

1. The *functional* or technical activities required to achieve the desired outcomes of the organization.
2. Responsiveness to the external *marketplace* (customers, suppliers, competitors, regulators, and so on) in which the organization has elected to compete.

No organization can select one focus to the exclusion of the other; the focus of employees must be simultaneous. Nonetheless, organizational leaders may choose to emphasize one over the other, and that emphasis is likely to change over time in response to the dynamism of the competitive environment and the strategic choices of the organization. It is therefore important that leaders understand the impact that various structural choices will have on the focus of employees and, consequently, on their behavior. Organization structure is a mechanism for helping to achieve the desired focus. Therefore, when a new strategy calls for a new focus, it is likely that the structure of the organization will need to change.

Choices of Organizational Structure

Building a Vocabulary of Change
Organizational structure the formal manner in which employees are subdivided into units and divisions as a way of focusing efforts on the required activities of the company.

Organizational structure refers to the formal manner in which employees are subdivided into units and divisions as a way of focusing their efforts on the required tasks of the company.

Structures impact behaviors by defining the context for work. The change implementation question, therefore, becomes two fold:

1. *What* structures to use?
2. *How* and *when* do we change structures?

Let's examine the *what* question first: what are the structural options available to leaders?

A quick look at an organizational chart reveals the choices that leaders have made concerning structure. A chart may show, for instance, functional units such as manufacturing, marketing, and engineering. Another chart might include product-oriented divisions, such as Macy's regional divisions. Far more complex charts might find lines of responsibility crisscrossing both horizontally and vertically, linking functions with product lines and perhaps even geographic regions.

Although structure is often thought of in terms of boxes and lines—who holds what title and who reports to whom—the key question is really one of focus

THEORY INTO PRACTICE

Organization structure is more than just boxes and lines; it is a way to focus the activities of employees.

FOCUS ON FUNCTIONAL EXCELLENCE In their earliest founding stages, organizations typically exist in a prestructural state. When Open Markets, Inc. (OMI), a software tools and development business started, for instance, 12 employees shared office space in a Cambridge, Massachusetts, basement. They had no job titles but only the most general definition of individual responsibilities. The tasks that needed to be accomplished were simply shared.[1]

At some point, as organizations evolve, leaders adopted a more formal structure to add greater order, stability, and focus. "As we've grown," noted an OMI employee, "some people feel it is difficult not knowing who your boss is, who will evaluate your performance, where to go for help. As we get larger, we need a little more structure."[2] At OMI, employees naturally assumed responsibilities for the various functional activities of their organization: software development, of course, but also marketing, sales, vendor relationships, finance, and administration.

THEORY INTO PRACTICE

As organizations move beyond the small, start-up stage, they are likely to adopt a simple functional structure: people with similar skills performing related activities are placed in functional departments.

Building a Vocabulary of Change
Functional structure a formal design choice that groups people together in units based on common tasks and specialized skills.

Over time, as an organization continues to grow, individuals with like-minded interests, inclinations, and competencies find a home among one or another of these functional activities. In doing so, an organization can change by adopting a **functional structure**: a structure meant to focus activities on the functional or technical tasks of the organization. Exhibit 6-1 depicts a prototypical functional organization chart for an Internet portal provider.

By changing to a functional structure, organizations seek to bring discipline and efficiency to an operation. Functional structures help the organization achieve efficiencies of operation and standardization of offerings. Functionally structured organizations are in a position to fine-tune the product and service offerings, making sure the customer, "gets the most for the least."[3]

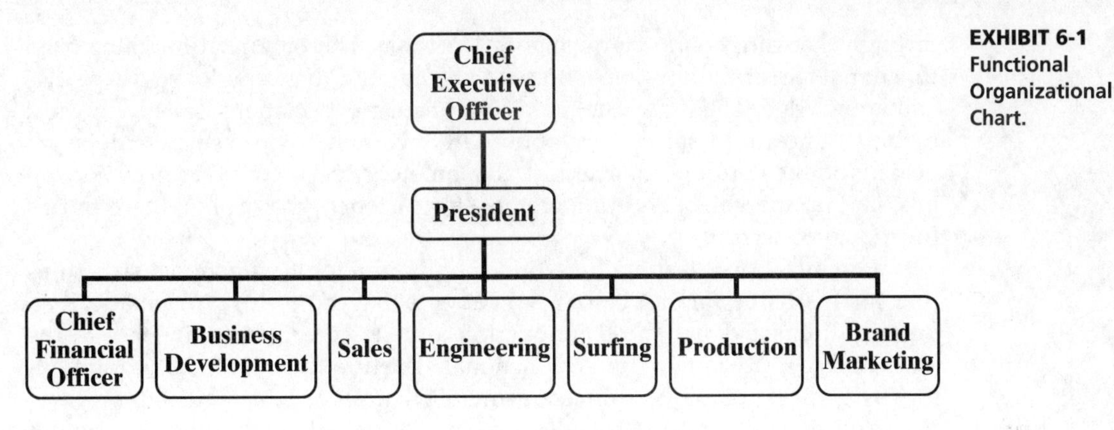

EXHIBIT 6-1 Functional Organizational Chart.

THEORY INTO PRACTICE

Use functional structures to shape the development of technical skills and expert knowledge on the part of employees.

No matter how functionally oriented an organization might be, there must also be some simultaneous capacity to respond to the marketplace. Functional structures attempt to achieve that responsiveness through a well-ordered sequential process.

In a functionally structured manufacturing firm, for example, we can follow the sequence:

1. Ideas from the marketplace enter the organization through the marketing department.
2. Engineers translate those ideas into designs.
3. Production transforms designs from concept to reality.
4. Products are delivered to customers via the sales department.
5. The financial department attends to such matters as profit margin and return on investment.

It is the responsibility of the general manager who sits atop the functional structure—sometimes a CEO, a senior vice president, or a managing director—to assure that the appropriate level of coordination among these sequential functional activities is achieved.

Because leaders call upon structures to focus employee behaviors, it is important to ask: Just what kind of employee behaviors can functional structures be expected to reinforce?

Let's start with the rigorous development of in-depth technical expertise. This development is enhanced by a functional career path that typically moves employees upward through a specific department. The organization hires individuals who enter at a low level of a function, then move vertically upward through that function as performance warrants. The organization gains from functional career path by developing and retaining their employees' expertise and knowledge. The individual gains clear career expectations, speedy upward mobility, and rapid salary escalation. Organizations whose success depends heavily on the depth of their technical competencies—accounting firms, hospitals, law partnerships, and universities, for instance—typically adhere to this functional pattern.

Organizational leaders may find that by moving to functional structures they inadvertently prompt behavioral patterns that can prove problematic. If an organization seeks enhanced innovation and speedier responsiveness to the marketplace, leaders may find a functional structure to be limiting and inhibiting. By focusing employees on achieving efficiencies and incremental improvements in existing products and services, functional structures may render employees less likely to be able to respond quickly with new and innovative offerings.

Much of the behavioral problem inherent in functional structures relates to low levels of coordination among employees, especially employees across different functional units. Functionally trained and developed individuals may find coordinated efforts with individuals from other departments to be difficult. Over time, insulated units tend to develop their own ways of thinking, unique patterns of working, speaking, conceptualizing time, and even defining effectiveness.[4]

In functional structures, employees have little opportunity to develop the competencies required of working together across departmental boundaries. At its worst, a kind of "us against them" mentality can evolve as employees battle each other across functions rather than uniting against common (external) competitors. The skills of the general manager may not be sufficient to overcome these structural barriers and achieve the required coordination.

THEORY INTO PRACTICE

Organizations seeking to create seamless coordination across functions may find that the silos erected through functional structures get in the way.

Organizational change efforts may seek to deal with the challenges raised by a functional structure. The particular challenge is to enhance marketplace responsiveness. One of the most common ways of achieving that focus is to adopt a divisional structure.

FOCUS ON MARKETPLACE RESPONSIVENESS As organizations grow in both size and complexity, they often seek greater external focus. Most typically, they turn to a **divisional structure** as a way of reinforcing behaviors that respond to the marketplace.

Building a Vocabulary of Change
Divisional structure a formal design choice that groups people together in units based on common products, services, or customers.

All activities associated with a particular product or families of products are brought together in a divisional unit. A general manager, often a senior vice president, divisional president, or managing director, sits atop each unit. That structure is depicted in Exhibit 6-2 for a prototypical software developer.

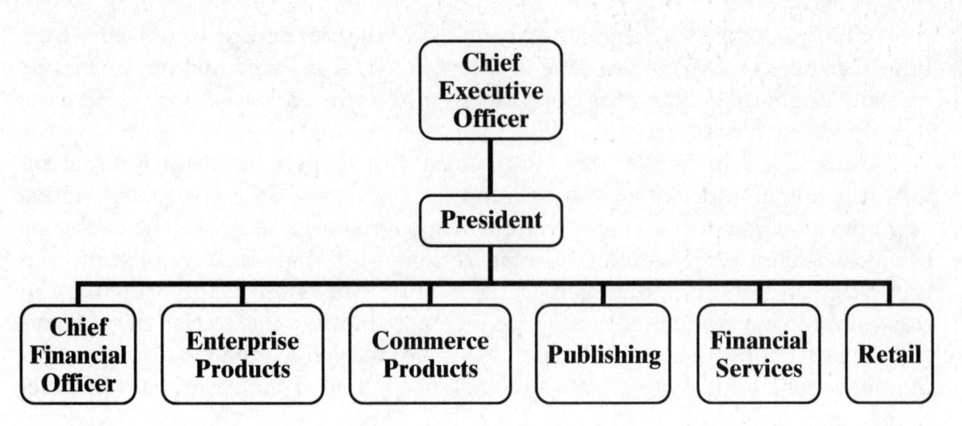

EXHIBIT 6-2
Divisional Organization Chart.

Another divisional option is to adopt a geographically focused structure. To reinforce geographic responsiveness, a fast-food chain, which is essentially a single-product operation, can create separate geographic divisions. McDonald's non-U.S. operations are subdivided into four regions: Asia/Pacific/Middle East/Africa, Canada, Europe, and Latin America. The company does so because executives believe that important differences exist in these multiple regions—in customer tastes and expectations, in supplier relationships, in government regulations, and in financial and labor markets—that require a differentiated response.

As we saw in the case of Macy's, regional structures may also be called upon to bring greater focus on local markets even within the same country. Differences in taste, style, and customer preferences do exist across regions. By creating 69 geographic districts, Macy's enhanced local autonomy which allowed for local responsiveness. The districts were not entirely autonomous, however, with corporate headquarters in Cincinnati still providing some centralized support functions.

THEORY INTO PRACTICE

Divisional structures enhance coordinated focus on the marketplace but make integration across highly autonomous divisional units difficult to achieve.

The object of the divisional structure, whether it is based on products, customer groups, or geographic locations, is to reinforce a market focus. Product divisions pay close attention to the expectations and needs of customers for their particular offerings, while geographic divisions can attend to the special requirements and habits of the customers in their regions.

It is precisely that focused attention on the external marketplace that, it is hoped, allows companies organized divisionally to meet the challenge of coordination faced by functionally structured companies. By concentrating on a clearly defined and understood market segment, divisions seek to win by offering new products and services. Rapid responsiveness to shifting market realities is the goal.

Changing from a functional to a divisional structure is not cost-free. Functional organizations seek the economies of scale; divisional organizations can be thought of as doing the opposite. In pure form, each functional activity is repeated in each division.

Adopting a divisional structure is meant to shape market-focused behaviors. It is not, in and of itself, any guarantee of true responsiveness. Remember, each product division is a self-contained functional organization. The problems often associated with functional organizations—internal focus, poor coordination, sluggish response time—can accrue over time in a product division. In multidivisional organizations, problems of coordination may arise across and between divisions. In order to respond to such problems, organizational leaders may now seek a kind of collaborative balance between functional and product divisions.

THEORY INTO PRACTICE

Functional silos can exist within divisional structures.

Building a Vocabulary of Change
Matrix structure a formal design choice that groups people by both function and product or product and geographical region.

DUAL FOCUS Leaders opt for a functional structure in order to emphasize efficiencies and depth of technical know-how and experience. A shift to divisional structures helps reinforce external focus on the marketplace. However, many organizations cannot make an either/or choice between internal and external focus. As the external environment becomes increasingly complex, organizational leaders need to consider increasing the complexity of their internal structures.

One choice available to organizations is the **matrix structure**. Exhibit 6-3 depicts one type of matrix structure. In that organization, both divisional and functional structures exist in an overlapping fashion, allowing for dual focus.

EXHIBIT 6-3 Matrix Organizational Chart.

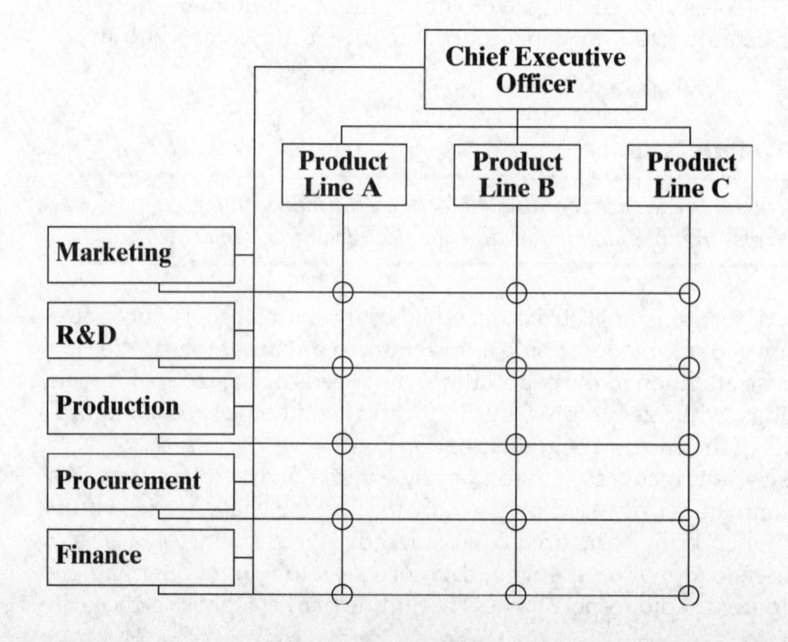

The requirement for dual focus might also arise from geographic demands. ABB built a geographic matrix through three regional groupings—Europe/Middle East/Africa, the Americas, and Asia—while simultaneously seeking segment focus through power, transmission and distribution, and industry and building systems divisions. Strategic focus again lies at the heart of the organization's challenge. While functional and product divisions prioritize their focus, matrix structures seek dual focus, attempting to move both quickly and efficiently.

THEORY INTO PRACTICE

Organizations can move to a matrix structure to help support dual focus—on technical expertise and marketplace responsiveness.

The most striking—and for many people the most troubling—feature of the matrix is the lack of a single reporting relationship. Consider the matrix structure depicted in Exhibit 6-3. Assume you are a market analyst housed in product line C. Who is your boss: the manager of product line C or the head of marketing? The answer, of course, is: both. In order to achieve the desired complexity of focus, you will be reporting to and expected to be responsive to both simultaneously.

The notion of dual reporting relationships violates one of people's most deeply held assumptions about the desirability of a clear and unified chain of command in organizations. By breaking that clear chain of command, matrix structures require employees to deal with competing, even conflicting directions from multiple bosses. Ambiguity, tension, even conflict—these are all likely outcomes of a matrix. That likelihood undoubtedly accounts for the high failure rate—perhaps as high as 70 percent—reported by organizations who have attempted to implement a matrix.[5]

Despite their obvious complexities and ambiguities, when matrix organizations reflect the complexities and ambiguities in their external environment, they can enable greater responsiveness. Because most organizations "have to do business with multiple customers, multiple partners, multiple suppliers, and compete against multiple rivals can multiple areas of the world," writes Jay Galbraith, they will need a structure that allows them to deal with multiple constituencies.[6] In order to respond to multiple constituencies, IBM currently maintains not two but *three* overlapping structures: products (hardware, software, and business solutions), customer groups (large corporations, governments, health care facilities, etc.), and geographic regions.

THEORY INTO PRACTICE

Matrix structures will be most effective in organizations that can manage ambiguity, tension, and conflict well.

Despite the difficulties inherent in managing a matrix, it is often necessary in order to compete effectively in today's highly fragmented competitive environment. Organizations that are able to make a matrix function effectively will enjoy a great competitive advantage.

Building a Vocabulary of Change
Supply Chain activities called upon by the organization to produce and delivery products and services to the custormer.

Building a Vocabulary of Change
Horizontally linked structure a formal design choice that groups people along the supply chain activities and processes that produce, market, deliver, and service the firm's offerings.

FOCUS ON THE SUPPLY CHAIN The advent of sophisticated information technology and the geographic dispersion of technological excellence and knowledge have encouraged organizations to focus on their supply chain. Organizations develop competitive advantage and create shareholder wealth through an interdependent sequence of activities known as the **supply chain**.

The supply chain can be defined as "the separate activities, functions, and business processes that are performed in designing, producing, marketing, delivering, and supporting a product or service."[7] **Horizontally linked structures** focus employees on the interrelated activities of the supply chain.

Horizontally linked structures usually supplement rather than replace existing functional or product structure in an organization. Dell Computers, a pioneer in supply chain linkages, relies on what founder Michael Dell calls "virtual integration." Dell focuses its attention on "how we can coordinate our activities to create the most value for customers."[8] Companies as varied as Zara, Wal-Mart, Southwest Airlines, and Shouldice Hospital call upon horizontally linked structures to coordinate supply chain activities in order to provide customers with a unique experience and their companies with a unique competitive advantage.

Zara, a fashion chain owned by Spain-based Inditex (which also owns and operates Pull & Bear, Massimo, and Dutti, among other retail formats), has succeeded by organizing activities around its supply chain. Starting with a clearly stated strategy—a focus on the ever-changing tastes of trendy young shoppers—Zara created raw material and design teams that could deliver their newly designed products into Zara retail stores within 3 to 15 days.[9] An organization chart for Zara is presented in Exhibit 6-4.

More traditionally structured apparel companies, where activities in the supply chain are separate and unlinked, often take up to a year to move from design to sale. Given the dynamic tastes of the rather fickle consumer base for fashion, slowness often leads to unused inventory, price-slashing sales, and waste.

EXHIBIT 6-4
Horizontally Linked Structure at Zara.

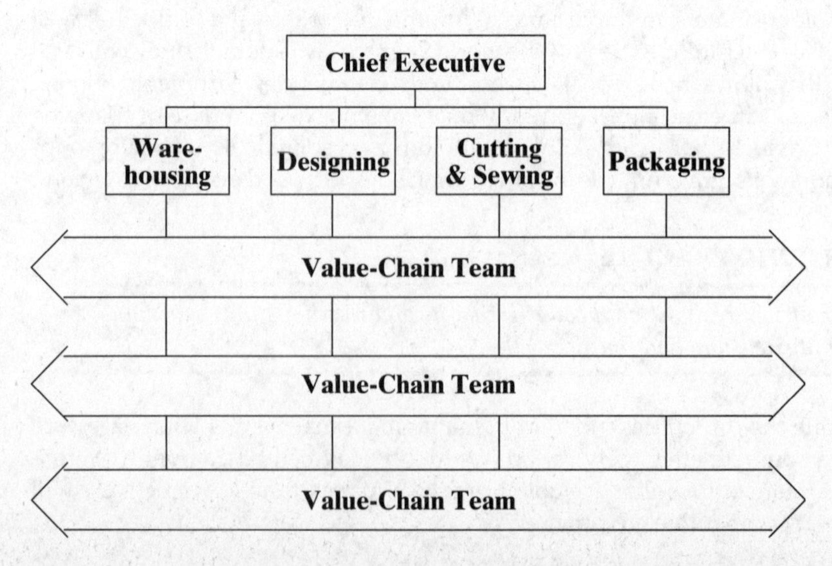

THEORY INTO PRACTICE

Organizations can use cross-functional teams to achieve linkages across the various and interdependent activities of their supply chain.

Organizations that have pioneered horizontally linked structures typically started with a clear strategic focus on their supply chain. It has been far more difficult for older, traditionally organized companies to respond. Delta's effort to create its own low-cost airline, Song, to compete with Southwest Airlines fell flat. Marks & Spencer tried and failed to compete with Zara for the young, fashion-trendy customer. Kmart has repeatedly slashed prices to compete with Wal-Mart while undermining its own profitability.

The difficulty seems to lie not in any formal structural change but in the organizational context that supports and reinforces the structure. Long-standing functional arrangements have cemented patterns of employee behavior that remain unchanged despite efforts to create horizontally linked activities.

No structure, whether it is horizontally linked, matrixed, or divided into divisions or functions can, in and of itself, provide an organization with distinctive competitive advantage for the simple reason that structures are not and cannot be distinctive.

The Role of Structural Intervention in Implementing Change

When Lou Gerstner took the reins of an ailing IBM, he made a strategic decision: derive competitive advantage from the size and scope of his global operation.[10] Rejecting suggestions that he spin IBM off into a number of smaller companies, he sought instead to create an integrated global organization.

Gerstner's initial challenge in pursuit of that strategy was to integrate IBM's overseas operations with the base of the company. What was often known within IBM as a "religion of decentralization" had led to highly autonomous country general managers who reported to powerful regional executives. The head of IBM France, say, ran what amounted to a largely independent operation.

IBM's decentralized structure worked wonders for the company. Country managers could focus on their own regions and grow the business based on local responsiveness. But if local responsiveness was the benefit of decentralized structures, the cost was low collaboration. Employees in non-U.S. operations had come to think of themselves as working in and for their own home country company. *I work for IBM France, not IBM.* Little connection existed between the country-based operations and the corporate entity.

IBM customers provided the trigger for change. Global customers such as American Express complained about interacting with what seemed like different mini-IBMs in each country rather than one IBM with a global presence. Give us one face for IBM globally, they said, not many faces for each IBM national operation.

Gerstner agreed that the lack of global interaction posed a problem: "Each country had its own independent system. In Europe alone we had 142 different financial systems." The status quo simply did not allow for the seamless global responsiveness that Gerstner's new strategy and IBM's global customers demanded. "Customer data could not be tracked across the company. Employees belonged to their geography first, while IBM took a distant second place." This, Gerstner believed, *had* to change and change fast if his strategy of global integration was to succeed.

As a former employee at the global consulting firm McKinsey & Company, Gerstner had experienced what he believed to have been an effective approach to globalization. Customer-focused global teams transcended national borders, allowing seamless responsiveness to global customers. To help IBM achieve that same global seamlessness, Gerstner turned to Ned Lautenbach, head of non-U.S. sales. Gerstner and Lautenbach would pursue their strategy with a globally focused, customer-centered organization.

Gerstner announced a new structure. Twelve customer groups (such as banking, government, and insurance) and one small and medium-sized company group would take over all IBM accounts, including responsibility for budgets and personnel. The restructuring reassigned most employees in non-U.S. operations to a specific group; they would now report to the global leaders of their industry group rather than to their country general managers.

The response from country general managers was overwhelmingly negative. *It will never work* and *You will destroy the company* were statements that expressed their resistance. Some country general managers responded by simply ignoring the new structure. One regional executive unilaterally decided to block all communications between Gerstner and the field.

It took three years of what Gerstner called a "painful and sometimes tumultuous process" before the new global strategy could be driven into IBM's multinational structure. "Regional heads clung to the old system," reflects Gerstner, "sometimes out of mutiny, but more often out of tradition." Only after "massive" shifts in resources, systems, and processes—not to mention the removal and replacement of numerous country managers who could not or would not make the transition—did the new structure take hold.

The fierce resistance that greeted Gerstner's attempt to realign IBM's global structure with its new strategy was, in part, a predictable response to his calling on the restructuring lever too early in the change process. After articulating a strategic focus and creating a supportive context, leaders can call upon structural interventions to reinforce new patterns of employee behavior. Organizations seeking greater customer responsiveness may move from a functional to a divisional function. If the firm's supply chain is failing to deliver competitive advantage, then the company may adopt a horizontally linked structure.

Just because structural interventions are useful in shaping employee behavior does not mean that changing structure is an effective opening tool for change. Effective change implementation, in fact, calls upon structural intervention not to *drive* change but to *reinforce* new patterns of behavior that have been created through earlier-stage interventions.

Returning to Lewin's theory of change (Chapter 2), adopting a new structure is part of the refreezing stage, not the unfreezing stage. For that reason, structural changes are most effective when used in Step 4.

THEORY INTO PRACTICE

Think of structural change in terms of Lewin's refreezing, not in terms of unfreezing.

To understand the power of appropriate sequencing of interventions in impacting effective implementation, let's look at IBM. That company's highly decentralized divisional structure allowed responsiveness to multiple national markets served by this giant corporation. Global customers such as American Express now demanded greater coordination across national boundaries. *We're a global company,* customers were telling IBM. *We expect* you *to be a global supplier. We don't want to be dealing with multiple national mini-IBMs with little capacity to provide consistent and seamless service.*

Gerstner's new strategy for IBM counted on taking advantage of the company's depth and scope. He drove that renewed strategy by creating a global matrix structure: customer-based groups laid over a geographically divisionalized organization.

Gerstner's reasoning seemed solid: global responsiveness could be coordinated by global customer-group executives. That was the approach that Gerstner had experienced at McKinsey. It worked well there, so why not at IBM as well?

The problem Gerstner ran into had far less to do with the efficacy of the idea than the implementation process he called upon to introduce that idea. The structural change occurred early in the process of transforming IBM. Gerstner had failed to unfreeze attitudes by creating dissatisfaction with the status quo. Used to a high level of autonomy, country managers resisted. That resistance grew, in part, from their own habits, competencies, and preferences. It also grew from the process used to introduce change.

The country managers themselves had not been part of the diagnosis that led to the change, nor had the country and industry group managers worked collaboratively to develop well-defined roles, responsibilities, and relationships among the two groups; nor had IBM provided training on how to enact these new, complex roles. In essence, Gerstner jumped from a diagnosis formulated by a handful of corporate executives—mainly him and Ned Lautenbach—to a new structure.

Faced with fierce resistance on the part of country managers, he removed and replaced a number of them. Despite all his formal authority and the power of his vision for a truly global IBM, it took three years of what Gerstner himself called pain and tumult before the desired new behaviors began to take hold in the organization.

This is not to say that pain and tumult can be avoided entirely in implementation. The point, rather, is that the approach of using structural change as a driver rather than a reinforcer helps create heightened levels of resistance, some of which might have been avoided.

Structural change typically unfolds as a top-down intervention. It is the task of leadership, after all, to design the architecture of the organization in order to enable outstanding performance. However, if structural change takes place late in the change process, restructuring will not be experienced as a unilateral imposition from above.

Remember the old adage: People don't resist change; they resist being changed. If structural change occurs early in the process, it will be experienced by employees as being changed. If new structures are used to reinforce new behaviors, employees are more likely to support the change.

THEORY INTO PRACTICE

When structural change occurs early in a change process, employees can be confused by its purpose, unsure of what new competencies are being required, and unwilling—or unable—to make appropriate alterations in behavioral patterns.

USING INCENTIVES TO SUPPORT NEW BEHAVIORS

Compensation represents one of the strongest, perhaps most immediate tools that can be called upon to change patterns of employee behavior. Do we need a more performance-driven culture? Let's place employees on a pay-for-performance incentive. Need to attract young, highly skilled employees to our start-up business? Let's dangle huge stock offerings. Having trouble implementing activity chain process teams? Let's try team-based performance bonuses.

Organizations expend a huge amount of resources on pay—time, energy, not to mention money (anywhere from 40 percent to 70 percent of sales revenues). What value are they gaining in return for that expenditure? How successful are monetary incentives in shaping and altering employee behaviors?

The answer may seem obvious: *Of course* money can shape and alter behaviors. The real question, however, relates to long-term effectiveness. What role can compensation play in efforts to implement organizational change? To answer that question, we need to understand both the nature of pay's impact on behavior as well as the choices available to organizational leaders.

Focusing Pay on Performance

Building a Vocabulary of Change
Pay for performance pay that is tied to performance in the form of either a merit raise to base pay or an incentive bonus that does not increase base pay.

As the competitive business environment increasingly pressures organizations to achieve ever-improving performance, companies have rushed to adopt some sort of pay-for-performance plan. **Pay for performance** devotes at least some portion of an individual's pay (ranging anywhere from 3 percent to multiples of 100 percent) to measurable performance outcomes.

Pay for performance can take one of the two forms: *merit pay,* which raises base salary based on performance, and *incentive bonuses,* which offer regular but onetime payouts on the basis of performance. Bonuses do not alter base salary. They are considered onetime payments because they are not guaranteed. Substandard performance in the following year can reduce or eliminate the bonus.

Virtually every organization in the United States claims to have some kind of a merit pay system already in place. Incentive bonuses have become more popular over the past two decades. As a percentage of total payroll costs, bonuses rose from 4 percent in 1991 to 9 percent in 2000.[11]

Most organizations select a mix of performance pay in order to shape employee behavior. GE, for example, calls for a blend of different bonuses to motivate executives, as indicated in the following company statement:

- Salary and Bonus—We pay salaries that are designed to attract and retain superior leaders, and we pay annual bonuses to reward exceptional performance.
- Stock Options and Stock Appreciation Rights—We award these to provide incentives for superior long-term performance and to retain top executives because the awards are fortified if the executive leaves before they become fully exercisable five years after grant.
- Restricted Stock Units (RSUs)—We grant RSUs to more closely align executives' interests with investors' long-term interests, to retain top executives because the awards are paid out only to executives who remain with the company for extended periods.
- Long-Term Performance Awards—We use these to provide a strong incentive for achieving specific performance measurements over multiyear periods.[12]

Organizations seek a mix of rewards in order to help ensure alignment between employee behaviors and their strategic goals.

One question to be raised in introducing or redesigning a pay-for-performance plan relates to level of aggregation: at what level of outcome should a pay-for-performance incentive be targeted—the individual, the group or team, or the organization? Pay for *individual* performance dominates the design of compensation in the United States. Exhibit 6-5 summarizes the various forms of individual pay-for-performance plans.

THEORY INTO PRACTICE

Individual incentives will be most effective in shaping behavior when the individual controls the outcomes being measured and rewarded, when the outcomes are tied to improved performance, when the evaluation of an employee's contribution is perceived as being valid, and when the difference between rewards for high and low performance is significant.

EXHIBIT 6-5
Forms of Individual Pay-for-Performance Plans.

Form	Description
Piece rate	Employee earns all or part of a wage based on number of units produced
Commission	Salesperson earns all or part of a wage based on number of units sold
Merit pay	Employee earns raise to base wage based on performance evaluation
Bonus	Employee earns extra payment based on performance

Although individual pay-for-performance incentives seem to hold great potential for shaping behavior, a number of challenges constrict that potential impact. The first question that can be raised about a pay-for-performance plan relates to the degree to which individuals have *control* over the outcomes that are being measured and rewarded. Without a significant and clear relationship between individual effort and outcome, a pay-for-performance incentive can drain the system of its full behavioral impact.

A second question relates to whether the incentive system has targeted appropriate *measures of performance* on which to base the reward. Failure to include *all* outcomes that are important for outstanding performance can lead to dysfunctional consequences. The more effectively the system impacts behavior, in fact, the more likely it will be that singling out one aspect of performance for measurement will give that aspect disproportionate attention.

For an individual pay-for-performance plan to impact behavior, the pay increment tied to outstanding performance must be perceived as being *significant*. To have a behavioral impact, the additional reward for that behavior should be 10 percent to 20 percent higher than the reward received absent the behavior. Raises, however, often amount to a relatively small amount of total compensation, making their potential to impact behavior weak. The "significance range" can be reduced considerably—down to 3 percent to 5 percent—if raises are accompanied by public recognition and praise.[13] Concerns over secrecy and confidentiality, however, often blunt an organization's willingness and ability to accompany merit raises with public acknowledgment.

Finally, in order to be effective, pay for performance must be based on *valid judgments* about individual performance. Distortions often creep into the evaluation process, leading participants to question the validity of resulting assessments. That lack of trust in the evaluation process presents itself as one of the key reasons. U.S. employees report high levels of dissatisfaction with the implementation of their companies' pay-for-performance plans. Less than one-third of surveyed U.S. employees believe a direct link exists between pay and performance, despite company claims of a merit pay plan.[14]

Despite the numerous questions that can be raised about the limitations of individual pay-for-performance incentives (summarized in Exhibit 6-6), such plans are nonetheless becoming more popular. Although there is evidence that managers in non-U.S. countries are far more skeptical of the positive arguments U.S. managers make concerning the performance benefits of discretionary bonuses, such bonuses are becoming increasingly popular around the world.[15]

Team-based pay-for-performance plans are becoming more popular in direct relationship to the rising reliance on team effort. Among performance incentives aimed at nonexecutive employees, in fact, team-based plans have become the most popular.[16] Under such a plan, teams can share a performance bonus equally or allocate to individual members based on an evaluation of their contribution. Team-based bonuses enhance team performance, although the effect is relatively weak.[17] A caveat is in order, however. Team-level bonuses can hurt collaboration *among* and *between* teams.

Performance appraisals are inherently subjective, with supervisors evaluating subordinates according to their own preconceived biases

Emphasize individual rather than group goals that may lead to dysfunction conflict in the organization

Encourage a short-term orientation (the performance period being evaluated) at the expense of long-term goals

Merit pay raises become an annuity on which employees continue to draw regardless of future performance

The often lengthy time lag between actual performance and reward undermines perceived connection between the two

Many jobs cannot be individually isolated and precisely measured without taking into account complex interdependencies

Pay differentials between performance levels tend to be relatively small and therefore of questionable behavioral value

Actual payout of program often determined by organizational factors beyond the control of individual employees and only indirectly related to actual performance

EXHIBIT 6-6
Factors That May Undermine Effectiveness of Individual Pay-for-Performance Plans.

Based on Luis R. Gomez-Mejia, David B. Balkin, and Robert L. Cardy, *Managing Human Resources* (Englewood Cliffs, NJ: Prentice-Hall, 1995), p. 404 and Edward E. Lawler III, "Pay Strategy: New Thinking for the New Millennium," *Compensation and Benefits Review* 32 (January–February 2000), pp. 7–12.

THEORY INTO PRACTICE

Organizations call upon team-based performance bonuses to enhance the effectiveness of teams, but the bonus may undermine collaboration between teams.

Because strategic renewal focuses on organizational performance, *organization-level* incentives often supplement or replace individual bonuses. Traditionally, organizations have offered organization-wide incentive bonuses only to executives and upper management on the assumption that their actions are more closely tied to overall organizational performance than employees at lower levels. However, some organizations have adopted a different perspective. Part of Archie Norman's strategic renewal at Asda was to offer an organization-level performance bonus to all employees, encouraging everyone to keep focused on the same measures of overall effectiveness.[18]

THEORY INTO PRACTICE

Bonuses based on the overall performance of the organization make a symbolic statement recognizing the shared purpose and responsibility of all employees and organizational units.

Stock options are intended to tie the total compensation package of individuals to the performance of their organization.[19] The goal, as articulated by the board of directors of eBay, is to "align the interests of directors and executives with the interests of stockholders."[20] Favorable tax laws have made these plans more popular in the United States than elsewhere, although a number of multinational firms—PepsiCo, Bristol-Myers Squibb, DuPont, and Merck among them—have offered stock options to virtually all of their employees worldwide.[21]

The actual effectiveness of these various organization-level performance bonuses is unclear. Some sort of incentive tied to organization-level performance is a frequent characteristic of high-performance companies.[22] What is less certain is whether the organization-level performance bonus results *in* or *from* outstanding performance. The cause-and-effect relationship between specific behaviors and organizational outcomes may be far too vague, especially in large organizations, to create a powerful incentive on the part of individual employees.

Undoubtedly, the degree to which organization-wide bonuses are accompanied by communication and feedback on firm performance, as well as the empowerment of employees to impact performance, will enhance the plan's motivational impact. Tying all employees' pay packages in some significant way to the same organizational-level outcomes may help in both a symbolic and real way to communicate a mutuality of interests and concerns.

Building a Vocabulary of Change
Extrinsic reward rewards (pay, promotion, praise, and so forth) provided by the organization to employees.

Intrinsic and Extrinsic Rewards

Incentive pay, regardless of the specific design, is an **extrinsic reward**: a reward external to the individual and provided by the organization. Money is the most obvious and prevalent example of an extrinsic reward. Motivational theory tells us that extrinsic rewards, although powerful, may not be terribly effective in driving long-term behavioral change.

THEORY INTO PRACTICE

By relying heavily on extrinsic rewards to shape employee behavior, organizations risk driving out the intrinsic rewards that might be associated with the work; as a result curiosity, creativity, and problem-solving behaviors may be lessened.

Building a Vocabulary of Change
Intrinsic reward rewards (feelings of pride, satisfaction, and self-esteem) that accrue to the individual based on the performance of a task.

Commitment to adopt new behaviors comes from *within* individuals. If the goal of change is to create motivation—as internalized desire on the part of employees—to adopt new behaviors, then organizational leaders need to consider intrinsic rewards as well. An **intrinsic reward** is a positive outcome naturally associated with a behavior.

Intrinsic rewards—a sense of accomplishment, learning, and growth, for example—are provided in a constant and ongoing way as individuals interact with their environments. Intrinsic rewards, according to Edward Deci, motivate exploration, play, curiosity, and puzzle solving.[23] For that reason, intrinsic rewards can be more helpful in building commitment to new behaviors, especially when the desired new behaviors are based on creativity and problem-solving activities.

No organization can rely solely on either extrinsic or intrinsic rewards to support new patterns of behavior. The challenge is that the two approaches to shaping behavior do not easily coexist. Overreliance on extrinsic rewards, pay in particular, can actually *dampen* internal motivation.[24] Employees may, and often do, find themselves behaving in a certain way *because* of the money attached to the behavior rather than an internalized desire to undertake the behavior. And the more attractive the reward is to that employee, the more likely it is to drive out internal motivation.

Not all extrinsic rewards work against internal motivation and creativity. Praise, which is an extrinsic reward, can enhance motivation by helping individuals feel competent and self-determining. Even pay can be used in ways that do not drive out motivation: when pay is used to *attract* individuals to an organization, it does not have a negative impact on motivation.

Rewards such as bonuses that are *not* tied a priori to specific outcomes but are presented after the fact in recognition of particularly creative effort are likely to lead to higher creativity in the future. The creativity benefit of such after-the-fact bonuses is enhanced when those bonuses are coupled with constructive feedback and tied to creative outcomes rather than any particular or specific methodology for achieving those outcomes.[25] Even so, intrinsic rewards are the primary factors contributing to creativity; extrinsic rewards more typically encourage routine behavior.

THEORY INTO PRACTICE

Bonuses provided "after the fact"—without being announced or promised beforehand—can be used to reinforce desired new behaviors.

The opportunity as well as the challenge for a manager is to provide motivation that is, in essence, internal to employees. Design decisions that allow employees to participate in decision making enhance the developmental opportunities of work, thus providing a key intrinsic motivation. Providing employees with autonomy and performance feedback enhances employees' sense of self-efficacy and ego satisfaction. In these cases, the organization is creating an environment where employees are more likely to find intrinsic motivation in their work.

Building a Vocabulary of Change
Pay equity a perception by employees that their pay is fair and equitable in relationship to others: peers inside the organization and out as well as subordinates and superiors in the hierarchy.

Pay equity is also vital to the achievement of intrinsic motivation. Only employees who believe that their pay level is fair and equitable—compared to peers both inside and outside the organization, to subordinates, and to superiors—will be intrinsically motivated by the desire to learn, to develop, and to grow.[26] Job evaluation plans endeavor to create a sense of internal equity, and regular salary surveys can help achieve external equity. Just as importantly, organizations that provide employees with regular and candid feedback about performance and contribution can help ensure congruence between pay levels and perceptions of fairness.

THEORY INTO PRACTICE

Organizations will not be able to call on intrinsic motivation unless employees feel that they are being paid equitably.

Sequencing the Introduction of Incentives

The temptation to introduce a new incentive plan early in change implementation is powerful but potentially harmful. Some brief examples of unintended consequences include:

- A community bank introduces a sales bonus designed to encourage more aggressive revenue generation on the part of employees. Customer service representatives now ignore the complaints of, and even occasionally hang up on customers once those customers have expressed a lack of interest in purchasing additional bank services or product offerings.
- After introducing a new executive bonus based on divisional performance, an organization finds its executives withdrawing shared resources from other divisions in order to maximize their own performance.
- A Silicon Valley–based software developer, which had relied heavily on stock options to attract employees, reels when its stock price drops sharply; high turnover deteriorates performance, which leads to even lower stock prices and leaves management with little to offer new employees by way of attraction.
- A plant manager halts a team-based incentive plan because of increasing rivalry among teams.
- A school system finds its "Teacher of the Year" bonus award designed to enhance performance instead leads to dissension and distrust among its formerly collegial faculty.

When applied early, new pay incentives can either fail to alter long-standing patterns of behavior or, even more troubling, change patterns of behavior in an unintended, even unwelcome way.

In the above examples, new incentives were put into place before a thorough diagnosis of the existent patterns of behavior in the organization; before a carefully, strategically guided, and participative effort was made to redesign roles, responsibilities, and relationships among employees; and before human resource development worked to imbue the organization with required new competencies. Management turned to incentives as a quick fix: an intervention that would immediately shape employee behavior. That is exactly what they did, of course, but not in a desired way.

THEORY INTO PRACTICE

Introducing new incentives early in a change implementation process risks negative consequences.

When it comes to integrating new incentives into change implementation, leaders face two types of choices: *what* and *when*.

What choices relate to decisions concerning the design of their incentives:

- At what level of performance will incentives be set?
- How large will potential incentive earnings be in relationship to base salary?

- To what extent will the incentives emphasize short-term or long-term performance or some blend of the two?
- How far up and down the hierarchy will incentives be offered?

The goal of the *what* questions is to make design choices that reinforce the behaviors sought of the strategic renewal and organizational change.

The *when* question relates to when incentives will be introduced in a sequence of transformational interventions. Michael Beer has suggested that pay changes be thought of as a "lag" intervention: one that follows other interventions and is not called upon to drive new behaviors.[27] Failure to diagnose and redesign first increases the likelihood that the new incentives will misfire, leading to unintended and perhaps negative consequences.

TECHNOLOGY AND BEHAVIOR CHANGE

Most employees, whether in high- or low-tech companies, in manufacturing or services, or in small or large organizations, have experienced the impact of new technology. Advances in computers and connectivity, in particular, have revolutionized the use of information.

Technology refers not just to the actual hardware but also to the processes and interactions of human behavior required to convert raw material into finished offerings, to turn raw data into actionable information that can guide behaviors. Although the technology itself may be stunningly innovative, the use to which that technology is put does not always alter patterns of employee behavior; it may simply automate existing patterns of behavior.

Building a Vocabulary of Change
Technology the processes, mechanics, and interactions of human behavior required to convert raw material into finished offerings.

Making a Choice

Richard Walton articulated what he referred to as the choice inherent in the introduction of new technology into a work setting.[28] One of the most fundamental choices managers face when introducing new technology, he noted, is whether to apply that technology in a way that merely automates existing processes or in a manner that transforms those processes.[29]

Using new technology to automate existing processes essentially leaves the status quo in place. *I used to get information through paper memos,* a manager in an automated workplace might say. *Now I get the same information over our network.* Or, *When it comes to introducing and supporting new products, those guys in Japan never got on board before we had SAP, and they still don't know even though we now have SAP.* One company—a state-run mass transit operation—forbid employees from sending e-mails, regardless of their contents, to anyone in other departments or functions without going through their boss. Functional silos remained intact.

THEORY INTO PRACTICE

When introducing new technology, organizational leaders face a choice: to use that technology to automate existing processes or to use new technology to support transformed behaviors.

The second option for introducing new technology is one that applies technology in such a way that supports transformed behaviors and alters the required skills. Some executives resist the transforming strategy for fear of losing control and disrupting required discipline. "There has been a fear of letting it out of our hands," said one corporate vice president in reflecting a widespread resistance to the use of IT to share performance data up and down the company. "That is why information is so carefully guarded ... Traditionally, we have thought that such data can only be managed by certain people with certain accountabilities and, I hesitate to say, endowed with certain skills or capabilities."[30] But other leaders, including the chief of staff of the U.S. Army, see the transforming strategy as a way of supporting the end of "business as usual" and the institutionalization of new behaviors.

Sequencing New Technology in Change Implementation

No one questions that new technology can have a powerful, transformative impact on the manner in which work is conducted, becoming a vital contributor to outstanding performance. However, as with other "hardwiring" interventions, organizational leaders must deal not just with the *what* question—what new technologies can we call on—but the *how* and *when* questions as well. How will the new technologies be introduced and when will they be added to the mix? Effective change implementation calls on new technology to enable and reinforce new behaviors.

THEORY INTO PRACTICE

New technologies can be introduced as a way to support desired behavioral changes.

Conclusion

Leaders find interventions designed to alter the hardwiring of their organization—structures, systems, and technologies—especially appealing. That appeal flows from the well-reasoned theory that structure and systems impact behavior. Because behavior must be altered as part of the change effort, the thinking goes, why not call upon new structures and systems early in the implementation effort to drive that change?

Time and time again, such interventions end up in disappointment. Instead of encouraging new behaviors, structural change can provoke resistance, even sabotage. (Lou Gerstner ran into both at IBM.) Any change, when imposed from above, risks energizing resistance from the very employees whose behavior needs to change.

The impact of incentive and technology changes coming too early in the implementation process runs an even greater risk. Leaders run the risk not just of failing to alter long-term patterns of behavior but of altering patterns of behavior in an unintended, even unwelcome way. That risk is enhanced when implementation starts from an inadequate and noninclusive diagnosis or from inadequate training to ensure employees are capable of exercising the new behaviors.

When formal structures are changed in Step 4 of the implementation process, they are experienced as reinforcers of new behaviors. Desired patterns of new behavior are now recognized and supported, and become built into the new hardwiring of the organization.

Discussion Questions

1. In comparing the efforts at Macy's and IBM, how do you explain the differences in the way managers reacted to the organizational changes?
2. It has been said that, given the growing complexity and dynamism of the world of business, *all* organizations will have to adopt some type of a matrix structure. Do you agree or disagree with that argument? Explain.
3. What is it about incentive systems that makes them so attractive to leaders attempting to implement organization change? Can you think of examples when it would be useful to create new incentives early in a transformation process?
4. Can you think of examples from your own experience—at work or in the classroom—where the manner in which your performance was being measured and rewarded worked *against* the goals you were trying to achieve?

Case Discussion

Read "Making the Problem Worse," and prepare answers to the following questions:

1. What went wrong? How can you explain how the technology actually led to more rather than fewer mistakes?
2. What theories of change implementation would have helped the administrators at the Springfield General Hospital solve the problem of medication mistakes?
3. How might you have gone about solving the problem at Springfield General? To what extent, if any, would new technology have been helpful?

MAKING THE PROBLEM WORSE

It's likely that many people simply skipped the morning newspaper on Thanksgiving 2010. Had they scanned the front page, however, they may have noted a headline: "Hospitals Make No Headway in Curbing Errors, Study Shows." The article did not make encouraging reading. After 10 years of efforts designed to reduce hospital errors, a study found "that harm to patients was common and that the number of incidents did not decrease over time."[31] To help understand this matter, we can look at one hospital that made an effort to avoid mistakes, and, in doing so, made matters worse.

Springfield General

The chief administrators at the Springfield General Hospital (a disguised name), a large urban teaching hospital, were determined to use technology to solve a nagging and disturbing problem: medication mistakes.[32]

The Problem Prescribing errors, confusion over drugs with similar names, inadequate attention to the synergistic effects of multiple drugs and patient allergies—those and other related errors that are lumped together under the label "adverse drug event"—kill or harm more than 770,000 patients annually in U.S. hospitals. In added health care costs alone, adverse drug events add several hundred billion dollars a year. And the most common type of error—the simplest to understand and, seemingly, to correct—is "handwriting identification": poor or illegible handwriting by the prescribing physician.

The Solution Administrators at Springfield General called upon a computerized physician order entry (CPOE) system to solve the problem. CPOE worked to ensure safety and accuracy by the following steps:

- All physician prescriptions for medicine and treatment would be entered into the hospital's IT network.
- Those computer entries would be available to all hospital staff, including both treatment and pharmacy staff.
- The system would catch all prescription errors: incorrect dosages, duplicate requisitions, patient allergies, and even adverse impact statements of multiple medications being prescribed to a patient.
- The system would also display the patient's complete medical history as well as the latest clinical guidelines for treatment.

Ample evidence existed that CPOE can and has been used to reduce both errors and costs.

The Results Surprisingly, the results at Springfield General were stunningly disappointing. Not only did the CPOE system not eliminate errors, it actually *increased* adverse drug events.

A subsequent study identified a number of problems:

- Incorrect Dosage Information—"House staff often rely on CPOE displays to determine minimal effective or usual doses. The dosages listed in the CPOE display, however, are based on the pharmacy's warehousing and purchasing decisions, not clinical guidelines. For example, if usual dosages are 20 or 30 mg, the pharmacy might stock only 10-mg doses, so 10-mg units are displayed on the CPOE screen. Consequently, some house staff order 10-mg doses as the usual or 'minimally effective' dose."
- Discontinuation Failures—"Ordering new or modifying existing medications is usually a separate process from canceling (discontinuing) an existing medication … medication-canceling ambiguities are exacerbated by the computer interface and multiple-screen displays of medications … viewing one patient's medications may require 20 screens."
- Patient Confusion—"It is easy to select the wrong patient file because names and drugs are close together, the font is small, and, most critical here, patients' names do not appear on all screens. Different CPOE computer screens offer differing colors and typefaces for the same information, enhancing misinterpretation as physicians switch among screens. Patients' names are grouped alphabetically rather than by house staff teams or rooms. Thus, similar names (combined with small fonts, hectic workstations, and interruptions) are easily confused."

How could this have happened?

Endnotes

1. Janis L. Gogan and Lynda M. Applegate, *Open Market, Inc.: Managing In a Turbulent Environment* (Boston, MA: Harvard Business School Publishing, 1996).
2. *Ibid.*, p. 13.
3. Quoted from Raymond E. Miles and Charles C. Snow, *Fit, Failure, and the Hall of Fame: How Companies Succeed and Fail* (New York: Free Press, 1994), p. 14.
4. Paul R. Lawrence and Jay W. Lorsch, *Organization and Environment: Managing Differentiation and Integration* (Boston, MA: Harvard Graduate School of Business Administration Division of Research, 1967).
5. Jay R. Galbraith, *Competing with Flexible Lateral Organizations* (Reading, MA: Addison-Wesley, 1994), pp. 101–102.
6. *Ibid.*, p. 13.
7. Arthur A. Thompson, Jr., and A. J. Strickland III, *Strategic Management: Concepts and Cases,* 13th edn (Boston, MA: McGraw-Hill Irwin, 2003), p. 129.
8. Dell is quoted in Joan Magretta, "The Power of Virtual Integration: An Interview with Dell Computer's Michael Dell," *Harvard Business Review* (Mar.–Apr. 1998), p. 75.
9. Ludo Van der Heyden, *Marks & Spencer and Zara: Process Competition in the Textile Apparel Industry* (France: INSEAD, 2002).
10. Based on Louis V. Gerstner, Jr., *Who Says Elephants Can't Dance? Inside IBM's Historic Turnaround* (New York: Harper Business, 2002), pp. 86–87.
11. Michelle Conlin and Peter Coy, "The Wild New Work Force," *Business Week* (Dec. 6, 1999), pp. 39–41.
12. Quoted in V. G. Narayanan and Lisa Brem, *Executive Compensation at General Electric* (Boston, MA: Harvard Business School Publishing, 2004), p. 8.
13. Thomas B. Wilson, *Innovative Reward Systems for the Changing Workplace* (New York: McGraw-Hill, 1993), p. 49.
14. Peter V. LeBlanc and Paul W. Mulvey, "How American Workers See the Rewards of Work," *Compensation and Benefits Review* 30 (Jan.–Feb. 1998), pp. 24–28; Jamie Hale and George Bailey, "Seven Dimensions of Successful Reward Plans," *Compensation and Benefits Review* 30 (July–Aug. 1998), pp. 72–73.
15. *Compensation and Benefits Review* 29 (Mar.–Apr. 1997), p. 7; *Compensation and Benefits Review* 29 (Nov.–Dec. 1997), p. 18. The Hewitt Associates survey results are reported in Kenan S. Abosch, "Variable Pay: Do We Have the Basics in Place?" *Compensation and Benefits Review* 30 (July–Aug. 1998), pp. 12–22. A comparison of executive attitudes toward bonuses in the United States, France, and the Netherlands can be found in Johannes M. Pennings, "Executive Reward Systems: A Cross-National Comparison," *Journal of Management Studies* 30 (Mar. 1993), pp. 261–273.
16. *Compensation and Benefits Review* 29 (Nov.– Dec. 1997), p. 18.
17. This was the conclusion of a study of cross-functional process teams in the U.S. electronics manufacturing industry. See Ann Majchrzak and Qianwei Wang, "Breaking the Functional Mind-Set in Functional Organizations," *Harvard Business Review* (Sept.–Oct. 1996), pp. 93–99.
18. The percentage and amount differed based on hierarchical level.
19. For a good summary of the many stock option plans available, see David G. Strege, "Employee Strategies for Stock Based Compensation," *Compensation and Benefits Review* 31 (Nov.–Dec. 1999), pp. 41–54.
20. "Stock Ownership Guidelines for Directors and Executive Officers," eBay Investor Relations.
21. Calvin Reynolds, "Global Compensation and Benefits in Transition," *Compensation and Benefits Review* 32 (Jan.–Feb. 2000), p. 29.
22. Jeffrey Pfeffer, *The Human Equation: Building Profits by Putting People First* (Boston, MA: Harvard Business School Press, 1998), pp. 80–85.
23. Edward L. Deci, "The Hidden Costs of Rewards," *Organizational Dynamics* 4 (Winter 1976), p. 62.
24. Edward L. Deci, "Effects of Externally Mediated Rewards on Intrinsic Motivation," *Journal of Personality and Social Psychology* 18 (1971), pp. 105–115, and "Intrinsic Motivation, Extrinsic Reinforcement, and Equity," *Journal of Personality and Social Psychology* 22 (1972), pp. 113–120.

25. Teresa M. Amabile, *Creativity in Context* (Boulder, CO: Westview Press, 1996).

26. This is a conclusion based on equity theory. See George C. Homans, *The Human Group* (New York: Harcourt, Brace, 1950); Leonard R. Sayles, *Behavior of Industrial Work Groups: Prediction and Control* (New York: Wiley, 1958); Elliott Jacques, *Equitable Payment* (New York: Wiley, 1961); George C. Homans, *Social Behavior: Its Elementary Forms* (New York: Harcourt, Brace, 1961); J. Stacy Adams, "Toward an Understanding of Inequity," *Journal of Abnormal and Social Psychology* 67 (1963), pp. 422–436; J. Stacy Adams, "Inequity in Social Exchange," in Leonard Berkowitz, ed., *Advances in Experimental Social Psychology,* Vol. 2 (New York: Academic Press, 1965).

27. Tom Ehrendfeld, Maggie Coil, Donald Berwick, Tom Nyberg, and Michael Beer, "The Case of the Unpopular Pay Plan," *Harvard Business Review* 70 (Jan.–Feb. 1992), p. 22.

28. Richard E. Walton, "Social Choice in the Development of Advanced Information Technology," *Human Relations* 35 (1982), pp. 1073–1083.

29. Shoshona Zuboff, *In the Age of the Smart Machine: The Future of Work and Power* (New York: Basic Books, 1984).

30. Quoted in Zuboff, *In the Age of the Smart Machine,* p. 239.

31. Denise Grady, "Hospitals Make No Headway in Curbing Errors, Study Shows," *New York Times* (Nov. 25, 2010), p. A1.

32. This case study is based on research published in Ross Koppel, Joshua P. Metlay, Abigail Cohen, Brian Abaluck, A. Russell Localio, Stephen E. Kimmel, and Brian L. Storm, "Role of Computerized Physician Order Entry Systems in Facilitating Medication Errors," *Journal of the American Medical Association* 293 (2005), pp. 1197–1203. The hospital is not identified in the article.

CHAPTER

7 Leading Change

At every stage of transformational change, from initial diagnosis to formal design changes, leaders intervene to oversee and orchestrate implementation. This reliance on the effective orchestration by leaders in a change process applies not just to top executives but also to leaders throughout the organization. Implementation depends not just on oversight and orchestration by individual leaders. Effective change demands the coordinated efforts of multiple leaders.

Although the role of leaders in implementation underlies much of what has been addressed earlier, this chapter will offer more focused attention on that leadership role. In particular, the chapter will:

- Define effective leadership
- Explore the difficulty of enacting effective leadership
- Delineate the tasks associated with leading change
- Analyze the requirements for developing future leaders in an organization

First, we will examine the efforts of the chief executive officer (CEO) of Cisco Systems to promote collaboration across the organization. As you read this introductory case, ask yourself:

- What triggered the demand for collaboration at Cisco?
- What steps has John Chambers taken to promote and sustain collaboration?
- Can a CEO be successful in promoting collaboration if, like Chambers, he or she demands that executives collaborate and then removes those who cannot and will not make the change?

COLLABORATION AND LEADERSHIP AT CISCO SYSTEMS

"I believe that only those companies that build collaboration into their DNA by tapping into the collective expertise of their employees—instead of just a few select leaders at the top—will succeed ... This sounds easy, but it is incredibly complex."[1]

That is what John Chambers, CEO of Cisco Systems, told an interviewer in 2008. A year later, he was even more adamant that collaboration, teamwork, and a supportive technology would be the hallmarks of the company's future. "If they're not collaborative," he said, speaking of potential future employees, "if they aren't naturally inclined toward collaboration and teamwork, if they are uncomfortable with using technology to make that happen both within Cisco and in their own life, they're probably not going to fit in here." And yet, as Chambers was the first to admit, he was not always so comfortable with teamwork and collaboration himself.

Cisco, widely recognized as "*the* Internet behemoth," designs, manufactures, and sells Internet-protocol networking and other byproducts related to the communications and IT industry, and provides services associated with those products and their use. Founded in 1984 by a Stanford-based husband-and-wife team (seeking a way to connect the computer systems in their two departments), Cisco grew so rapidly that, at the height of the Internet bubble (2000), its market value made it the third most valuable company in the world (behind Microsoft and GE). Chambers became CEO in 1995 and helped drive that growth. When the bubble burst in 2001, Cisco experienced what Chambers called "a near death experience." Layoffs and cutbacks helped Cisco survive, but Chambers was determined to do more: Cisco would thrive by understanding market trends and responding earlier than its competitors, or even its customers.

Chambers came to believe that the only way to stay ahead of the markets was by "tapping into the collective expertise of all our employees." That meant building cross-functional collaboration and teamwork throughout the entire organization. An elaborate network of councils and boards brought together "groups of people with relevant expertise" who could "work together to make and execute key decisions supported by networked Web 2.0 technologies." All well and good, but Chambers also realized that neither he nor his top executives were quite prepared to make the transition themselves. "I'm a command-and-control person," Chambers admitted. "I like to be able to say turn right, and we truly have 67,000 people turn right." His top executives were the same.

At first, Chambers found that his top executives did not much like the process of collaboration and would have "opted out" if allowed. "But I didn't give them a choice in the matter," he noted, "I forced people to work with others they didn't get along with." He also tied executive bonuses to collaborative efforts and let about 20% of his management team go. "It's not that they weren't successful working on their own or that they weren't good people," he explained. "They just couldn't collaborate effectively."

UNDERSTANDING LEADERSHIP

Building a Vocabulary of Change
Leadership actions that mobilize adaptive behavior within an organization.

Cisco CEO, John Chambers was committed to building collaboration as a way of keeping his company agile and responsive to a rapidly shifting competitive and technological environment. In demanding collaboration within his top team, aligning rewards with desired new behaviors, and removing and replacing those who could not or would not make the transition, he was exercising leadership. **Leadership** can be understood as a set of activities or behaviors that mobilize adaptive behavior on the part of members of the organization.[2]

THEORY INTO PRACTICE

Think of leadership as an intervention into the organization designed to impact the behaviors of others.

Thinking of leadership as an intervention designed to mobilize adaptive behaviors focuses attention away from the particular individuals who reside at the head of an organizational hierarchy. Instead of examining the traits or personalities of individual leaders, leadership involves actions and behaviors. The effectiveness of leadership will be judged not by personalities and traits but by the impact those actions and behaviors exert on the change process.

THEORY INTO PRACTICE

Effective leadership can be exercised at all levels of an organization.

Effective leadership can be found in three separate but interrelated notions. First, effective leadership shapes the behaviors of others in the organization. No matter how talented an individual may be or what personal traits that individual may possess, she alone will be unable to create and sustain outstanding performance. How employees react in response to the actions of leaders will determine the effectiveness of leadership. No individual is an effective leader unless and until employees behave in effective ways. When an organization is attempting transformational change, the behavior of leaders is meant to impact changes in the behavior of others.

THEORY INTO PRACTICE

Effective leadership shapes the behaviors of employees.

Second, the term *mobilize* implies that the mechanism used to help shape behavior will be internalized motivation. Leader actions that result in compliant reactions on the part of employees—following orders and adhering to rules in order to achieve extrinsic rewards and/or to avoid negative consequences—fail that definition of effectiveness. Mobilizing employees involves creating an internalized commitment to achieving the new goals of the organization. Leadership behavior that creates dependency or alienation on the part of employees undermines mobilization; by definition, then, it is ineffective.[3]

The third aspect of effective leadership—mobilizing *adaptive* behavior—suggests that not all behaviors resulting from the actions of leaders are equally desirable. The distinction is between leadership and the exercise of power. Formal leaders may exert a powerful influence over followers without exercising effective leadership. Powerful individuals can induce followers to take actions that may be harmful to the organization (for example, Richard Fudd at Lehman Brothers) and, ultimately, to themselves. As powerful and influential as these individuals are, they are not exercising effective leadership. Leadership is

Building a Vocabulary of Change
Formal leader a designated individual who is granted authority, usually based on hierarchical position, in an organization.

effective when employee behavior is shaped in a way that supports the long-term best interests of employees and the organization.[4]

THEORY INTO PRACTICE

The exercise of power is not the same as leadership.

THE TASKS OF LEADERSHIP

Leaders often attempt to impose change on their organization. The results are often disappointing and frustrating. Effective leadership is not about imposing new directions and demanding new behaviors. Instead, effective leaders energize an organization for change, build commitment to new directions, and then put into place a process that will translate such commitment into action.[5]

THEORY INTO PRACTICE

Strong, demanding leaders don't always succeed at leading change.

Although all organizations and circumstances differ, it is possible to suggest there are five core tasks that lie at the heart of effective leadership. Those tasks, summarized in Exhibit 7-1, place greater emphasis on what the leader does rather than who the leader is.

Building a Vocabulary of Change
Organizational purpose a clearly articulated and well-defined ambition for the organization.

Develop and Communicate Purpose

Leadership starts by identifying and articulating organizational purpose. **Organizational purpose** is something broader than strategy. Worldwide Pants, a television production company founded by late-night host David Letterman, has a clear purpose: *whatever makes Dave laugh.*[6]

Purpose involves a "clearly articulated, well-defined ambition" for the organization, an ambition that engenders "strong, enduring emotional attachments" among employees and remains constant over time.[7] By articulating a clear

EXHIBIT 7-1
Core Tasks of Change Leadership.

Develop and articulate *clear and consistent sense of purpose and direction* for the organization

Establish *demanding performance* expectations

Enable *upward communication*

Forge an *emotional bond* between employees and the organization

Develop *future change leaders*

and consistent purpose, leaders enhance the effectiveness of change implementation in a number of ways:

- A common sense of direction and goals allows decentralized decision making and greater autonomy over enacting that purpose.
- Autonomy places decision-making authority in the hands of employees who are best able to respond, and respond quickly, to a dynamic environment.
- Additionally, common purpose enhances the ability of an organization to achieve required levels of coordination and teamwork.
- Leaders at operational levels can formulate strategy to help advance that purpose and then change the strategy in response to or anticipation of a dynamic environment.

Organizational purpose provides a steady framework that helps shape strategic responsiveness (summarized in Exhibit 7-2).

THEORY INTO PRACTICE

A widespread and common understanding of organizational purpose allows employees to exercise greater autonomy in moving the change effort in its desired direction.

Establish Demanding Performance Goals

In his study of the most effective U.S. leaders who have led their companies from "good to great," Jim Collins observed a trait they all had in common. The most effective leaders shared a "ferocious desire" to achieve outstanding performance for their companies. They were, says Collins, "fanatically driven, infected with an incurable need to produce *results*."[8] Effective change efforts are firmly rooted in that focused drive to achieve outstanding performance.[9]

THEORY INTO PRACTICE

Effective change efforts are built on a drive to achieve outstanding performance.

EXHIBIT 7-2
Shared Purpose Helps Change Implementation.

Supports decentralized decision making	Common sense of direction and goals allows employees at multiple levels to make decisions that further overall purpose of organization
Supports enhanced autonomy	Employees at all levels understand purpose and goals and can respond quickly and effectively to dynamic environment
Supports coordination	Employees working toward a common goal better able to coordinate their efforts

Building a Vocabulary of Change
Stretch goals clearly articulated and challenging performance expectations.

Jack Welch talked about **stretch goals** as a way of keeping employees focused on outstanding performance during a transformation. During his tenure as head of General Electric (GE), Welch's emphasis was largely on financial goals. Welch's successor, Jeff Immelt, refocused expectations to emphasize innovation and customer responsiveness as GE's new stretch targets.

Establishing demanding performance goals supports change by focusing employee motivation and commitment on the goal of achieving outstanding performance.[10] It is that interconnection between achieving outstanding performance and employee commitment to change that makes this a core task of change leadership. It is the conviction that, given high performance goals—coupled with the requisite levels of autonomy and resources—employees will adopt the behaviors required to meet those goals.

Enable Upward Communication

As we saw in Chapter 5, Vineet Nayar, CEO of HCL, believed the only way to spur innovation within his company was to "invert the pyramid." That image conveyed his sense that traditional hierarchical structures placed barriers between employees and managers. New ideas need to come from the front lines of the organization, and Nayar worked to ensure that there was an open flow of communications from those levels to the management.

Building a Vocabulary of Change
Upward communication the flow of information from lower to higher hierarchical levels in an organization.

Effective leaders communicate *downward* to make sure employees at all levels understand in a clear and consistent way the purpose and direction of the firm. But effective organizations need **upward communication** as well. The simple fact is that employees further down the organizational hierarchy are well positioned to know things vital to the organization. Employees possess "local knowledge" about customers, competitors, and how the products and services of the organization meet the shifting needs of the marketplace that need to be communicated upward in an organization.

Through their everyday interaction with customers, suppliers, and peers, employees develop experience-based, deep knowledge.[11] If that knowledge is not allowed to impact decision making in a direct and immediate way, organizations can find themselves in trouble. Employees can communicate upwardly both the need for change and the degree to which management's response is addressing that need. That is why a vital task of effective leadership is to enable upward communication.

THEORY INTO PRACTICE

Effective leadership involves listening, engaging, and learning as well as communicating.

Knowledge possessed by employees at lower hierarchical levels puts them in an excellent position to understand the degree to which the change goals articulated and pursued by upper management are both being implemented and achieving the desired results. In Chapter 1, we saw that the top management team that ran ASDA, the U.K. grocery chain, learned the hard way that not enabling upward communication can lead to difficulties during a change process.

THEORY INTO PRACTICE

Particularly in situations of strategic renewal and change, formal leaders need to learn about how their effects are proceeding through a process of mutual engagement with employees at all organizational levels.

ASDA's leaders formulated a new strategy for the chain, previously known as a discount store for working-class customers. They would move upmarket to capture highly profitable wealthy shoppers. As they directed that new strategy from above, however, store managers experienced a troubling reality: Old, loyal customers were discarded without being replenished from this new, desired niche. Upper management failed to create mechanisms to allow store managers to communicate upwardly that the chain's strategy was seriously flawed. Top management never learned—at least until the company faced bankruptcy—that their new strategy was not working.

To help ensure that knowledge lodged at lower hierarchical levels is captured, discussed, and acted upon, leaders can enable upward communication by three steps:

1. Top executives can *acknowledge,* both to themselves and to the organization, that they do not know everything that needs to be known about the organization and its competitive environment. That acknowledgment needs to include the explicit recognition that they need to learn from lower-level employees.

2. Executives can *create channels* for information to flow upward in an uncluttered and unfiltered way. These channels often take the form of direct contact and communication between upper management and lower-level employees. Taken by themselves, such tactics—management-by-walking-around, internal comment, and suggestion cards, "graffiti walls" where employees' comments are posted—may seem superficial and programmatic. They can and do become real when upper management seriously seeks and values such input.

3. Executives can also *push decision-making authority down* to lower levels, allowing employees to exert authority and take responsibility for the organizational–environmental interface.

For change implementation to stay on track, knowledge of whether interventions are working must be communicated upward and shared in a timely and candid way with top management.

THEORY INTO PRACTICE

Effective leaders take specific steps to ensure that communications move both upward and downward.

Forge an Emotional Bond Between Employees and the Organization

Organizations consist of individuals who possess skills, competencies, and knowledge. Their connection to the organization is, in part, instrumental. They exchange those skills, competencies, and knowledge for the rewards provided by the organization. To transform an organization from a collection of individuals (even highly talented individuals) into a coordinated, interdependent unit requires a bond that transcends instrumentality. A deeper **emotional bond** provides a robust source of support for change when a company enters a transformational period.[12] One of the key tasks of change leadership, therefore, is to forge just such an emotional and personal attachment between employee and employer.

Building a Vocabulary of Change
Emotional bond a relationship between individuals and their organizations based on a deeply felt commitment to the organization's purpose and goals.

Organizational leaders can use their position to personify an emotional attachment among employees. Herb Kelleher, Southwest Airline's CEO for nearly three decades of profitability, helped create and sustain a bond that employees came to refer to explicitly as "love" (Love Field in Dallas, after all, served as Southwest's hub airport).[13] He involved himself in virtually every aspect of the business, from handing out onboard peanuts to dropping in on maintenance workers at 3 AM in Southwest hangars with coffee and doughnuts. That involvement had both a symbolic and operational aspect to it: providing employees with direct access to a CEO with whom they were on a first-name basis while simultaneously offering employees an up-close-and-personal opportunity to see and experience Kelleher as the human embodiment of the company's values and principles.

THEORY INTO PRACTICE

If employees are committed to their organization emotionally as well as instrumentally, they are more likely to engage in required behavioral changes.

An emotional bond encourages employees to coordinate their efforts, communicate more honestly and freely, take the risks required of creativity, and manage conflicts in ways that benefit the organization. By locating a sense of purpose and meaning within the organization's mission and goals, employees are ready and willing to make sacrifices on behalf of the organization, to act in ways that are informed by the organization's core values and renewed strategies, and to alter behaviors in ways that enhance the company's performance.

The instrumental exchange of effort for reward cannot be overlooked in any organization. The drive to acquire—that is, the desire of individuals to boost their share of scarce resources—is fundamental to human nature. But it is not the *only* fundamental human drive. People also have a need to bond, to form networks, to be part of mutually reinforcing relationships.[14]

Leaders who fail to create the opportunity for emotional bonding will find it difficult to generate high levels of commitment to change. "It's hard to get excited about 15 percent return on equity," said a manager in a transforming organization.[15] Outstanding financial performance is a necessary, even appealing aim of change, but there needs to be more. Emotional bonds are much more than niceties of a pleasant business environment; they support outstanding performance and create a work context open to change.

Develop Future Leaders

Companies that retain market domination over long periods tend to develop leaders internally.[16] Paying attention to the development of leadership assures a strong pipeline of individuals capable of supporting transformation, both now and in the future. Jack Welch spent more of his time at the helm of GE on senior executive development than any other matter. GE, in fact, became so good at developing leaders that it was a major—probably *the* major—supplier of CEOs to other Fortune 100 companies.

Some have argued that leadership is an inherent trait; that leads are "born, not made." Consultant Ron Morris observes, "Did you not pretty much know who the 'leader' of your Cub Scout pack was way back in 1955? He was the guy leading, was he not?" Nobody teaches leaders how to lead. While individuals may learn confidence and resourcefulness, "leadership is an art, and therefore it simply cannot be taught."[17] However, most observers accept the argument that leadership can be developed. "The truth is that leaders are made, not born," says consultant John Baldoni. "Leadership is developed by learning and refining a set of skills—skills that anyone, including you and me, can learn and develop."[18]

THEORY INTO PRACTICE

Given a combination of experience, training, and circumstances, a wide array of individuals can be effective leaders.

Failure to address the requirement for effective leadership can prove disastrous. Paul Lawrence and Davis Dyer documented how the U.S. steel industry suffered from inadequate development of leaders.[19] Whether it was U.S. Steel, Bethlehem Steel, or the other companies that dominated the industry for decades, leadership development followed a common pattern. Future executives typically entered their organizations at a low level, worked their way up through a single function, then assumed top positions without the requisite skills to exercise effective leadership. Inadequate, poorly developed leadership drained the capacity of those companies to respond to the tide of global competition in the 1980s and 1990s. Nonadaptiveness in an organization or even an industry can be traced in no small part to the manner in which leaders are developed.

THEORY INTO PRACTICE

Inadequate attention to leadership development can hurt a company, even an industry.

EXHIBIT 7-3 Organizational Barriers to Effective Leadership Development.

Based on John P. Kotter, *The Leadership Factor* (New York: Free Press, 1988).

Practice	Barrier
Rapid upward mobility	Prevents individuals from having to live with consequences of their actions and learning from their successes and failures.
Movement within a single function	Individuals never gain knowledge of total organization, particularly of how subunits fit together.
Short-term performance pressures	Individuals get better at tactical and operational management than at long-term strategic and visionary leadership.
Recruitment for specific technical skills	Internal employee pool is thin on individuals with real leadership potential.

With narrowly focused functional managers rather than broadly based leaders, organizations become nonresponsive. It is virtually impossible to mobilize adaptive behavior on the part of others when the individuals who sit atop the hierarchy are themselves engaging in nonadaptive behavior. The lack of time, resources, and attention paid to the development of future leaders can ultimately undermine a company's ability to maintain outstanding performance. Rapid upward mobility is only one of the traditional development practices that can undermine the development of individuals capable of effective leadership (summarized in Exhibit 7-3).

THEORY INTO PRACTICE

Rapid upward movement of personnel through the hierarchy can work to hurt an organization's ability to develop effective leadership.

In order to learn how to lead change effectively, John Kotter suggests future leaders experience a number of situations:

- Work through coalitions rather than relying on hierarchical authority.
- Formulate visions and strategies rather than planning and managing budgets.
- Communicate purpose and build commitment rather than issuing reports and creating policies.
- Think in long-term time horizons rather than immediate results.
- Work with an organization's culture and not its formal structures.[20]

Approaching leadership development in a strategic manner while understanding that effective leaders can be "made" through experience, feedback, assessment, and training will provide a source of future leadership and support change.

BEYOND INDIVIDUAL LEADERSHIP

The exercise of leadership is not limited to any one individual in an organization. Given the realities of today's business environment, the notion that any one individual can change an entire organization is inadequate. An increasingly dynamic competitive environment, especially when coupled with the growing complexity of organizations themselves, requires that for transformational change implementation to be effective, leadership must be exercised by many people on multiple organizational levels.

Reliance on one person to be the leader of change might actually undermine the effectiveness of a change effort. Think of the following potential consequences of overreliance on an individual leader:

- High levels of dependency can displace individual and group initiative.
- That dependency, in turn, can slow decision making.
- Providing the candid feedback required of effective transformation can become a risky, to-be-avoided venture.
- A dominant leader, particularly one who sees the exercise of leadership on the part of others as a direct threat, might be unable to build the sense of teamwork and shared responsibility required to sustain a coordinated change effort.

Dominant individual leaders can create an internal dynamic that builds dependency while stifling initiative, innovation, teamwork, and change. Instead of being centralized within an individual, change leadership can be exercised both vertically and horizontally in the organization. Vertically means that organizations allow and encourage leadership to be exerted up and down the formal hierarchy. Horizontally means that leadership is exercised across the organization, in multiple divisions and units. Changing an organization—at multiple levels and across numerous units—is a challenge that requires distributed rather than individual leadership. Dominant individual leaders may allow—even inadvertently encourage—others to back away from the exercise of change leadership.

THEORY INTO PRACTICE

Dominating individual leaders can actually hurt an organization's ability to change.

Moving from individual to shared leadership is desirable, but it is not easily achieved. The attitudes, decision-making style, and skill sets of top executives can all reinforce individual rather than shared leadership. Start with attitudes. Top executives often conceive their roles in independent rather than *inter*dependent terms, leading them away from the sense of shared responsibility so vital to teamwork. Especially when an organization has grown largely through acquisition, top executives can conceive their roles as highly autonomous individuals, resenting efforts to "impose" on them a sense of collective responsibility.

The management style of the chief executive can also influence the behaviors of other organizational leaders. The key variable here is the degree to which the chief executive insists on a tight hold over the reins of decision making. Shared leadership requires decentralized decision making. In a highly centralized situation, the chief executive controls the decision making, while other top executives engage in what is essentially political behavior aimed at preserving one's own position, turf, and power. Responsiveness to a highly dynamic environment requires that multiple leaders be involved in decision making, particularly around the question of how the organization's purpose and strategy are to be implemented.

Finally, top managers often have a difficult time engaging in disagreement and debate among gthemselves over important strategic issues.[21] Executives often carry with them an assumption concerning disagreement and debate that also works against the desire to enhance employee influence. That view can be stated quite simply: Consensus is good, argument is bad. In what has been labeled the "unity view" of organizations,[22] managers often believe that diversity of opinions, debate, and conflict are best avoided.

The Challenge of "Walking the Talk"

Reflecting on his experience reversing the lagging fortunes of Nissan Motors, Carlos Ghosn talked about the importance of aligning leaders' actions with words. "Top management is highly visible," he noted. "What we think, what we say, and what we do must be the same." Discrepancies between words and actions, he warned, could "spell disaster."[23] A discrepancy between words and actions can undermine change implementation by spreading suspicion and distrust among employees.

Ghosn addressed the requirement for leaders to align what they say with what they do.

Effective change implementation requires high levels of commitment among employees, a strong sense of shared purpose and partnership, and a climate of trust that supports candid communication, open inquiry, and joint problem solving.

During his first two years as president of Johnsonville Sausage, Ralph Stayer's effort focused on the behaviors of his direct reports. He hoped to instill a heightened sense of confidence, autonomy, initiative, and creativity among his top executives. Frustrated by his inability to achieve those goals, Stayer initially blamed *them*: They were simply not rising to the challenge. It took Stayer two years to understand that the failure was *his*, not theirs—that is, his behaviors were inconsistent with his stated objectives:

> I didn't really *want* them [his direct reports] to make independent decisions. I wanted them to make the decisions I would have made. Deep down, I was still in love with my own control. I was just making people guess what I wanted instead of telling them.[24]

It was not until he aligned his actions with his goals and allowed real decision making on the part of his top executives that he was able to shape a real problem-solving team.

Conclusion

It is often said in organizations that if you are not leading change, you are not leading. That expression captures the central role of leadership to a change effort.

The intervention of leaders is critical in determining the effectiveness of an organization's change implementation. In order to mobilize adaptive behavior on the part of organizational members, leaders engage in six core tasks, starting with the articulation of a sense of purpose and direction for the organization coupled with demanding performance goals. Employees can then adapt to changing circumstances by finding new and innovative ways of meeting the performance expectations while aligned with the company's purpose and direction.

Communication channels, especially upward communication, support new behaviors and help ensure that leaders will learn from employees at all levels about the effectiveness of their efforts. Building employee commitment to the organization enhances the internalized motivation so critical in a change effort, which, in turn, helps energize learning and adaptation. Developing future leaders and creating effective teamwork at the top will greatly enhance an organization's ability to adapt, change, and maintain outstanding performance.

Just as a leader cannot run an organization on her own, no individual leader can change an organization. Effective change leadership requires collaborative partnership among those individuals who hold positions of formal authority and employees at other organizational levels who can participate in the process of leading change. Entering into such a partnership involves formal leaders ceding their unilateral control and allowing for a kind of shared authority in which multiple parties participate. The goal, of course, is to enhance the likelihood that change will produce results that benefit the organization as a whole.

Discussion Questions

1. What leadership steps did John Chambers take to ensure that Cisco remained flexible and adaptive?
2. It is said that if you are not leading change, you are not leading. Do you agree or disagree with that statement? Explain.
3. Why is upward communication so difficult to achieve in organizations? Explain the barriers that exist and how leaders might overcome them.
4. Why is a strong emotional bond with the company especially important in times of change? What specific steps can leaders take to create such a bond?
5. Do you agree that traditional approaches to leadership development can hurt a company's effort to develop effective change leaders? Explain.

Case Discussion

Read "Leading Change—Carlos Ghosn at Renault and Nissan," and prepare answers to the following questions:

1. What are the strengths and weaknesses of Carlos Ghosn's approach to change leadership at Nissan? To what extent has he succeeded in mobilizing adaptive behavior on the part of employees?
2. Using the core tasks of leadership (Exhibit 8-1), evaluate Ghosn's change leadership at Nissan.
3. What are the beliefs and values of Ghosn concerning leadership and change? Show how those beliefs and values have been enacted at his various leadership positions.
4. Has Ghosn "walked the talk" on his leadership style, that is, aligned his actions with his words?

LEADING CHANGE—CARLOS GHOSN AT RENAULT AND NISSAN

> "There is no business executive in the world I would rather see at the helm of Renault. Carlos has a golden touch. First at Michelin, then at Nissan—everywhere he has been he has turned disaster into success. He is very strong, very forceful, and very positive."
>
> "Look, I cannot deny his past successes. But really, what has he done? He has relied almost exclusively on slash-and-burn techniques to cut costs and return these companies to profitability. But how long can that last? He has not brought any new ideas to the running of business: just cut costs. He is now returning to a profitable Renault. I'm unsure of what he can do now."
>
> "I think you both are missing the point. Ghosn's past has been impressive, no doubt about it. But why is he trying to run two companies at the same time? Does he believe too much his own press? The way it is now, he cannot focus properly on either Nissan or Renault."

Three French executives offering contrasting reflections on Carlos Ghosn upon his return to Renault in April 2005.

Whatever qualms some executives may have felt about Carlos Ghosn (name is pronounced to rhyme with "phone"), senior management at France-based Renault harbored no such misgivings.[25] In April 2005, chairman Louis Schweitzer announced that Ghosn would return to Paris to assume control of Renault. Over the past five and a half years, Ghosn had engineered a remarkable turnaround at Nissan Motors, headquartered in the Ginza district of Tokyo. He had moved from Paris to Japan as part of the 1999 Renault–Nissan alliance. Ghosn's return to Paris, however, would not remove him from oversight of Nissan. He vowed to serve as a dual CEO—leading both Renault and Nissan, dividing his time evenly between the two.

Ghosn's career involved a number of remarkable leadership opportunities: Michelin Brazil, Michelin North America, Renault, Nissan, and now the Renault–Nissan alliance. But no story is more dramatic or exemplary of his approach to change management than his tenure at Nissan.

Nissan Motor Company

As part of a 74-firm Japanese *zaibatsu*—a powerful, interconnected industrial combination that included Hitachi, Nippon Mining, and Nissan Chemical—Nissan leveraged its considerable assets into becoming Japan's number two automaker (behind Toyota).[26] Nissan began exporting their Datsun cars to the United States in 1958 and 17 years later became the top-selling import in the U.S. market. Their sporty Datsun 240Z, known as the Z car, gained an especially loyal following based on its reputation as "the ultimate thrill machine, an unbeatable combination of rakish lines, raw horsepower and affordability that young Japanese and American guys found impossible to resist."

A number of management missteps kicked off a debilitating and long-lasting decline starting in the 1980s. Executives changed the company's brand name in the United States from the popular Datsun to the completely unfamiliar Nissan. Additionally, they allowed their popular Z car to drift and decline with little infusion of innovative technology. Less obvious but even more troubling was Nissan's inability to find flexibility in its relationship with suppliers. Their cost of parts ranged from 15 percent to 20 percent above domestic competitors. Aggressive competition from Honda in the United States forced Nissan to take a $1,000 discount on their cars.

Sales declined, but costs did not. Despite several announced restructuring plans, Nissan executives achieved little real improvement. "Powerful trade unions, a societal taboo against layoffs and institutional inertia stalled any real changes." After the company borrowed money from the government-owned Japan Development Bank to stay afloat, executives decided to court potential partners. Talks with both DaimlerChrysler and Ford proved fruitless. France-based Renault agreed to an alliance. As a precondition of the alliance, Nissan executives agreed that Renault's second-in-command, Carlos Ghosn, would come to Japan as COO under CEO Yoshikazu Hanawa. The agreement was announced on April 15, 1999—and the Ghosn era at Nissan began.

Carlos Ghosn

Ghosn was born in Brazil in 1952 to a French mother and Lebanese father. He moved to Lebanon at the age of six to attend a French Jesuit school. He received his college education in Paris, first at the Ecole Polytechnique and then at the Ecole des Mines de Paris. Representatives from Michelin, a privately held French tire company, approached Ghosn in March 1978 while he was still a student. They were looking for French-educated engineers who could speak Portuguese (Ghosn's first language) to help them build a market in Brazil. Ghosn accepted their offer and worked his way through several manufacturing positions in France, South America, and the United States before joining Renault.

Ghosn at Renault

In October 1996, Ghosn joined Renault when CEO Louis Schweitzer offered him the number two position (with potential succession to the top position). Ghosn had already developed a philosophy of change leadership at Michelin based on three premises:

- Assume nothing (find answers within the company).
- Work fast.
- Earn trust and respect with strong results.

At Renault, his formal assignment was to run engineering, manufacturing, and purchasing. However, Ghosn's main responsibility was to cut costs.

Renault Ghosn's early analysis of Renault's problems led him to conclude that the company culture emphasized narrow, functionally based thinking at the expense of a larger strategic view:

> The company was organized into completely separate departments, like silos. The heads of the departments often turned them into baronies or fiefdoms. This was an enormous problem, because I felt the road to recovery

> lay in implementing cross-functionality. And advocating cross-functionality is tantamount to challenging certain practices that belong to certain functions. But I believed that cross-functionality was fundamental to our success … We had to break down some high walls and reorganize the company so that everyone worked together.

Relying on cross-functional teams, Ghosn came up with a plan to reduce costs by $4 billion in three years.

His plan, which included closing Renault's plant in Vilvoorde, Belgium, with its 3,500 jobs, earned him the lasting nickname: "le cost killer." Ghosn claimed to have no problem with his reputation:

> Businesses have always tried to reduce costs … I don't see how one can manage a business without keeping one eye glued to expenses. It's a fantasy to think otherwise. … There have been very few successful extravagant captains of industry.

Renault returned to profitability in 1997.

Within the company, Ghosn earned a reputation as a tough, demanding boss who set "brutally high standards." At the same time, executives considered him a consensus builder with a "knack for getting straight to the heart of tough problems and … an ability to motivate others by setting ambitious but realistic targets." Ghosn avoided personal confrontation. "To my knowledge," he said, reflecting on his entry into the Renault executive suite, "there were no personal conflicts, because by definition I'm not a confrontational man. I try to manage pressure where I find it. I don't make scenes or attack people. I'm firm, but not confrontational."

Renault–Nissan Alliance Throughout the 1990s, Renault sought a partnership with another carmaker in order to expand its market reach. Early attempts had been disastrous. The company proved unable to close a potential deal for Volvo. Their purchase of U.S.-based AMC cost Renault billions of dollars before selling that unit off to Chrysler. Schweitzer and Ghosn, however, remained convinced that the company needed a partner to help it break out of the confining European market (85 percent of all company sales were in Europe) and seek robust sales in Asia and North America.

After Nissan's merger talks with DaimlerChrysler fell through, Ghosn pursued serious negotiations with the Japanese carmaker. As the companies engaged in talks, a difference in style and culture—Renault's highly legalistic style clashed with Nissan's preference for broad-based discussion—threatened to undermine potential agreement. Ghosn proposed cross-company teams to look at all opportunities for synergistic effort, creating 11 teams of members from similar jobs in the two companies. Once the companies approved the alliance, these teams allowed Ghosn to have a head start on what needed to be done at Nissan.

The 1999 alliance called for Renault to acquire a 36.8-percent stake in Nissan. "We are not merging," noted Renault's CEO Louis Schweitzer, "we are creating a binational company." At the time, Nissan had $19.9 billion in debt and losses of $250 million for the year. The company had posted losses seven out of the previous eight years. Their domestic market share had sunk from 34 percent in 1974 to under 19 percent in 1999, their global market share from 7 percent to under 5 percent.

Ghosn at Nissan

Upon his arrival in Japan, Ghosn announced that his goal was not to advance the interests of Renault but rather "to do everything in my power to bring Nissan back to profitability at the earliest date possible and revive it as a highly attractive company." He realized the delicate position in which he found himself:

> In corporate turnarounds, particularly those related to mergers or alliances, success is not simply a matter of making fundamental changes to a company's organization and operations. You also have to protect the company's identity and the self-esteem of its people. Those two goals—making changes and safeguarding identity—can easily come into conflict; pursuing them both entails a difficult and sometimes precarious balancing act. That was particularly true in this case. I was, after all, an outsider—non-Nissan, non-Japanese—and was initially met with skepticism by the company's managers and employees. I knew that if I tried to dictate changes from above, the effort would backfire, undermining morale and productivity. But if I was too passive, the company would simply continue its downward spiral.

The challenge, he said, was to save the business without losing the company.

While he was not the first Westerner to take the reins of a Japanese auto company (an American had led Mazda after Ford purchased the company), the local press still wondered how a Westerner would fit in and be able to adjust. Ghosn held no such concerns:

> By focusing on specific business objectives, people don't have time to worry about cultural differences or politicking (which is obviously a very dangerous thing in an alliance or merger). This focus on results instead of politics gives you a much greater opportunity to create a success in an alliance or merger if the turnaround works. Realistically, though, it can jeopardize the whole merger or alliance if it doesn't work.

He believed that by focusing on performance, he could bypass concerns for cultural differences.

By inclination, Ghosn avoided making sweeping changes in the makeup of his executive committee. He said he would make personnel changes only after giving people a "reasonable time" to change. "I do it, but only when necessary. I consider it a waste. It is more of a challenge to me to change people from within. It is more long-lasting and beneficial—more powerful—to change people than to change persons." Within two years of his arrival, however, Ghosn did remove a number of key executives for failure to meet performance targets. Accountability, he repeated over and over, *must* start at the top.

Ghosn insisted on consistency between the stated beliefs of top executives and their actions:

> Top management is highly visible. What we think, what we say, and what we do must be the same. We have to be impeccable in ensuring that our words correspond to our actions. If there are discrepancies between what we profess and how we behave, that will spell disaster. Included in this is our accountability. We must be committed to the responsibilities we've agreed to. When we don't deliver, we have to face the consequences. The Japanese culture is a very proud culture. Our workers and managers want to succeed. For that matter, so do the unions inside Nissan. They want to be proud of their company and their management. They need management to manage. And good management involves accountability.

Leaders, in his view, must do what they say and say what they do.

Early Diagnosis

Between April and late June 1999, Ghosn toured Nissan plants, subsidiaries, and dealerships in Japan, the United States, Europe, and Taiwan. He had learned from his experience at Michelin to start change without any preconceived ideas:

> This is extremely important in management. You must start with a clean sheet of paper because the worst thing that you can have is prefabricated solutions … you have to start with a zero base of thinking, cleaning everything out of your mind.

Performance numbers told him a great deal about Nissan but not the underlying causes of their problems. "You have to go out in the field to see what's going on." Ghosn engaged in a process he called "deep listening," speaking to over 5,000 people:

> I asked people what they thought was going right, what they thought was going wrong, and what they would suggest to make things better. I was trying to arrive at an analysis that wouldn't be static but would identify what we could do to improve the company's performance. It was a period of intensive, active listening. I took notes. I accumulated documents that contained very precise assessments of the different situations we had to deal with, and I drew up my own personal summaries of what I learned. In the course of those three months, I must have met more than a thousand people.

Ghosn's diagnostic tour built a good deal of hope and high expectations.

Almost immediately, Ghosn announced three changes based on decisions he had arrived at on his own:

1. The "official language" of Nissan would become English and all top management meetings would be held in English. Executives who did not learn English immediately would have to leave the company.

2. The Japanese press would be invited to attend Nissan shareholder meetings as a way of making Nissan's current problems and future plans transparent to the public.
3. The position of regional president for Europe and North America was replaced with four cross-functional management teams.

By early July, Ghosn reached some conclusions about Nissan. Perhaps the most surprising was the lack of urgency among Nissan executives: "For a company that has been losing money for seven years out of eight, there is not enough of a sense of urgency. People should be banging their heads on the walls everywhere." Increasing a sense of urgency was on his mind when he announced his diagnosis to the press and, more importantly, to employees within the company. In an "all-hands" presentation carried across the company via closed-circuit television, Ghosn listed strengths and weaknesses:

The fact that he spoke directly to employees was especially important to Ghosn:

> Now, it's impossible to resurrect a failing company without first diagnosing its problems and then making sure everyone in the enterprise knows the results of your diagnosis. If there's a reticence about sharing the results, there can be no shared sense of urgency ... You have to identify the problem and circulate your diagnosis. When we pointed out in public that some of Nissan's products were not all that attractive, we got a lot of criticism ... But it was this very statement, the frank admission that some of the products in our line weren't appealing, that allowed us to straighten things out, even if what we said may have had a short-term negative effect.

Ghosn was enacting what he considered to be his primary role: "The only power that a CEO has is to motivate. The rest is nonsense."

Cross-Functional Teams

To enrich his diagnosis and specify action plans, Ghosn returned to cross-functional teams:

> In my experience, executives in a company rarely reach across boundaries. Typically, engineers prefer solving problems with other engineers, salespeople like to work with fellow salespeople, and Americans feel more comfortable with other Americans. The trouble is that people working in functional or regional teams tend not to ask themselves as many hard questions as they should. By contrast, working together in cross-functional teams helps managers to think in new ways and challenge existing practices. The teams also provide a mechanism for explaining the necessity for change and for projecting difficult messages across the entire company.

Ghosn pulled together nine cross-functional teams to examine all aspects of the business operation: from business development to manufacturing and logistics to supplier relationships to organizational structure. Each had ten members, all from middle management. Teams could also create subteams to help them collect data. In total, the effort involved about 500 people. Ghosn gave the teams three months to review the company's operations and make recommendations.

Only three explicit rules governed the activities of the teams. First: "Nothing is off limits to discuss and explore. Teams are not to be hindered by traditions or avoid sensitive corporate issues." Second: "Teams had no decision-making power. That was left in the hands of the executive committee." And third: "Only one issue is non negotiable: the return to profit."

Ghosn was tough and demanding on team members. When the purchasing team, for example, came back with a plan to reduce costs by 10 percent over three years, Ghosn's response devastated them. "Ghosn rejected our recommendations outright," recalled a team member. "He told us they were not aggressive enough. He told us to come back with recommendations that will yield 20 percent savings over the next three years." Far from being discouraged, the group went back to work. After what was recalled as "a wrenching two weeks of hard work and tough negotiations," the group met Ghosn's expectations with recommendations that, in retrospect, seemed obvious.

"Mr. Ghosn is always challenging us to make higher commitments and targets," said an executive. "We [constantly] talk about challenge and stretch." Added another executive, "I have never worked for anyone who is so demanding."

Nissan Revival Plan

With the recommendations from the nine cross-functional teams Ghosn and the executive committee pulled together what became known as the Nissan Revival Plan (NRP). In October 1999, Ghosn announced that plan to the press, to the employees, and to the public. He started his presentation by saying, "The key facts and figures about Nissan point to a reality: Nissan is in bad shape." The highlights of his action plan included:

- Reduce operating costs by $10 billion.
- Cut the number of parts and material suppliers in half.
- Create new product investment and rollout, including launch of 22 new models by 2002—capital investment increased from 3.5 percent in 1999 to 5.5 percent in 2002.
- Reduce global head count by 21,000.
- Reduce number of vehicle assembly plants in Japan from seven to four.
- Reduce number of manufacturing platforms in Japan from 24 to 15.

"The combination of growth and cost reduction will allow Nissan to achieve a consolidated operating profit of 4.5 percent or more of sales by FY 2002." Revival would depend on more than cost cutting, he emphasized. "While cost cutting will be the most dramatic and visible part of the plan, we cannot save our way to success."

In the question-and-answer period that followed his presentation, a reporter asked if Ghosn was prepared to take responsibility for the company's performance. If Nissan is not profitable in 2000, Ghosn responded, he and the entire executive committee would resign. Committee members had made that agreement privately but had not expected Ghosn to make it public. In hindsight, Ghosn thought it was an important statement. "To say Nissan will be profitable or I'll quit ... this struck a chord. [Fellow] executive committee members were obviously surprised when they heard of my remark."

The NRP contained several significant departures from traditional Japanese approaches to management. Nissan's relationship with suppliers, for example, represented the *keiretsu* system that linked large manufacturers, like Nissan, to its suppliers often through cross held stock. "The *keiretsu* was like a big family," noted a reporter. "In the 1980s it was considered one of the key components of the success of Japanese manufacturing, as the cozy relationships ensured that manufacturers were delivered high quality parts, manufactured to specification, as they were needed." With suppliers now placing Nissan at a considerable cost disadvantage, Ghosn targeted the system. The number of suppliers would be cut in half, and they would be expected to cut costs by 20 percent by 2003.

Additionally, all purchasing would be centralized. Said Ghosn, "Purchasing represents 60 percent of our total costs, or a minimum of 58 percent of our net sales. Today, Nissan buys parts and materials on a regional basis, or even in certain areas on a country basis. This will stop immediately." From that point onward, purchasing would be centralized and globalized.

Traditional human resource policies would also be changed. Said Ghosn:

> Like other Japanese companies, Nissan paid and promoted its employees based on their tenure and age. The longer employees stuck around, the more power and money they received, regardless of their actual performance. Inevitably, that practice bred a certain degree of complacency, which undermined Nissan's competitiveness.

Nissan's seniority system would be abandoned, along with their approach to pay:

> In the traditional Japanese compensation system, managers receive no share options, and hardly any incentives are built into the manager's pay packet ... We changed all that. High performers today can expect cash incentives that amount to more than a third of the annual pay packages, on top of which employees receive company stock options.

The revival plan sent shock waves not just through the company but through the entire nation. Japan's stock market reacted by dropping Nissan's price a full 20 percent. Ghosn was not alarmed:

> To be able to make changes, it is necessary to do some hard things. If you do those things, it does not mean that you do not value people. In my opinion, the reverse is true. People who do not tell the truth do not respect people. My concept of respect for people starts with telling the truth and establishing the facts of a situation.

Telling the truth and establishing the facts of a situation—those were to be the hallmarks of Ghosn's approach.

Results and More Plans

Nissan achieved the results promised in the NRP a full year ahead of time. Ghosn became president of Nissan in 2000 and CEO in 2001. At that time, he announced a new plan, named NISSAN 180:

> Through NRP we transformed a struggling company into a good company; through NISSAN 180, we will transform a good company into a great company. The achievement of NISSAN 180 will rely on four pillars: more revenue, less costs, more quality and speed and a maximized alliance with Renault.

Once again, Nissan made good on its promises. "The story of Nissan's revival is now complete."

Moving Up

In April 2005, Ghosn officially returned to France to run Renault, announcing that he would continue to oversee Nissan. "I won't be a part-timer, but one CEO with two hats." Forty percent of his time, he said, would be spent in Japan (with Toshiyuku Shiga serving as Nissan COO), 40 percent in France, and the rest globally. In fact, Ghosn played a *third* role as well. The alliance board of directors—the body designated to oversee the strategy of the alliance as well as any and all activities undertaken jointly by Renault and Nissan*—had been headed jointly by the CEOs of Renault and Nissan, as well as five senior executives from each. With Ghosn now serving in both CEO roles, he became, in essence, the chairman of the joint board.

"It is very flattering," said Ghosn of his emergence as a kind of global superstar, "but at the same time you know that you are as good as your last quarter results or your last six-month results or your last year results. I know very well the rules. As long as you perform, you are good. Your management is as good as your performance."

Rough Seas at Renault

As he had done at Nissan, Ghosn set ambitious plans for Renault, emphasizing the introduction of 26 new models by 2009. As the market awaited the arrival of the redesigned compact Megane and other models, Renault sales slipped, while competitors Fiat and Volkswagen grew. Profits at Nissan declined for three straight quarters, and the Renault stock price took a beating. After selling off one-and-a-half million Renault shares, a fund manager expressed a concern. "The near term looks weak," he said, "and we remain concerned that Carlos Ghosn is still running both Renault and Nissan." Ghosn, however, reassured employees, customers, and the market. "My record," he said simply, "is to do what I said I was going to do."

*Joint activities included shared purchasing, shared research on fuel cell technology, shared factories in Mexico and Brazil, and shared car platforms.

Endnotes

1. John Chambers quoted in "The HBR Interview: John Chambers," *Harvard Business Review* (Nov. 2008), p. 77. Information used for this case comes from that interview, as well as Matt Richtel, "A Cheerleader for a Company in a Midlife Funk," *New York Times* (June 23, 2002), and Adam Bryant, "In a Near-Death Experience, a Corporate Rite of Passage," *New York Times* (Aug. 2, 2009).
2. This definition of leadership as mobilizing adaptive behavior is offered by Ronald A. Heifetz, *Leadership Without Easy Answers* (Cambridge, MA: Belknap Press, 1994).
3. *Ibid.*, p. 20.
4. John P. Kotter, *The Leadership Factor* (New York: Free Press, 1988), p. 17.
5. See Bert Spector, "From Bogged Down to Fired Up: Inspiring Organizational Change," *Sloan Management Review* 30 (Summer 1989), pp. 29–34.
6. Jacques Steinberg, "They Know All the Stupid Sitcom Writer Tricks," *New York Times* (Sept. 11, 2005), sec. 2, p. 90.
7. Christopher A. Bartlett and Sumantra Ghoshal, "Changing the Role of Top Management: Beyond Strategy to Purpose," *Harvard Business Review* (Nov.–Dec. 1994), p. 82.
8. Jim Collins, *Good to Great: Why Some Companies Make the Leap . . . and Others Don't* (New York: Harper Business, 2001), p. 30. Emphasis in the original.
9. See Michael Beer, Russell A. Eisenstat, and Bert Spector, *The Critical Path to Corporate Renewal* (Boston, MA: Harvard Business School Press, 1990).
10. Edwin A. Locke and Gary P. Latham, *Goal Setting: A Motivational Technique That Works!* (Englewood Cliffs, NJ: Prentice-Hall, 1984).
11. Dvora Yanow, "Translating Local Knowledge at Organizational Peripheries," *British Journal of Management* 15 (2004), pp. 9–25.
12. Roderick D. Iverson and Parimal Roy, "A Casual Model of Behavioral Commitment: Evidence from a Study of Australian Blue-Collar Employees," *Journal of Management* 20 (1994), pp. 15–41; Roderick D. Iverson, "Employee Acceptance of Organizational Change: The Role of Organizational Commitment," *International Journal of Human Resource Management* 7 (Feb. 1996), pp. 122–149; Jon R. Katzenbach and Jason A. Santamaria, "Firing Up the Front Line," *Harvard Business Review* (May–June 1999), pp. 107–117.
13. Information on Southwest Airlines is from Jody Hoffier, *The Southwest Airlines Way* (New York: McGraw-Hill, 2003), and James L. Heskett, *Southwest Airlines 2002: An Industry Under Siege* (Boston, MA: Harvard Business School Publishing, 2003).
14. Paul R. Lawrence and Nitin Nohria, *Driven: How Human Nature Shapes Organizations* (San Francisco, CA: Jossey-Bass, 2001).
15. Quoted in Beer, Eisenstat, and Spector, *The Critical Path to Corporate Renewal*, p. 85.
16. James C. Collins and Jerry I. Porras, *Built to Last: Successful Habits of Visionary Companies* (New York: Harper Business, 1994).
17. Ron Morris, "Great Leaders Are Born; Great Managers Are Made," *Techyvent Pittsburg*, (Nov. 7, 2005).
18. John Baldoni quoted at *www.johnbaldoni.com*.
19. Paul R. Lawrence and Davis Dyer, *Renewing American Industry* (New York: Free Press, 1983).
20. John Kotter, *Leading Change* (Boston, MA: Harvard Business School Press, 1996).
21. See Kathleen M. Eisenhardt, Jean L. Kahwajy, and L. J. Bourgeois III, "How Top Management Teams Can Have a Good Fight," *Harvard Business Review* (July–Aug. 1997), pp. 77–86.
22. Gibson Burrell and Gareth Morgan, *Sociological Paradigms and Organizational Analysis* (London: Heinemann, 1979).
23. Victoria Emerson, "An Interview with Carlos Ghosn," *Journal of World Business* 36 (Spring 2001), p. 9.
24. Ralph Stayer, "How I Learned to Let My Workers Lead," *Harvard Business Review* (Nov.–Dec. 1990), p. 66.
25. This case is based on the following publications: Michael A. Cusumano, *The Japanese Automobile Industry: Technology and Management at Nissan and Toyota* (Cambridge, MA: Council on East Asian Studies, 1985); Emily Thornton, "Remaking Nissan," *Business Week*, (Nov. 15, 1999), p. 70; Stephane Farhi, "Ghosn Sees Fast Start at Nissan," *Automotive News* 73 (Apr. 5, 1999), p. 1; S. Strom, "In a Change, Nissan Opens Annual Meeting to Press," *New York*

Times (June 26, 1999), p. C2; Chester Dawson, "The Zen of Nissan," *Business Week*, (July 22, 2002), p. 142; Carlos Ghosn, "Saving the Business Without Losing the Company," *Harvard Business Review* (Jan. 2002), Michael Yoshino and Masako Egawa, *Nissan Motor Co., Ltd., 2002* (Boston, MA: Harvard Business School Publishing, 2002); Michael Yoshino and Perry L. Fagan, *The Renault-Nissan Alliance* (Boston, MA: Harvard Business School Publishing, 2002); David Furlonger, "Back from the Brink of Failure," *Financial Mail* (June 28, 2002), p. 102; Carlos Ghosn, speech at INSEAD Global Leader Series, September 24, 2002; Tim Larimer, "Japan, Nissan and the Ghosn Revolution," *Chazen Web Journal of International Business* (Spring 2003), p. 5; David Magee, *Turnaround: How Carlos Ghosn Rescued Nissan* (New York: HarperCollins, 2003); Brian Bremmer, "Nissan's Boss," *Business Week* (Oct. 4, 2004), p. 50; Carlos Ghosn and Philippe Ries, *Shift: Inside Nissan's Historical Revival* (New York: Currency, 2005); "Nissan Reports Record Results for FY04," *Japan's Corporate News* (May 25, 2005), p. 1 (*www.japancorp.net/Article.Asp?Art ID=9931*) James Brooke, "Nissan's Mr. Fix-It Is the Talk of Detroit," *New York Times* (Nov. 19, 2005), p. C4; Laurence Frost, "Renault's Chief Losing Support as Share Price Drops," *International Herald Tribune* (Sept. 8–9, 2007), p. 13.

26. For background on Nissan, see Michael A. Cusumano, *The Japanese Automobile Industry: Technology and Management at Nissan and Toyota* (Cambridge, MA: Council on East Asian Studies, 1985).

CHAPTER

8 Going Green

In recent years, there has been a virtual stampede of executives proclaiming their desire to "go green"; that is, to reduce or eliminate the negative impact of their business activities on society and the planet. For some, this proclamation amounts to little more than a public relations gimmick. Others, though, are genuinely committed to meeting the needs of their shareholders, customers, employees, host communities, and even the larger global community. These executives are looking at the processes their companies use to develop, manufacture, distribute, and perhaps even recycle their own products. They are seeking to develop products and services in ways that are compatible with what is being called "sustainability." For these businesses, there are many technical questions: how to reduce waste, produce more efficiently, and so forth. They also face another, perhaps less obvious challenge. Going green is about more than new tools and techniques; it also involves organizational transformation.

We are not focusing here on companies founded on positive values concerning the social responsibility of business and the need to be a steward of a just and healthy planet. Patagonia, Ben & Jerry's, Newman's Own, and the Body Shop are examples of companies in which the founders embedded values of social responsibility into the company's culture. These types of companies, however, are *not* the focus of this chapter.

Instead, the chapter looks at companies that were founded on a different set of assumptions and values. These companies viewed regulations concerning the environment and the treatment of employees from a compliance perspective. Rules were to be either followed, or occasionally even circumvented.

When a company with one strategy and set of values decides to "go green," it will need to engage in a change effort.* And it is a change that is transformational in nature. The chapter will focus on the organizational transformation involved in going green. In particular, the chapter will:

- Present the key concepts of sustainability and the triple bottom line
- Examine going green as an organizational transformation

*In this chapter, "going green" and "sustainability" will be used interchangeably.

- Articulate the steps that are part of that particular transformation process
- Delineate the role of leadership in creating and maintaining a green culture within an organization

Before doing so, we will examine an attempt by a large athletic shoe company to go green. As you read this introductory case, ask yourself:

- What was the trigger event for Nike?
- What steps did Nike take to transform itself?
- How successful has Nike been in its effort to go green?

NIKE JUST DOES IT

In *Newsweek's* 2010 ranking of the most "green" companies in the United States, Nike sat at number 10 overall, topping the list of all consumer products companies.† As impressive as that achievement may seem, what made it all the more remarkable was that almost 20 years earlier, Nike was being held up as the "poster child" for corporate *ir*responsibility in a global economy.[1] A 1992 exposé in *Harper's Magazine* cited Nike as an example of the dark side of globalization. Nike prospered by shutting U.S. factories and exporting work to Indonesia, China, Malaysia, and other "Third World" countries. Nike had even abandoned the factories in South Korea when the government recognized the right of workers to form unions and strike.

At first, company executives reacted defensively. "We believe that we look after the interests of our workers," said a Nike spokesman. "There's a growing body of documentation that indicates that Nike workers earn superior wages and manufacture product under superior conditions." When that response failed to quell the storm, executives sought to be reassuring. "We have uncovered these issues clearly before anyone else, and we have moved fairly expeditiously to correct them."

Denial, however, took the company only so far.

Over time, a new, more proactive approach emerged. Nike would reconsider its corporate practices. The company now committed itself to fair labor practices, zero waste and toxins, a closed-loop system that reused all products, and "sustainable growth and productivity." An internal audit demonstrated that annual footwear production generated $700 million in waste. By 2020, the company pledged, all that would be eliminated.

It was "very difficult to really grasp and understand what we were attempting," noted Darcy Winslow, general manager of Nike's Women's Fitness division, "much less get buy-in on it." Early efforts to promote the so-called triple bottom line ("people/planet/profits") failed to garner much enthusiasm on the part of either employees or top management. Nike's founder and board chairman Phil Knight seemed genuinely interested in improving the brand's image, but the language of sustainability was alien within Nike's highly competitive, performance-driven culture. Discussions with supply chain partners (both

†*Newsweek* looks at environmental impact, green corporate policies, and the company's reputation among corporate social responsibility experts.

suppliers on one end of the supply chain and manufacturers on the other‡) were earnest but perfunctory. The company's small Corporate Social Responsibility (CSR) function had little clout with line managers. The whole effort was seen as somewhat peripheral to the business of designing and selling athletic shoes around the world.

That approach began to change in 2002. Said Winslow, "We started to create an overarching strategy of what it meant to be a more sustainable company." All goals were now translated into dollars and cents impact. In 2009, the CSR department became the Sustainable Business and Innovation (SBI) department. That name change embedded the sustainability effort more explicitly in the company's drive for innovative products. In a company statement, Nike said, "Sustainable Business and Innovation is an integral part of how we can use the power of our brand, the energy and passion of our people, and the scale of our business to create meaningful change." The company announced its Considered Design process for new product development, requiring that issues such as recycling and waste not be after-thoughts to product design. Rather, they were to be taken into consideration at the very earliest stages of new product development.

The move from CSR to Sustainable Business and Innovation was more than just a name change. The vice president of SBI was placed on Nike's strategic leadership team in order to participate in decision making concerning mid- and long-term plans. The department's staff was housed *within* product and geographic groups, reporting matrix-style to both line managers and the vice president.

Other organizational changes intended to fuel Nike's sustainability effort included:

- The creation of internal audit teams to track labor practices and waste in facilities around the world.
- Active lobbying by company representatives to influence labor standards and regulations in the countries where manufacturing activities were occurring.
- Changing the incentive offered to supply chain partners away from cost savings, placing heavier emphasis on local labor conditions.
- Reengineering inventory control systems in order to avoid last minute rushes which encouraged supply chain partners to circumvent Nike's sustainability standards.

Products began to emerge that were designed at the outset—the Trash Talker, for instance, made entirely with recycled materials (trash)—to be eco-friendly. The company opened shoe recycling centers, using the material not only for its own shoes but also to be donated to schools and communities for use in building tracks.

To be sure, Nike possessed some advantages in its change to green. For one, the founder and chairman remained committed and actively involved. Then too, Nike's customer base tended to be young, active, and affluent: aware of social

‡Nike outsourced all manufacturing and assembly; the company mainly performed design and marketing.

issues and willing to pay for green products. Celebrity product sponsors, most notably Michael Jordan, were excited to have their names associated with sustainability efforts. And Nike's "Just Do It" corporate slogan captured a company commitment to remaining a market leader.

MOVING TOWARD THE SUSTAINABLE CORPORATION

Building a Vocabulary of Change
Sustainability voluntary actions taken by organizations designed to meet the needs of the present generation without compromising the needs of future generations.

Although many definitions of **sustainability** or going green exist, one of the most widely accepted involves organizations taking voluntary steps to meet the needs of the present generation without compromising the needs of future generations.[2] The inclusion of the term "voluntary" is important. Going green is not the same as **compliance:** actions of an organization designed to meet requirements imposed by law.

THEORY INTO PRACTICE

Corporate sustainability involves voluntary efforts on the part of organizations.

Building a Vocabulary of Change
Compliance actions of an organization designed to meet requirements imposed by law.

The issue of business organizations going green is one that is mired in significant controversy. To start with, what is the proper role of business in our society? Do businesses have a stewardship role over the planet or should the focus of corporate activity be solely on enhancing profitability? Some of the key points of that debate, which has been going on for decades, are summarized in Exhibit 8-1. Even when businesses accept a degree of responsibility, questions can be raised such as: what is the nature of that responsibility, and how should it best be enacted?

EXHIBIT 8-1
Is This a Proper Role for Business?

It may surprise you to know that debates about the social obligations of businesses go back decades. The first dean of the Harvard Business School, Wallace Donham, insisted that business executives had a responsibility not just to their enterprise but to the society in which their businesses operated. In a 1927 speech, he argued that the "development, strengthening, and multiplication of socially-minded" executives was "the central problem of business." In the aftermath of World War II, Harvard readjusted its curriculum in order to help business students develop "an integrated social and economic philosophy."[3]

There have been equally spirited augments against the notion that business has a larger social and environmental responsibility. Harvard Business School professor Theodore Levitt suggested that the dubious notion of a larger responsibility for business detracted attention from the main job of corporations. "The business of business is profits"; anything else was a dilution of effort. American business leaders would stand "a much better chance of surviving if there is no nonsense about its goals—that is, if long-run profit maximization is the one dominant objective in practice as well as theory." Nobel Prize winning economist Milton Freedman added his voice in a famous 1970 article titled, "The Social Responsibility of Business Is to Increase Profits."[4]

THEORY INTO PRACTICE

There is still much that is controversial about going green.

Although the debate has been ongoing for years, the most recent pressure for businesses to look at their impact on the environment can be traced to 1984, when an India-based subsidiary of Union Carbide experienced an environmental, social, and economic disaster. A chemical leak from its plant in Bhopal resulted in thousands of deaths and the devastation of the community. What was widely considered to be the worst industrial catastrophe in history sparked a succession of international organizations—led by the United Nations—to look at an appropriate balance between the economic requirement for development and growth, societal needs for human dignity and rights, and environmental needs for sustainability.[5] Very quickly, the role of business institutions attracted attention both as contributors to the "problem" (placing financial returns above concerns for people and the planet) and for their potential to lead the way to a solution.

THEORY INTO PRACTICE

The Bhopal chemical leak of 1984 proved to be a major trigger event in looking at the social and ecological responsibilities of companies.

Another turning point occurred in 1993 when Paul Hawken, cofounder of Smith & Hawken's, a garden supply company, published *The Ecology of Commerce*. "Quite simply," Hawken wrote, "our business practices are destroying life on earth."[6] Business had been handed a "blank check" to ignore its social responsibilities, he insisted. But business was also uniquely positioned to implement solutions. To forge a path forward, business could find a "third way" between promoting growth and enhancing the planet.

That attention led to the identification of the **triple bottom line** in which social, ecological, and economic dimensions are all taken into *equal* account. The idea of the triple bottom line is that corporations do not have to choose among these outcomes. It is a win-win-win in which each of the three—people, planet, profits—can gain by working together.

Building a Vocabulary of Change
Triple bottom line an approach to defining performance that takes into account social, economic, and ecological dimensions and assumes that the three are mutually reinforcing.

Like much else in the field of sustainability, the notion of a triple bottom line attracts controversy. Some critics suggest that, although the approach is sound in principle,—that is, the ability of corporations to balance people, planet, and profits—it is unlikely to occur in practice. At the end of the day, profits will always trump people and the planet.[7]

THEORY INTO PRACTICE

Although there is a great deal of controversy about the triple bottom line, it is an important step toward aligning business with sustainability concerns.

Others suggest that the basic approach is fundamentally, even fatally flawed. Profitability is far easier to measure than the other two components, and the concept of good "people" outcomes is vague and open to a wide variety of ideological rather than scientific interpretations.[8] For those reasons, it is difficult to assess if a company is complying with its people bottom line.[9]

Many companies begin their path to sustainability by focusing on "low-hanging fruit": relatively easy ways of reducing energy consumption and waste as ways of saving money. Other companies aim at complying with ever more stringent environmental laws or reducing their liability for environmental damage.[10] There is also a phenomenon of companies simply relabeling products and services as "green." For instance, a bank that was moving toward online services tagged the effort "Eco-banking." A railway freight company promoted its service as energy saving compared to trucking. This so-called **greenwashing** refers to a public relations effort to claim environmental virtue for actions the company was already taking.

Building a Vocabulary of Change
Greenwashing public relations efforts aimed to claim environmental virtue without making any substantive organizational change.

THEORY INTO PRACTICE

"Greenwashing" is a public relations effort that does not involve organizational transformation.

A 2009 report on business and sustainability issued by the Boston Consulting Group, together with the *MIT Sloan Management Review,* found that most executives believe sustainability is now and will continue to be important to their business.[11] However, a significantly smaller number are actively pursuing sustainability initiatives. The companies were driven by three factors:

1. Government regulations
2. Consumer preferences
3. Employee interest

Government legislation was more significant for U.S.-based companies, while consumer preferences were more of a driving factor in Europe.

THEORY INTO PRACTICE

Government regulations are the main motivation for going green in the United States; in Europe, the major factor is customer preferences.

Simon Zadek has suggested that organizations travel through five stages of responsiveness to issues of sustainability:[12]

- Defensive stage: company denies claims that they are responsibility for negative outcomes.
- Compliance stage: company accepts responsibility and costs of following rules and legislation as "the cost of doing business."
- Managerial stage: company integrates sustainability objectives into the management goals at multiple levels of the organization.

- Strategic stage: sustainability issues become fully integrated into a company's business strategy.
- Civil stage: company representatives promote wider efforts on behalf of sustainability.

Of course, most companies have not yet evolved to the managerial stage, let alone the civil stage.

THEORY INTO PRACTICE

When it comes to going green, most organizations follow a predictable path, starting with denial and compliance before becoming managerial, strategic, and civil.

The Performance Advantage of Sustainability

The 2007 Boston Consulting Group/*Sloan Management Review* report surveyed executives concerning the expected benefits from sustainability efforts.[13] Leading the list, by a huge margin, was improved company/brand image, with cost savings, competitive advantage, employee satisfaction, and innovation as other perceived benefits.

One of the most frequently mentioned performance advantages of going green is the impetus it provides for innovation. Interface founder Ray Anderson said his company's commitment to sustainablility offered "an incredible fountainhead of inspiration."[14] An excellent example of such innovation can be seen at Bloomberg, a company that provides investors with financial data. Bloomberg leveraged its internal ecological commitment, BGreen, into a new product: providing environmental, social, and governance (ESG) performance investment analysis tools to socially responsible investors.[15] Exhibit 8-2 summarizes the performance advantages of going green.

EXHIBIT 8-2 Performance Advantages of Going Green.

Advantage Gained:	By:
Lowered cost of operating	Elimination of waste
Reduced exposure to risk	Inoculating against future law suits
Increased innovation	Impetus for new products/services
Improved recruitment	Enhanced image of green company makes it more attractive to potential employees
Enhanced employee motivation	Creates sense of excitement and purpose for employees
Market differentiation	Appealing to sustainability-conscious consumers

THEORY INTO PRACTICE

In addition to cost savings and image building, going green offers "an incredible fountainhead for innovation."

Although sustainability can and does result in improved performance, the relationship between investment in green innovation and payoffs is not a simple straight line up. As Dean Schroeder and Alan Robinson have demonstrated with their "Green Payback Curve," the bottom-line impact of green investment goes through predictable stages:[16]

- Phase 1: Early efforts target "low-hanging fruit" and result in "quick and certain" financial payback.
- Phase 2: At this point, projects target areas of investment in which financial returns are in the future.
- Phase 3: Investments made in Phase 2 now sharply improve financial performance.

Interface's Ray Anderson was confident in the business case for sustainability:

> Costs are down, so it's saving money. Products are better, which means the top line is better. People are motivated and galvanized, which means employees' morale and engagement is up. And the goodwill of the marketplace is astonishing. I don't know what else provides this kind of business case: costs are down, products are better, people are motivated, and customers are receptive—and we're winning market share.[17]

"Any notion that companies need to make a tradeoff between financial and environmental performance was simply a false choice," insisted Anderson. There is no trade-off.

THE PROCESS OF CHANGING TO GREEN

In Chapter 1, we saw how organizational change is typically initiated in response to a trigger event; a shift in the environment that creates a need for altered strategies and new patterns of employee behavior. For Nike, it was the adverse publicity associated with Nike's labor practices that prompted CEO Phil Knight to put the company on a different path. Such trigger events can be dramatic in nature—Brazilian oil giant Petrobras suffered through three major disasters within a year of each other, including an oil rig explosion that killed 11 employees, before seeking to enhance its safety and maintenance performance—or subtle. Let's take the case of Ray Anderson, CEO of Interface.

Ray Anderson started Interface Flooring Systems, headquartered in Georgia, in 1973.[18] Interface's main product was carpet tiles, a high-end offering aimed at commercial customers that generated over $1 billion in global sales by the late 1990s. Carpeting was mainly made of nylon, a highly durable but also nonrecyclable product that ended up in landfills and takes 20,000 years to degrade. Interface followed standard industry practice, recycling no more than 4 percent of its production. The company grew to become the world's leading commercial provider.

The turning point for Anderson and Interface came at the confluence of two seemingly minor events. In the mid-1990s, Interface's research department invited Anderson to deliver a talk to a global meeting of employees focused on the company's environmental efforts. That invitation was prompted by queries from customers—what was Interface doing for the environment?—that grew out of the cultural–political climate of the decade. Anderson was reluctant to attend such a meeting. After all, his only vision for an environmentally responsible company was quite simple: "obey the law, comply, comply, comply." Certainly, the notion that his company or any other could be harming the environment while complying with environmental regulations never crossed his mind.

At the same time, and purely by coincidence, Anderson was reading Paul Hawken's *Ecology of Commerce.* "It changed my life," said Anderson. "It hit me right between the eyes. It was an epiphany." Anderson was inspired to begin a transformation, which he referred to in his typically understated manner, as a midcourse correction. "I'm dedicating the rest of my life to creating a company that can grow and prosper without doing harm to the earth."

Of course, not all potential trigger events actually trigger any significant change. Nike's Phil Knight could have attempted to paper over charges of labor abuse with public relations efforts, and Ray Anderson could have continued with his compliance-based vision of environmental responsibility. Much depends on company leadership. Jack Welch, for instance, fought community and government attempts to have General Electric (GE) contribute to the cleanup of the Hudson River. His successor, Jeffrey Immelt, on the other hand, launched "Ecoimagination" designed to commit GE to developing "tomorrow's solutions such as solar energy, hybrid locomotives, fuel cells, lower emission aircraft engines, lighter and stronger durable materials, efficient lighting, and water purification technology."

Once the trigger event motivates a reevaluation of values, goals, and strategies, companies seeking to go green undergo a transformation that follows a set of sequential interventions:

- Set the vision
- Diagnose the status quo
- Alter first informal and then formal design elements.

Ultimately, the leadership of the organization will need to bear the responsibility for setting a green culture in which sustainability becomes interwoven into the fabric of the organization.

Set the Vision

For existing organizations, going green represents a new direction: not just a new strategy but a new way of thinking about strategy. Not surprisingly, then, it seems quite helpful for organizational leaders to set the path and define the territory. In that regard, going green starts when top leadership offers a vision about what is meant by going green:

THEORY INTO PRACTICE

Going green starts with a visionary statement from top leadership.

- When Jan Stenberg, then CEO of Scandinavian Airlines (SAS), committed his company to be an early mover in addressing environmental concerns related to airplane emissions, he explained: "A sound environmental profile is profitable. But it is more than that. It is our contribution to a sustainable society and to future generations.[19]
- In 2002, Jeff Immelt, CEO of GE, launched the company's ecoimagination campaign in order to achieve his goal of building a "great and good" company.[20]
- Interface's Ray Anderson made clear that his commitment to sustainability was not just about pollution. His vision of sustainability involved "taking nothing from the earth that is not rapidly and naturally renewable, and doing no harm to the biosphere."
- The leadership team at Subaru's automobile plant in Lafayette, Indiana set as their goal "zero-landfill" in the production of 1,000 cars per day.[21]

The vision sets a consistent strategy that helps avoid the complaint of one executive that, when it came to sustainability, his company had "too many unaligned programs and messages."

The power of the vision to motivate, unify, and excite, comes not just from its boldness but also from its alignment with the strategy of the company itself. Compare Coca Cola pledging donations to the Boys and Girls Clubs of America to Nike's effort to recycle athletic shoes and donating them to schools and communities to be used as the material for tracks.[22] Michael Porter and Mark Kramer differentiate between "generic" social issues and issues that are more directly related to the activities of a company or the social environment in which the company operates. Take the issue of HIV/AIDs. That may be a generic issue to a large American retailer but a strategic issue to pharmaceutical company thinking about investing in the development of a treatment or a South African-based mining company whose employees are directly affected.[23]

Green visions have three characteristics in common:

1. They articulate some specific territory in which the organization can contribute to sustainable development.
2. They state a belief that going green and performing well is mutually reinforcing rather than mutually exclusive.
3. They vow a commitment to a long-term social responsibility that transcends the performance of the company.

Typically, Porter and Kramer conclude, "the more closely tied a social issue is to a company's business, the greater the opportunity to leverage the firm's resources—and benefit society."[24]

THEORY INTO PRACTICE

To be effective, green visions embed and connect the firm's commitment to sustainability with its business mission; that way, going green is seen as strategic, not peripheral.

Diagnose the Current Situation

In 2005, Wal-Mart's image as a "good neighbor" was slowly but significantly eroding in the public mind.[25] Sure, the company delivered on its promise of everyday low prices, thereby saving consumers money. But a question was raised: at what costs? A popular documentary movie, *The High Cost of Low Price,* suggested the social costs of Wal-Mart's labor practices—low wages, dependence on part-time workers and even illegal immigrants, lack of health care—passed on the true labor costs to society.[26] Wal-Mart's image was damaged, and customers were noticing and responding.

Although Wal-Mart had reacted defensively to such attacks in the past, CEO Lee Scott now considered a new approach. He would address in a positive way Wal-Mart's impact on the environment with particular attention to "energy, waste, and products." A team of executives and high potential employees were brought together to recommend targets and steps. That team did not work on its own, however. In addition to hiring consultants, the team worked with Conservation International and Environmental Defense, and relied on data supplied by the Union of Concerned Scientists.

Kicking off sustainability efforts with diagnosis helps focus employees on what needs to change. Because sustainability involves a larger commitment to the community in which the organization exists, diagnostic efforts will need to focus not just on the company but also on the other businesses in the supply chain. The employee team at Wal-Mart learned how little impact the company could have without addressing its supply chain. Said one member: "If we had focused on just our own operations, we would have limited ourselves to 10 percent of our effect on the environment and, quite frankly, eliminated 90 percent of the opportunity that's out there."[27]

THEORY INTO PRACTICE

Early diagnostic efforts will need to include not just the company itself, but also its supply chain partners.

Supply chain partners are the companies that provide services, goods, or raw materials that are needed to design, produce, market, deliver, and support a company's offer. In the case of McDonald's, for instance, supply chain partners provide meat, buns, potatoes, and other key ingredients of the product. In order to promote sustainability across its supply chain, McDonald's created the Supply Chain Working Group in 2006.[28] The mission was to create a sustainable supply chain "that profitably yields high quality, safe products without supply interruption while creating a net benefit for employees, their communities, biodiversity, and the environment."[29] The group developed a set of social/economic, environmental, and animal welfare guidelines intended to drive the effort.

Once the diagnosis identifies areas of opportunity, the organization can address its own systems, altering informal design first before moving to formal design.

Alter Informal Design Elements

In the introductory case, we saw Nike make an implementation mistake that is often committed in change efforts. The company made a formal design change too early in the process. In response to the CEO's call to refurbish the company's image, Nike created a new department structure: the CSR function. The office had little real impact. The commitment to sustainability had not yet been embedded in Nike's strategy. Going green represented not a business reality but a corporate nicety. No wonder line managers treated the office's commitment to social responsibility as a peripheral matter.

Organizational design, as defined in Chapter 4, refers to the arrangements, both formal and informal, that an organization calls upon to help shape employee behavior. In effective change implementation, informal redesign—altering roles, responsibilities, and relationships—proceeds formal change. Formal design changes—measurements, structures, pay, and so forth—follow later in the sequence of interventions in order to reinforce and institutionalizes new behaviors.

Going green requires new patterns of employee behavior. Perhaps the most significant change is that going green is inherently a collaborative effort.[30] That collaboration is both horizontal (cross-functional) and vertical (cross-hierarchical levels). Horizontal collaboration occurs within the organization when employees from different functions and units combine their efforts. It also occurs when employees collocate with supply chain partners.

THEORY INTO PRACTICE

Informal design changes associated with going green start with building high levels of collaboration.

Remember Nike's Considered Design process? The idea of considering sustainability at the earliest possible stage of product development has become increasingly common the past several years.[31] Considered Design requires that organizations abandon their traditional silos and functional boundaries. Instead of the traditional step-by-step sequential approach to product design, all participants in the product—from raw material suppliers to design engineers, manufacturers, logistical experts, and market professionals—come together at the outset of a process at work together to develop, produce, merchandise, deliver, and recycle green products.

Collaboration will also need to occur vertically, that is, across hierarchical boundaries. Companies that have moved toward sustainability find that many of the most important innovations come not from top executives but from front-line employees. Bloomberg's BGreen initiative—an effort started in 2007 to reduce the company's carbon blueprint—grew out of an employee suggestion.[32] Interface's Ray Anderson acknowledged that the very basis of his company's green mission has been empowered employees. Mission Zero, he said, "empowered our people to dare to risk, working in teams, and challenging everything that we were doing. In other words, challenge the status quo.[33]

Alter Formal Design Elements

Formal resign can be used to reinforce and institutionalize new behaviors. In the case of Nike, we saw a number of formal design changes:

- Placing the head of the newly created SBI department on the company's strategic leadership team and staff members within the different business lines.
- Altering incentives offered to supply chain partners to align with company goals focused on improving local labor conditions.
- Reengineering inventory systems in order to eliminate last-minute rushes and the potential abuses in standards that such rushes might produce.

One of the most significant formal design changes that occur in the process of going green involves the manner in which the firm measures performance. That change has both an internal and external aspect to it.

INTERNAL MEASUREMENT Amanco, a leading Latin American building solutions company, is part of the Grupo Nueva holding company. At the group's urging, Amanco management committed the business unit to the triple bottom line, specifically:

1. Create economic stability in the long run.
2. Generate value through a system of CSR.
3. Generate value through environmental management.[34]

One of the questions that faced Amanco was about measurement. There were, in fact, two aspects of that question. First, what outcomes do we measure? And second, how do we ensure that we are achieving satisfactory results on environmental, social, and economic performance? To help provide an answer, Amanco turned to the balanced scorecard.

Building a Vocabulary of Change
Balanced scorecard (BSC) a tool for measuring multiple outcomes—financial performance, customer satisfaction, internal process excellence, and employee learning and growth—and the connection of those outcomes to the vision and strategy of the organization.

The premise for the **balanced scorecard** (BSC) is that financial returns need to be understood as one among several vital outcome measures (Exhibit 8-3). Financial measures of performance, wrote Robert Kaplan and David Norton, "are lag indicators that report on the outcomes from past actions. Exclusive reliance on financial indicators could promote behavior that sacrifices long-term value creation for short-term performance."[35]

The scorecard balances financial measures with three additional metrics:

1. Customer—To achieve our vision, how should we appear to our customers?
2. Internal Business Processes—To satisfy our shareholders and customers, what business processes must we excel at?

EXHIBIT 8-3
Balanced Scorecard.

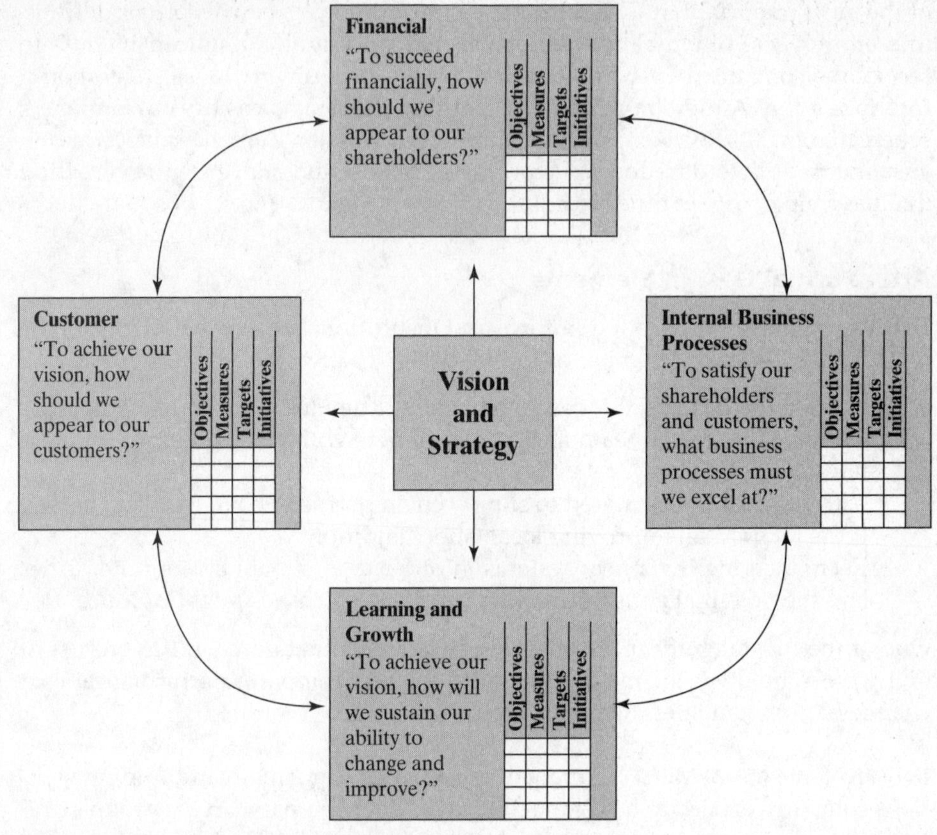

Source: http://www.balancedscorecard.org/basics/bsc1.html

3. Learning and Growth—To achieve our vision, how will we sustain our ability to change and improve?[36]

By focusing on multiple outcomes—customers, internal processes, and learning—the BSC can help managers escape the exclusive focus on a single outcome—mostly financial—and help ensure that their change interventions are having the intended results on the other key activities of their firm.

THEORY INTO PRACTICE

BSC is a tool for measuring the effectiveness of change efforts on multiple dimensions.

At the core of the BSC lies a clearly stated and widely understood vision and strategy for the organization. The vision and strategy determined in the earlier phases of change can now be used to drive *all* performance measures, financial measures included. Each perspective can be evaluated only in terms of objectives, measures, targets, and initiatives when that vision and strategy are clear and widely shared.

A growing number of companies, including Electricité de France, LVMH, and Lusotur, S.A., have called on the BSC to help them integrate sustainability objectives with their strategy.[37] In these cases, **green metrics**—specific objective measurements of social and environmental impact—are built into the scorecard. Wal-Mart, PepsiCo, and P&G also require their supplies to use a sustainability BSC in order to be approved by the corporation for use by their business units. In other cases, investment firms insist that potential clients provide them with a sustainability BSC in order to be rated as a socially responsible investment.

Building a Vocabulary of Change
Green metrics specific objective measurements of a firm's social and environmental impact.

THEORY INTO PRACTICE

A sustainability balanced scorecard can help an organization measure its performance on the triple bottom line.

There is no standard approach either to how companies utilize the BSC in going green or in what outcomes they measure.[38] Some companies place sustainability within the "internal business processes" domain. Others place sustainability "key success factors" and "key performance indicators" in all four dimensions. Still others add a fifth dimension to the traditional BSC, focusing on social and environmental indicators that link to the other four perspectives. The appropriate choice is based on the specific challenges facing each company.

The choice of outcomes to be measured will also be based on the company's strategy, its industry, and its social environment. Exhibit 8-4 presents the green metrics that are used by carpet tile manufacturer Interface.

Whatever the specific choices, sustainability BSC needs to meet two criteria to be effective:

1. It should be specific to the business unit utilizing the tool rather than genetic.
2. It should reflect the overall strategy of the firm so it is not seen as a mere add-on that can be ignored or slighted in difficult financial times.

EXHIBIT 8-4
Examples of Interface 2004 Measures of Sustainability.[39]

Environmental Sustainability
Cumulative avoided costs from waste elimination activities since 1995
Decrease in total energy consumption required to manufacture carpet since 1996 per m^2
Percentage of total energy consumption from renewable sources
Social Sustainability
Employee volunteer hours in community activities
Percentage of women in management positions

Source: Wendy Stubbs and Chris Cocklin, "An Ecological Modernist Interpretation of Sustainability: The Case of Interface, Inc.," Business Strategy and the Environment 17 (2008), p. 519.

The goal, of course, is to integrate sustainability into the overall management of the firm.

- Waste discharged per vehicle
- Electricity needed to make each vehicle
- Packaging material reused

EXTERNAL MEASUREMENT Given the increasing public interest in sustainability, it is not surprising that a number of external organizations have devised rankings of companies' social and environmental impact. The Dow Jones Sustainability Index, the FTSE4Good Index, and *Newsweek* magazine all offer ratings that are available to the companies and the public. External ratings are useful to organizations for three reasons:

1. They provide board members, executives, and employees with a perspective on the company's performance relative to others in the same industry.
2. They can be used as outcomes for the firm's sustainability BSC.
3. They provide information to concerned consumers and investors.

The ratings are not without problems, however. There can be significant differences across rating systems as to the criteria used and the relative weight assigned to each criterion. Additionally, they often rely on data supplied by the companies themselves.[40]

SHAPING A GREEN CULTURE

Building a Vocabulary of Change
Organizational culture the common and shared values and assumptions that help shape employee behavior and are typically passed down from current to future employees.

Sustainability efforts grow out of a value system or culture in an organization. **Organizational culture** refers to the common and shared values that help shape employee behavior and are typically passed down from current to future employees. Culture serves as the glue that binds an organization or, in the words of Terrence Deal and Allan Kennedy, "the way we do things around here."[41] Marcel van Marrewijk and Marco Wewe have suggested that a sustainability culture is built over multiple levels. At its most committed, a sustainability culture accepts that sustainability on a worldwide scale is required and that sustainability should be fully integrated and embedded in every aspect of the organization.[42] See Exhibit 8-5 for a summary of that cultural evolution.

THEORY INTO PRACTICE

Organizational culture can help embed a green mindset and shape employee behaviors.

Founders—think of Yvon Chounard of Patagonia, Ben Cohen and Jerry Greenfield of Ben & Jerry's, Paul Newman and A.E. Hotchner of Newman's Own, and Anita Roddick of the Body Shop—are the ones responsible for the original establishment of a culture. Once founders exit the company, it is the organizational leaders who have responsibility for shaping the culture. It is their decisions and actions that resonate throughout the company. Leaders can

EXHIBIT 8-5
An Evolving Sustainability Culture.[43]

	Culture of Compliance	Culture of Commitment
Ambition level	No ambition for sustainability but awareness of need to comply	Sustainability fully integrated and embedded into every aspect of organization aimed at contributing to quality and continuation of all societies
Motivation	Take on sustainability merely in order to improve reputation firm	Belief that everyone in the organization has a universal responsibility to both current and future generations
Criteria for decision making	How will it affect my personal reputation and that of the firm?	How will it affect the overall well-being of the planet?

examine four sets of behaviors that Edgar Schein says help create and embed culture in an organization.[44]

1. Leaders *make choices about what to pay attention to, what to measure, control, and reward*. What sustainability outcomes will the company measure and reward? If all the significant rewards flow to economic outcomes, it will be impossible to maintain a green culture.

2. Leaders *react to critical incidents and crises*. Whether it is Phil Knight responding to the drubbing Nike took in the press in the early 1990s or Ray Anderson responding to a speaking engagement just after reading Paul Hawken's book, the reaction of the leaders set the pace and direction for the company.

3. Leaders call upon the *"observed criteria" to allocate scarce resources*.[45] A CEO who extols the virtue of going green but slices budgets in order to meet short-term financial goals sends a signal about what the company values. The same can be said of a managing director who refuses to cut training budgets during a downturn emphasizes the extent to which the company values human resources. Making tough choices about resource allocation helps shape the values and resulting culture of an organization.

4. Leaders choose to *emphasize certain criteria in their recruitment, selection, and promotion of employees and future leaders*. Going green requires new skill sets, both technical and interpersonal, that can be considered in hiring and promoting employees.

Top executives are the most visible embodiment of their organization's culture. Their behaviors are apparent to both external stakeholders—customers, suppliers, labor markets, and the host community—and to employees. What leaders *say* matters; what leaders *do* matters even more. Key choices and decisions, more than speeches and documents posted on walls, embed values and spread culture.

THEORY INTO PRACTICE

The values and behaviors of leaders shape an organization's culture.

The question of developing leaders capable of moving their organizations toward sustainability has received a great deal of attention recently.[46] Perhaps an outstanding "green" leader such as Ray Anderson is simply an outstanding leader, sharing the same characteristics and displaying the same behaviors. However, there are a number of particular characteristics that can be associated with outstanding "green" leadership:

1. The ability to see and work at a high level of understanding. Outstanding green leaders are capable and motivated to look beyond their individual organization and understanding the interdependence between organizational performance and broader social, economic, and scientific issues.

Building a Vocabulary of Change
Sustainability mindset a positive openness to the complexities and opportunities of aligning people, profits, and the planet.

2. The development of a **sustainability mindset**. Green leaders will have a positive openness to the complexities and opportunities of aligning people, profits, and the planet.

3. The ability to engage in holistic thinking. Because effective sustainability efforts call for collaboration across an entire company, green leaders understand and acknowledge the degree to which all functions and units must coordinate their efforts.

4. The ability to engage in collaboration outside of the organization. Green leaders will need to engage in shared dialogue with a wide variety of external stakeholders: advocacy groups, scientific panels, and university experts as well as shareholders.

Building a Vocabulary of Change
Espoused values the set of values called upon by individuals to explain or justify their course of action or pattern of behavior.

Building a Vocabulary of Change
Enacted values the set of values that are implicit in that course of action or pattern of behavior.

Ultimately, effective green leaders will need to align espoused and enacted values. **Espoused values** are the values called upon by individuals to explain or justify their course of action or pattern of behavior. **Enacted values** are the values that are implicit in that course of action or pattern of behavior.[47] The triple bottom line calls for attention to people and the planet as well as profits, and effective green leaders behave in ways that are consistent with the goals they are proposing to their organization.

Like any excellent leaders, green leaders ultimately will need to have the capacity to learn. Learning is the process by which individuals receive data from the external environment, analyze that data, and adjust their thinking and behaviors accordingly. Green leaders will need to learn from their own experience and the experience of others. That learning consists not just of gathering knowledge, but also of applying insights into future actions.

Conclusion

Organizations often approach the challenge of going green from a technological perspective. There is certainly merit to employing innovative technology to make processes of production, distribution, and recycling more effective and less wasteful. But a full commitment to going green requires a broader perspective. Leaders set a vision and mold the culture. The sequential steps of effective transformation lead the organization through diagnoses, redesign, and new informal and formal systems. Human resources will be impacted in terms of the skills required to make green efforts effective. Finally, collaboration will be vital—both within the organization and across boundaries to include supply chain partners and external interest groups. By treating the challenge of going green as a transformational challenge, organizations will be better positioned to meet the goals of the triple bottom line.

Discussion Questions

1. Where do you stand on the various debates and controversies surrounding going green? Is protecting the plant a business responsibility or does it distract from their main purpose? Can every organizations really have a triple bottom line or will financial performance always outweigh other outcomes?
2. It is said that going green is now the main source of innovation within companies. Do you agree? How does sustainability support innovation?
3. The chapter argues that collaboration is the main behavioral change that needs to accompany going green. Do you agree? Explain.
4. Are excellent green leaders the same as excellent leaders or are important additional skills needed?

Case Discussion

Read "Changing to Green at an Oil Company (?)" and prepare answers to the following questions:

1. What triggered Gabrielli's commitment to going green at Petrobras?
2. How would you evaluate Petrobras' sustainability effort? What have they done well and or not so well in the transformation?
3. Do you agree with Gabrielli's assessment of the success of green policies at Petrobras? Explain.

GOING GREEN AT AN OIL COMPANY(?)

For many people, the notion of environmental sustainability does not fit well—if at all—with a giant oil company. This is an industry, it would seem, that thrives on the ever-increasing consumption of fossil fuels, not to mention environmental catastrophes such as oil spills. José Sergio Gabrielli de Azevedo, CEO of Brazil-based oil giant Petrobras since 2005, says he is determined to change that image.[48]

Gabrielli describes his personal politics as progressive and leftist, pointing to his 1970 arrest by the Brazilian army as he was protesting his country's then military dictatorship. After receiving a PhD in economics and joining the faculty of the London School of Economics, Gabrielli joined Petrobras in 2003 as Chief Financial Officer. His fast rise to the top was helped by his close personal and political ties with Brazil's ruling Workers' Party.

A State Company

Petrobras was founded by the government in 1953 under the nationalist slogan, "The petroleum is ours!" Petrobras held a monopoly until 1997, when the government gave up its complete ownership (although it still controls a majority of voting stock) and allowed for competition. Since then, the company has compiled a troubling history of disasters. In January 2000, a poorly maintained pipeline spilled oil into Guanabara Bay for two hours before the leak was detected. Six months later, a Petrobras refinery spewed millions of gallons of oil into two nearby rivers. A BBC news report referred to "an embarrassing level of incompetence" on the part of Petrobras managers. Then, less than a year later, a Petrobras drilling platform—the world's largest at the time—blew up, killing 11 employees and dumping 300,000 gallons of oil into the water.

Gabrielli saw that troubled history as a business problem to be solved as well as an environmental threat to be addressed. "From a purely financial perspective," he said, "environmental mismanagement was just bad business. From an investor relations perspective, ignoring the growing demand for transparency and sustainability was also bad business."[49] Plus, added Gabrielli, his personal values and political beliefs led him to move Petrobras into a position of environmental leadership.

Gabrielli Acts

In pursuit of his goal, Gabrielli took a number of steps:

- Increasing the budget of the company's health, safety, and environment programs
- Using the enormous market clout of Petrobras (which was the largest company in Latin America) to demand that all of its suppliers comply with best standards for environmental management
- Personally touring sites to check compliance with company standards
- Moving Petrobras' new refineries away from gasoline and toward biofuels
- Joining the Dow Jones Sustainability Index in order to invite external monitoring of and reporting on Petrobras' efforts
- Endorsing (and sitting on the board of) the United Nations Global Compact
- Personally blogging and tweeting in order to make the case for Petrobras' efforts directly to the public.

As evidence that these activities were changing the culture and operations of Petrobras, Gabrielli pointed to two facts:

- The company had gone eight years without a "major" environmental accident.
- The private consulting firm, Management and Excellence, ranked Petrobras as number one among the world's oil and gas companies for promoting sustainability.

Petrobras' 5-Year Strategic Plan, announced in 2010, called for additional investment in refining capacity. The company's goal was to make Brazil fuel independent by 2014. That independence, it was hoped, would be supplied by Petrobras' 2008 discovery of a major oil reserve coming from a vast deep water off-shore region known as the subsalt. Later that same year, however, the Gulf of Mexico oil spill—a British Petroleum rig exploded, killing 11 workers and pouring nearly 185 million gallons of oil into the Gulf—raised questions about the viability and the costs of future deep water drilling.

How Green *Is* Petrobras?

In 2010, *Newsweek* conducted an audit of the top ranking "green" companies in the world.[50] The highest ranking companies—IBM, Hewlett-Packard, Novartis, and Panasonic among them—received an overall score in the 90s. The highest ranking oil and gas company, French-based Total, received a score of 65. Petrobras' score was 48, placing it sixth in the list of oil and gas companies and 84th overall in the top 100 companies. In fact, five of the bottom ten on that list were oil and gas companies.

Endnotes

1. Information on Nike is from Jeffrey Ballinger, "The New Free-Trade Heel," *Harper's Magazine* (Aug. 1992), pp. 46–47; Simon Zadek, "The Path to Corporate Responsibility," *Harvard Business Review* (Dec. 2004), pp. 125–132; Stanley Holmes, "Nike Goes for the Green," *Business Week* (Sept. 25, 2006); Reena Jana and Burt Helm, "Nike Goes Green, Very Quietly," *Business Week* (June 22, 2009), p. 56; Maurice Berns, Andrew Townend, Zayna Khayat, Balu Balagopal, Martin Reeves, Michael Hopkins, and Nina Kruchwitz, *The Business of Sustainability: Imperatives, Advantages, and Actions* (New York: Boston Consulting Group, 2009); Marc J. Epstein, Adriana Rejc Buhovac, and Kristi Yuthas, "Why Nike Kicks Butt in Sustainability," *Organizational Dynamics* 39 (2010), pp. 353–356. The *Newsweek* rankings can be found at newsweek.com/feature/2010/green-rankings.
2. Susan Albers Mohrman and Christopher G. Worley, "The Organizational Sustainability Journey: Introduction to the Special Issue," *Organizational Dynamics* 39 (2009), p. 289.
3. Wallace B. Donham, "The Emerging Profession of Business," *Harvard Business Review* 5 (July 1927), p. 401; Wallace B. Donham, "The Social Significance of Business," *Harvard Business Review* 5 (July 1927), p. 406; Jeffrey L. Cruikshank, *A Delicate Experiment: The Harvard Business School, 1908–1945* (Boston, MA: Harvard Business School Press, 1987).
4. Theodore Levitt, "The Dangers of Social Responsibility," *Harvard Business Review* 36 (Sept.–Oct. 1958), p. 52; Milton Freidman, "The Social Responsibility of Business Is to Increase Profits," *New York Times Magazine* (Sept. 13, 1970).
5. This history is traced in John Elkington. "Towards the Sustainable Corpporation: Win-Win-Win Business Strategiues for Siustanable Development," *California Management Review* 36 (Winter 1994), pp. 90–100. Elkington is either the original source of the term "triple bottom line" or certainly the popularizer of the concept. See Elkington, *Cannibals with Forks: The Triple Bottom Line of 21st Century Business* (London: Capstone, 1997).
6. Paul Hawken, *The Ecology of Commerce* (New York: Harper Business, 1993), p. 3.
7. Some scientists argue that the Triple Bottom Line is inherently delusional and nonsustainable in that it assumes that growth and ecological concerns can be reconciled. Robinson's "Squaring the Circle" has an excellent, brief overview of this and other definitional debates.
8. See Andrew Manikas and Michael Godfrey, "Enabling Triple Bottom Line Compliance via Principle-Agent Incentive Mechanisms," *Global Journal of Business Research* 5 (2011), pp. 105–114. I have written elsewhere about the extent to which the definition of a "good" and "just" society is deeply ideological. That is a matter far beyond the scope of this text. However, anyone interested in pursuing the topic can look at Bert Spector, "'Business Responsibilities in a Divided World': The Cold War Roots of the Corporate Social Responsibility Movement," *Enterprise and Society* 9 (2008), pp. 314–336.
9. To review the Triple Bottom Line debate, you can go to Wayne Norman and Chris MacDonald, "Getting to the Bottom of the

'Triple Bottom Line,'" *Business Ethics Quarterly* 14 (2004), pp. 243–262, and Moses L. Pava, "A Response to 'Getting to the Bottom of the Triple Bottom Line," *Business Ethics Quarterly* 17 (2007), pp. 105–110.

10. See Minda Zellin, "The Greening of Corporate America," *Management Review* 79 (June 1990), pp. 10–18, and Harvey Meyer, "The Greening of Corporate America," *Journal of Business Strategy* 21 (Jan./Feb. 2000), pp. 38–43.

11. Berns et al., *The Business of Sustainability*.

12. Zadek, "The Path to Corporate Responsibility."

13. Berns, et al., *The Business of Sustainability*.

14. Quoted in Jennifer Robinson, "The Business of Sustainability," *Gallup Management Journal Online* (Oct. 3, 2009).

15. Christopher Marquis, Daniel Beunza, Fabrizio Ferraro, and Bobbi Thomason, *Driving Sustainability at Bloomberg L.L.* (Boston, MA: Harvard Business School Publishing, 2010). See also Ram Nidumolu, C. K. Prahalad, and M. R. Rangaswami, "Why Sustainability Is Now the Key Driver of Innovation," *Harvard Business Review* 87 (Sept. 2009), pp. 56–64.

16. Schroeder and Robinson, "Green Is Free," pp. 348–349.

17. Quoted in Jennifer Robinson, "The Business of Sustainability," *Gallup Management Journal Online* (Oct. 3, 2009).

18. For background on Interface, see "The Green 50: The Industrialist," *Inc. Magazine* 28 (Nov. 2006), pp. 80–81; Tom Andel, "Interface's Green Epiphany," *Logistics Management* 46 (June 2007), pp. 36–37; Lauren Hilgers, "Interface Sets the Pace for Going Green," *Plastics News* 20 (Oct. 6, 2008), p. 23; Wendy Stubbs and Chris Cocklin, "An Ecological Modernist Interpretation of Sustainability: The Case of Interface Inc.," *Business Strategy and the Environment* 17 (2008), pp. 512–523; Bruce C. Posner, "One CEO's Trip from Dismissive to Convinced," *MIT Sloan Management Review* 51 (Fall 2009), pp. 47–51; Kristy J. O'Hara, "About Face," *Smart Business Atlanta* (Jan. 2009), pp. 1518.

19. Quoted in Jennifer Lynes, *Scandinavian Airlines: The Green Engine Decision* (Ontario: Ivey Publishing, 2009), p. 3.

20. Philip Mirvis, Bradley Googins, and Sylvia Kinnicutt, "Vision, Mission, Values: Guideposts to Sustainability," *Organizational Dynamics* 39 (2010), pp. 316–324. Immelt is quoted from pp. 317–318.

21. Anderson quoted in "The Green 50: The Industrialist," *Inc. Magazine* 28 (Nov. 2006), p. 80. Information on Subaru is from Dean M. Schroeder and Alan G. Robinson, "Green Is Free: Creating Sustainable Competitive Advantage Through Green Excellence," *Organizational Dynamics* 39 (2010), pp. 345–352.

22. This point is made in Mirvis et al., "Vision, Mission, Values: Guideposts to Sustainability." The quotes concerning unaligned programs as well as the Coke example are from that article.

23. Michael E. Porter and Mark R. Kramer, "Strategy and Society," *Harvard Business Review* 12 (Dec. 2006), pp. 78–92. The issue of the South African mining company and AIDs is directly addressed in Margie Sutherland and Verity Hawarden, *Goedehoop: When Social Issues Become Strategic* (Ontario: Ivey Publishing, 2008). The Porter and Kramer quote is from p. 88.

24. Michael E. Porter and Mark R. Kramer, "Strategy and Society," *Harvard Business Review* 12 (Dec. 2006), pp. 78–92. The issue of the South African mining company and AIDs is directly addressed in Margie Sutherland and Verity Hawarden, *Goedehoop: When Social Issues Become Strategic* (Ontario: Ivey Publishing, 2008). The Porter and Kramer quote is from p. 88.

25. Information in Wal-Mart is from Erica L. Plambeck, "The Greening of Wal-Mart's Supply Chain," *Supply Chain Management Review* 11 (July–Aug. 2007), pp. 18–25, and Erica L. Plambeck and Lyn Denend, *Wal-Mart's Sustainability Strategy* (Stanford, CA: Stanford Graduate School of Business, 2008).

26. *Walmart: The High Cost of Low Price* (2004). Written and directed by Robert Greenwald. DVD. Weades Moines Video, 2004.

27. Plambeck and Denend, *Wal-Mart's Sustainability Strategy*, p. 4.

28. Information on McDonald's comes from Ray A. Goldberg and Jessica Droste Yagan, *McDonald's Corpporation: Managing a Sustainable Supply Chain* (Boston, MA: Harvard Business School Publishing, 2007).

29. *Ibid.*, p. 1.

30. Hillary Bradbury-Huang, "Sustainability by Collaboration: The SEER Case," *Organizational Dynamics* 39 (2010), pp. 335–344.

31. Per-Anders Enkvist and Hela Vanthourmout, "How Companies Think About Climate Change: A McKinsey Global Survey," *McKinsey Quarterly* (Feb. 2008); Marc J. Epstein, Adriana

Rejc Buhovac, and Kristi Yuthas, "Implementing Sustainability: The Role of Leadership and Organizational Culture," *Strategic Finance* 91 (Apr. 2010), pp. 41–47; Rosa Maria Dangelico and Devashish Pujari, "Mainstreaming Green Product Innovation: Why and How Companies Integrate Environmental Sustainability," *Journal of Business Ethics* 95 (2010), pp. 471–486.

32. Marquis, et al., *Driving Sustainability at Bloomberg L.L.*

33. Quoted in Jennifer Robinson, "The Business of Sustainability," *Gallup Management Journal Online* (Oct. 3, 2009).

34. Robert S. Kaplan and Ricardo Reisen De Pinho, *Amanco: Developing the Sustainability Scorecard* (Boston, MA: Harvard Business School Publishing, 2008), p. 5.

35. Robert S. Kaplan and David P. Norton, "Transforming the Balanced Scorecard from Performance Measurement to Strategic Management: Part I," *Accounting Horizons* 15 (Mar. 2001), p. 87.

36. Robert S. Kaplan and David P. Norton, "Using the Balanced Scorecard as a Strategic Management System," *Harvard Business Review* (Jan.–Feb. 1996), p. 3.

37. See Frank Figge, Tobias Hahn, Stefan Schaltegger, and Marcus Wagner, "The Sustainability Balanced Scorecard—Linking Sustainability Management to Business Strategy," *Business Strategy and the Environment* 11 (2002), pp. 269–284; Idalina Dias-Sardinha, Lucas Reijinders, and Paula Antunes, "Developing Sustainability Balanced Scorecards for Environmental Services: A Study of Three Large Portuguese Companies," *Environmental Quality Management* (Summer 2007), pp. 13–34; W.-H. Tsia, W.-C. Chou, and W. Hsu, "The Sustainability Balanced Scorecard as a Framework for Selecting Socially Responsible Investment: An Effective MCDM Model," *Journal of the Organizational Research Society* 60 (2009), pp. 1396–1410.

38. Marc J. Epstein and Priscilla S. Wisner, "Using a Balanced Scorecard to Implement Sustainability," *Environmental Quality Management* (Winter 2001), pp. 1–10.

39. Based on Wendy Stubbs and Chris Cocklin, "An Ecological Modernist Interpretation of Sustainability: The Case of Interface, Inc.," *Business Strategy and the Environment* 17 (2008), p. 519.

40. For a discussion of the problems inherent in the rating systems, see Aaron Chatterji and David Levine, "Breaking Down the Walls of Codes: Evaluating Non-Financial Performance Measurement," *California Management Review* 48 (Winter 2008), pp. 29–51.

41. Terrence E. Deal and Allan A. Kennedy, *Corporate Cultures: The Rites and Rituals of Corporate Life* (Reading, MA: Addison-Wesley, 1982), p. 4.

42. Marrevijk and Were, "Multiple Levels of Corporate Sustainability," p. 113.

43. This chart is based on a more detailed elaboration in Marrevijk and Were, "Multiple Levels of Corporate Sustainability," p. 113.

44. *Ibid.*, pp. 97–99.

45. *Ibid.*, p. 98.

46. Laura Quinn and Maxine Dalton, "Leading for Sustainability: Implementing the Tasks of Leadership," *Corporate Governance* 9 (2009), pp. 21–38; Patricia Hind, Andrew Wilson, and Gilbert Lenssen, "Developing Leaders for Sustainable Business," *Corporate Governance* 9 (2009), pp. 7–20; Nada K. Kalabadse, Andrew P. Kalabadse, and Linda Lee-Davies, "CSR Leaders Road Map," *Corporate Governance* 9 (2009), pp. 50–57; Anthony Middlebrooks, Lauren Miltenberger, James Tweedy, Grant Newman, and Joanna Follman, "Developing a Sustainability Ethic in Leaders," *Journal of Leadership Studies* 3 (Nov. 2009), pp. 31–43; Derek E. Crews, "Strategies for Implementing Sustainability: Five Leadership Challenges," *SAM Advanced Management Journal* 75 (Spring 2010), pp. 15–21.

47. Chris Argyris and Donald A. Schön, *Organizational Learning II: Theory, Method, Practice* (Reading, MA: Addison-Wesley, 1996), p. 13.

48. Information on Petrobras is from John Barham, "Brazil's Big Oil Man," *Latin Finance*, October 2005, pp. 18–20; "An Interview with José Sergio Gabrielli de Azevedo," *Oil and Gas Investor* (Oct. 2008), p. B4; José Sergio Gabrielli de Azevedo, "The Greening of Petrobras," *Harvard Business Review* (Mar. 2009), pp. 43–47; Peter Haldis, "Future Petrobras Refineries Will Produce Biofuels, Diesel, Not Gasoline," *Ethanol and Biodiesel News* (June 9, 2009); Geri Smith, "Petrobras Brandishes Its Corporate Blog," *Business Week* (Aug. 31, 2009).

49. Gabrielli, "The Greening of Petrobras," p. 44.

50. The *Newsweek* rankings can be found at newsweek.com/feature/2010/green-rankings.

INDEX